Resilience

ANNE DEVESON spent her childhood in Malaya, Australia and England, but for most of her adult life she has lived in Sydney. She is a writer, documentary film-maker and former head of the Australian Film, Television and Radio School, with a long involvement in social justice issues. Her films in Africa and Southeast Asia have won three UN Media Peace awards and her books include the bestselling *Tell Me I'm Here* — about her son's struggles with schizophrenia — which won the 1992 Human Rights Award for non-fiction and was shortlisted in five major literary awards. She is an Officer of the Order of Australia.

ALSO BY ANNE DEVESON

Lines in the Sand (2000)
Coming of Age (1994)
Tell Me I'm Here (1992, 1998)
Faces of Change (1984)
Australians at Risk (1978)

Resilience

Anne Deveson

ALLEN&UNWIN

Thank you for kind permission to reproduce the following: part of 'Some Advice to Those Who Will Serve Time in Prison' by Nazim Hikmet from *Poems of Nazim Hikmet*, translated by Randy Blasing and Mutlut Konuk. Translation copyright © 1994, 2002 by Randy Blasing and Mutlut Konuk. Reprinted by permission of Persea Books, Inc. (New York); part of 'Forgive, O Lord' from *The Poetry of Robert Frost* edited by Edward Connery Lathem, © 1969 by Henry Holt and Co., c 1962 by Robert Frost. Reprinted by permission of Henry Holt and Company, LLC; part of 'Comment' by Dorothy Parker, reproduced by permission of the National Association for the Advancement of Colored People. Every effort has been made to contact the copyright holders of non-original material reproduced in this text. In cases where these efforts were unsuccessful, the copyright holders are asked to contact the publisher directly.

First published in 2003

Allen & Unwin
83 Alexander Street
Crows Nest NSW 2065
Australia
Phone: (61 2) 8425 0100
Fax: (61 2) 9906 2218
Email: info@allenandunwin.com
Web: www.allenandunwin.com

National Library of Australia
Cataloguing-in-Publication entry:

Deveson, Anne.
   Resilience.

   Bibliography.
   Includes index.
   ISBN 1 86448 634 1.

   1. Resilience (Personality trait). I. Title.

155.24

Design by Greendot Design
Set in 12/14pt Bembo by Asset Typesetting Pty Ltd
Printed and bound in Australia by Griffin Press

10

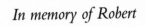

In memory of Robert

Acknowledgements

This book had its origins in a walk along the banks of the Yarra with two friends several years ago. My companions were Jackie Yowell, my publisher, and Jan Carter, who was then Professor of Human Resources at Deakin University. We were questioning our tendency in Western societies to label people as victims, and to focus on their problems, rather than working with their strengths and their resilience. Thus began a long conversation which is still continuing.

The book took me much longer than I anticipated to write, and at this point I warmly thank The Foundation for Young Australians who gave me a generous grant to help me write the book, and who were infinitely patient in spite of all my delays.

Of the many people who helped me with research and information, I'd especially like to thank Simon Champ; Richard Eckersley; Barbara Hocking; John Howard (no, not the Prime Minister); Petrea King; Paul Morgan; Alan Rosen; Jane Schwager; Fiona Stanley; Graham Vimpani; Ian Webster; Jane Woodruff and Leah Mann — who was CEO of The Queen's Trust before it became The Foundation for Young Australians. My thanks, as always, to Fiona Inglis at Curtis Brown for her ever-prompt support.

Varuna, the Writers' House, gave me a three-week fellowship in the Blue Mountains — which is always a joy for any writer — and Peter Bishop offered his usual wisdom and encouragement. Ken Methold also offered generous hospitality at his property at Capricorn Hill. And sundry kind friends sometimes hid me for days at a time so I could escape interruptions and the dreaded telephone. Phillipa White at Cure Cafe revived me with endless cups of her excellent coffee and put up with my papers sprawled across her table tops.

For most of the book I was fortunate to have weekly first-class research assistance and ideas from Liz Bradshaw. When she left to complete her doctorate, Sophie Alstergren cheerfully pitched in to help with last-minute research and hunting for missing files. Ted Markstein kept my computer ticking over, and cheerfully accepted frantic phone calls at all hours of the day and night.

Jan Carter, Jenya Osborne and Rosie Scott read the first complete draft of the book — which is always a hazard for any friend — and gave me honest and thoughtful appraisals. I much appreciated their help.

Jane Schwager, who introduced me to Robert Theobald, remained a dear kind stalwart friend throughout the months that I knew Robert, and particularly during the time of his illness and death. Many other friends gathered around me during this time. I would particularly like to thank my two children, Georgia and Joshua Blain who have always un-complainingly accepted the many dramas in my life and who continue to give me the most generous love and support.

I send greetings and thanks to my friends on the other side of the world — in Spokane, where Robert lived and died. I thank Bob Stilger and Susan Virnig, Michele and Ryan Holbrook, Francesca Firstwater, Amanda Butcher, Annie Stilger Virnig, and John, Justin, Colin and Kate Holbrook.

All these families took me into their homes and their lives with generosity and warmth.

Allen & Unwin, my publisher, bent over backwards to help — and gave me first-class professional support and patience. In particular I thank Christa Munns, senior editor at Allen & Unwin, both for her skills, and for her buoyancy and optimism. And Edwina Preston, text editor, who worked hideous hours towards the end, and gave me the kind of professional editorial assistance which writers crave but don't often get. I'd also like to thank Andrew Hawkins for his support in promoting the book.

Jackie Yowell, my publisher at Allen & Unwin, is an old friend — she was the one who initiated *Tell Me I'm Here*, in her Penguin days, many years ago. Jackie loves books, ideas, discussion, argument, so that as well as having a long-standing friend by my side, I also had someone whose professional work is outstanding.

Finally my thanks to someone who won't even know I am thanking her, Bibi, my all-forgiving dog. The fierce little cat, alas, died before this book was finished.

This book went to press at the start of a war that will have global reverberations for years to come. These are times when we will need all our resilience: at home with those we love, in communities which may be divided, abroad in a world made fearful, in our relationships with nations that may not share our views.

Resilience is about facing adversity with hope. We inhabit one world in which we are all deeply connected. I hope for the wisdom and justice which will bring us peace.

Anne Deveson
19 March 2003

Contents

Acknowledgements   *vi*

1. In the beginning   *1*
2. The defrocked economist   *14*
3. Everyday magic   *23*
4. Shaping brains   *41*
5. A great world to be in   *56*
6. Families — we all have 'em   *74*
7. It takes a community   *91*
8. Violence   *106*
9. The problem is the problem   *122*
10. Values — what happened?   *141*
11. The briefest joy   *152*
12. Shadows of illness   *164*
13. Freedom   *180*
14. A question of age   *189*
15. Spokane   *197*
16. The Wolverine Poochpack   *211*
17. Spirit   *223*
18. Yours truly, Annie   *233*
19. Across the gulf   *245*
20. If you love, you grieve   *258*
21. In retrospect   *266*

Notes   *269*
Reading suggestions   *287*
Index   *289*

In time the wind sags, and we hoist new sails
                    PINDAR'S ODES (PYTHION IV)

It may not be that resilience is elusive, but that it is invisible. What if it is something you feel, but you can't describe? What if resilience is something that happens, but you can't see? What if resilience is something that creates music in a life born deaf? What if resilience is something that warms you in your thoughts, but there is no language to share it? What if resilience is the poetry of life, and we are now just learning the alphabet?

JEANETTE L. JOHNSON
RESILIENCE AND DEVELOPMENT

1

In the beginning

When I think about resilience, I think about my mother. She is sitting opposite me at a kitchen table in Western Australia. It is summer, and already the heat is ransacking the freshness of the early morning. A fly-paper dangles above our noses and the flyscreens are rent in several places.

My mother is a beautiful woman in her early forties, head upright, shoulders back. Dark hair pulled into something known as a 'French roll'. She wears a red shirt and is drumming her fingers impatiently on the linoleum table-top. The rest of us are slumped in our chairs.

The year is 1942. Singapore has just fallen to the Japanese and we are refugees from the war in the Pacific. Three women and five children. Our fathers missing, possibly dead.

Two weeks earlier we were sent by the Red Cross to this run-down farm just outside Perth in Western Australia, with a suggestion we should try to live off the land. Our present job is to tend a large strawberry patch which either an optimist or an idiot has planted in a drought-stricken paddock. We are supposed to make the fruit into jam which we will then sell. As our mothers are used to all the comforts of a colonial life, and scarcely know how to boil an egg, I can see this is a dubious proposition. The day before they starched sheets which now hang on the line like huge pieces of cardboard, creaking in the hot, dry wind.

On this particular morning, we are being fractious, kicking the table legs, sullenly playing with our food. We whinge. We whinge about the heat, about the flies, about the fact the water tank is running dry and the milk has curdled. We whinge that everything is hopeless. My mother snorts in exasperation. 'It's bad enough *being* in shit, we don't have to lie down in it as well.'

She probably doesn't say 'shit', but 'a ghastly mess'. She is very English. She strides to the back door, grabbing a hoe which is propped up against the wall, and yells at us to join her: we have to get back to the strawberry patch. Then something unexpected occurs.

Up till then, my mother has simply been my mother. Someone who loves and comforts me when I am distressed, who corrects my manners, and who smells of Chanel No. 5 rather than fly spray. But still an appendage to most of my needs. Now for the first time I see her as separate from me and I realise that behind her fierceness, she feels daunted and miserable like the rest of us. That surprises me, but at the same time I feel better because it makes everything seem more real. I also know — with absolute conviction — that no matter what obstacles come our way, she will take action to get us through. If I were older, I would have said she was being *resilient*, but I am only eleven years old and scarcely aware of the word.

• • •

Many years later, when I became a journalist, I met people with the same capacity as my mother to overcome hardship with determination and guts. A burly man who had just experienced his second bushfire stood in the smoking ruins of his house, scratching his head at the devastation which surrounded him. When a television reporter waved a microphone under his nose and asked what he would do, he looked at her in amazement.

'Get a truck, shift the bloody iron and start again,' he said. 'What else would I do?' When I heard him, I wondered what exactly was this quality of resilience which carried him through once, and would do so again?

History is full of stories about people surviving the most horrendous disasters, but most of our struggles relate to every-day life. We battle with a serious illness; one of our children is at risk; we lose a job; we lose someone we love. Friends grapple with divorce — one person remains locked in anger, while the other lets go gracefully. Why? What is the difference between them? Are some people more resilient than others?

I am not sentimentalising resilience — the problems I am talking about can be tough. Like the story of a promising young Australian dancer, nineteen-year-old Marc Brew, who was injured in a car crash caused by a drunken driver. The accident killed his girlfriend, her brother and her brother's friend. Marc was left a quadriplegic. He had been dancing since he was seven years old and felt he had lost more than the use of his legs; he had lost his identity, his sense of self.

When he was lying in hospital, critically ill, he felt he had to make a decision whether to live or die. 'I was slipping away. I knew I was dying and I didn't want to die. I said, "Okay, I want to live." Then I thought, "Okay, how am I going to live the rest of my life? Am I going to be someone who feels sorry for myself?" I have a million and one excuses to be sorry for myself. I have a million and one excuses to become an alcoholic or a drug addict ... but life is too precious; the reality is, it can be over any time.'

So Marc lived, and learned to dance on wheels with the Infinity Dance Theatre, a pioneering dance troupe of disabled and able-bodied dancers in New York. Writing his story like this, in two short paragraphs, doesn't do justice to his courage, the agonies of endurance he went through, the small shifts he made towards recovery when recovery meant letting go of everything he once desired.

A memory returns of a young woman in a pink floral dress who is having a difficult time with her five-year-old son. He has cerebral palsy. His legs and arms are in constant spasm, and from his mouth comes a strange language only she can understand.

The young mother represents 'the handicapped' — a vague label once pinned on anyone with a disability, from mental illness to loss of limb — and she has come to give evidence before the Royal Commission into Human Relationships. The Commission was a visionary initiative of the Whitlam government, created to enable public discussion of social and technological changes affecting human relationships, and to determine how the State might help improve the quality of those relationships — especially in areas where policy and laws lagged behind change. I was one of three appointed commissioners, together with Justice Elizabeth Evatt and the Archbishop of Brisbane, Felix Arnott.

A few years earlier, this child with cerebral palsy would have been placed in an institution. His mother might not even have seen him. Now she had the care of her child, but the pendulum had swung in the opposite direction.

When he was born, she had been discharged from the hospital with her baby, a feeding formula and a tiny pink plate for the child's cleft palate. The only advice she received was to come back later to have the plate refitted. Her general practitioner prescribed her sedatives for depression, and she and her husband found their own way to the Royal Blind Society by asking a blind man they saw outside a supermarket. She had only learned accidentally from one of the nurses that her baby was blind. 'He's mentally retarded too,' the nurse had added, almost as an afterthought.

Now this young mother stood in front of us, glowing with defiance as she told the Commission of her experiences. A thin young woman, she kept pushing her wispy blonde hair behind her ears as she spoke.

'I won't give in,' she said. 'I won't ever give in. I owe it to my son. I love him, you know.'

So where did this young woman find such magnificent resilience? Did it come from the immense love she had for her son? How did she have the capacity to endure difficulty, when I have seen others in similar circumstances crumble from despair? Why does adversity sometimes lead to transformation and at other times only to more suffering?

If you ask me for some well-known examples of resilience, I think of people like Nelson Mandela, who lived through twenty-seven years of imprisonment with his integrity and convictions unshaken. He emerged to become one of the greatest statesmen of our time. How did this happen? How did he find — in jail — the wisdom and love to forgive his persecutors? How did he have the courage to believe South Africa could one day be a country of peace and justice for everyone, regardless of race?

All of us have to face suffering at different times in our

lives. It is part of the human experience and how we learn. Psychologist Polly Young-Eisendrath, in *The Resilient Spirit*, writes that hardship is one of the engines of human development. 'Until we reach our limits, we don't know how to overcome them. Until we feel our greatest fears directly, we don't know our courage.'

Nowadays, 'resilience' has come to mean an ability to confront adversity and still find hope and meaning in life. George Vaillant, a Harvard psychiatrist who has written widely on the subject, declares, 'We all know perfectly well what resilience means until we try to define it.'

Just up the road from where I live there is a cafe called *Cure*, which dispenses some of the best coffee in Sydney alongside homeopathic remedies — countless dark little bottles labelled with names like Belladonna, Arnica, Hypericum. The owner has a catholic attitude to life: caffeine or calendula, choose your cure. I decided to take the dog and ask a few fellow coffee lovers their definition of the word 'resilience'. It was early March.

A young woman in a black beret, who was struggling with three wriggling children, said wryly that resilience was 'rising above the shit' — I remembered the words of my mother all those years ago. A Buddhist meditation teacher observed that resilience was about transforming adversity into wisdom, insight and compassion. And a man who introduced himself as a biologist stated that resilience was about evolution and survival, the capacity of all life-forms to endure. (He was drinking a soy-milk decaffeinated latté.)

His comment made me wonder why our view of resilience is so anthropocentric. All life has inbuilt survival mechanisms; and, in one sense, the natural drive of the human mind and body towards regeneration is the same as the natural drive of all living things — possibly the least understood force on earth. As we chatted in the cafe, I thought of the aftermath of bushfires, recalling the sight — in the midst of burned and blackened trees — of a charred stump bearing a triumphant crown of green branches shooting out at absurd angles and against all the odds.

'Rrrresilience.' When I rolled the word round my tongue, it sounded darkly heroic. I said it slowly and it spoke of endurance and determination. I was becoming attached to the word. The dog thumped her tail.

Each generation probably claims it is the one that has endured the most suffering. Yet no one else can experience another's hardship, nor judge its effect. Who is to say that being killed by boiling oil in the Middle Ages was any more savage than a drenching of napalm in the twentieth century? Today's high-altitude bombing might seem more discriminating than gunpowder and canon — after all it is called 'precision bombing' — but when it rains down on the heads of hapless civilians, the result is the same: death and maiming. Over the centuries, virulent illnesses have decimated huge populations across the globe. Yet from these disasters emerge stories of great resilience and altruism — like that of the people of Eyam, a tiny village in seventeenth-century Derbyshire, who gave up their lives to save others from catching bubonic plague. The plague had started in London in the summer of 1665, and then found its way via a tailor-journeyman to Eyam. The village inhabitants, led by the vicar, prevented the further spread of contagion by quarantining their entire village (no one in, no one out). Ultimately, not many people survived.

When Australian author Geraldine Brooks wrote a novel based on this story, I found it fascinating to conjecture whether a similar situation could occur in contemporary times. A whole village willing to die for the common good? I decided it was unlikely. Even if the altruism was present, I doubted if modern society would have the discipline or social cohesion for such sustained self-sacrifice.

Yet I believe people have shown a different kind of courage and tenacity in battling the devastating global epidemic of HIV/AIDS. Forty million people in the world are now living with HIV/AIDS and nearly twenty-two million have died — a figure which equals almost the entire population of Australia. Initially, small groups of people struggled on their own to combat the disease, but then quickly realised that the containment of such a massive disaster required vast numbers of people working together.

In the early 1980s — before AIDS also became a hetero-sexual concern — HIV positive men and women not only had to deal with the desperate reality of their diagnosis, but with prejudice, ignorance and cruelty from the outside world. Children who had caught AIDS from blood transfusions were often refused entrance to schools; several families with HIV/AIDS had their houses torched; men and women who spoke publicly about their homosexuality risked losing their jobs, their friends, and sometimes the love of their families. The response to such dire outcomes was active resilience rather than despair: take risks, see what needs to be done, join together, work together. Campaigns were undertaken to fight governments and pharmaceutical companies to get cheaper drugs; to outlaw discrimination; to raise government and private funding for research; to engage in public education about the disease with messages like

'Kissing doesn't kill; greed and indifference do'. Behind this kind of resilience lies emotional honesty. Hiding from reality weakens a person; being open to it brings strength.

Australian Aboriginal leaders like lawyer Noel Pearson, who was part of the Indigenous Negotiating Team during the drafting of the *Native Title Act* in 1993, are following this path today when they confront the breakdown of values and relationships in Aboriginal societies, and question dependency on passive welfare. When I was a child at school in Western Australia, we were told that Aboriginal people would soon die out. We were not told the reasons why, nor were we told about the huge and cumulative damage which still resonates in Aboriginal lives today.

Aboriginal life expectancy continues to lag twenty years behind that of the wider population, a figure that has not improved in two decades, and is virtually without precedent on a world scale. Yet stoically, persistently, in the face of insults and procrastination, Aboriginal people continue their fight for justice. They use legal processes and make their position clear without violence. Who can forget the patience of Aboriginal leaders throughout those endless debates about rights to land, resources and self-determination in the 1990s. And when nothing seemed to have been achieved, the calm dignity with which they turned their backs on the Prime Minister at the Reconciliation Convention 1999.

Noel Pearson insists that resilience is crucial for his people in the Cape York Peninsula. He says that with resilience comes strength and action; without it comes weakness and victimhood.

• • •

One of my major concerns in writing this book was to look at what is happening to children in today's world. According to a United Nations Report in 2002, decades of hard-won gains in child development and education are unravelling. Unless they are properly attended to, huge problems get worse, not better.

Children in affluent Western societies are also facing difficulties. Professor Fiona Stanley, Director of Perth's Institute for Child Health and one of Australia's leading child health experts, believes children are growing up in what she calls a 'toxic society' — subject to social and economic pressures that are producing unhappy, unhealthy kids. She argues that we need to ponder why rates of suicide and asthmatic illness have trebled in thirty years and are higher now than at any time in Australia's history. Or why it is that so many teenage deaths are now due to road accidents and that Australia has one of the highest rates of youth suicide in the world. I read this and think about other signals of distress: about depression and the rising incidence of drug and alcohol abuse. I wonder if resilience is something we can help children develop so they can cope with problems that will inevitably confront them in their lives.

I agree with Canadian economist, John Ralston Saul, when he talks about our civilisation being in a long-term crisis, 'drifting further out into a cold, unfriendly, confusing sea'. Change is happening faster than we can understand or manage and if we are to ride out such bewildering and destructive times, we need to have the self-awareness and flexibility that resilience brings.

This is probably one of the reasons why resilience has become such a hot topic in the last few years. Ecologists now study the resilience of our natural environment and wonder if it will survive pollution and global warming. Doctors, faced with mounting health costs, try to understand more about resilience as a means of encouraging people to be well, not sick. Educators teach resilience in a wide range of contexts, including resilience classes in schools. The concept of resilience even made it to the pages of the *Harvard Business Review* in May 2002. In an article called 'How Resilience Works', Diane Coutu wrote, 'Resilient people and companies face reality with staunchness, make meaning of hardship instead of crying out in despair, and improvise solutions from thin air. Others do not. This is the nature of resilience, and we will never completely understand it.'

Diane Coutu may be right. There are many things we do not completely understand about resilience. Is it a fixed quality, something we either possess or lack? Or is it more subtle than that — a complex interplay between biology, psychology and environment? We do not live our lives in isolation. Our culture, our laws, our values profoundly affect our capacity for resilience.

If we send a young single mother to the far-flung reaches of suburbia, where there is no childcare, poor public transport and no community support, we have a recipe for breakdown. But imagine the reverse scenario: good community networks, childcare and transport would make the same woman's story vastly different. So if we fail to resource communities with tools which enable resilience, individual resilience may also suffer.

Apply mandatory sentencing laws to a fifteen-year-old Aboriginal boy who has stolen some pens and pencils valued at less than fifty dollars, jail him eight hundred kilometres away from his family — his mob — and wonder why he kills himself. Was his tragedy really brought about by a lack of resilience, or was it the consequence of draconian laws and the failure of our social responsibility to young people? These are not easy questions to answer, but they are important ones to ask.

As I write this book, I find myself thinking about my own resilience, wondering about the influence of my parents, and all the things I have experienced and learned. At several stages in my life I have had my own resilience put to the test. But even as I use these words, 'put to the test', I am disturbed, because this sounds as if I believe resilience is some challenge to be passed or failed — that only the strong are resilient, the weak fail.

When my eldest son Jonathan was diagnosed with schizophrenia, he was seventeen years old. His illness never responded to medication. Much of the time he was psychotic and for several years, I and my two younger children lived with his fear and ours. He died when he was twenty-four, saying the struggle with his illness had become too great to bear. There were times when I fought to save him and times when I had to retreat. So don't imagine this book is written by an expert in the practice of resilience. There are no experts. People do the best they can.

In my mind's eye, resilience is a cloak of many colours. My mother's was bold and brightly coloured. My father's resilience was quieter, woven with a self-deprecatory sense of humour. I'm not sure about mine: also brightly coloured, a bit torn, but it'll keep going for several more years.

I began working on this book at a time when I hoped I could forget about my own personal resilience for a while and look at the subject more broadly. I was well. I was enjoying my life. I had good friends. My two grown-up children were happily partnered and I had three small grandchildren with whom I had fallen hopelessly in love. It seemed safe to tempt the gods. But out of the blue my life took an unexpected twist.

'We must expect everything,' wrote the Roman philosopher Seneca almost two thousand years ago, 'there is nothing which Fortune does not dare.'

2

The defrocked economist

It happened like this. One afternoon in early March, when the pavement tar bubbled from late summer heat, and swimmers flopped past my windows on their way to the beach, a friend rang urging me to drop everything and interview a man called Robert Theobald. She knew I was writing this book and Theobald was a high-profile international lecturer who was well known for his work on resilient communities. He was about to return to the United States.

I had already heard of Robert Theobald, who had a large following in Australia. He described himself as a 'defrocked economist', and for over forty years had challenged the Western world's commitment to rising productivity and consumerism, passionately arguing that people and communities were more important than the accumulation of goods and wealth. He believed that our best response to the growing turbulence of the world was to develop resilient communities and resilient ecological systems. All the same, I baulked at my friend's suggestion. I wasn't yet ready to interview anyone. I was finishing a novel, and recalling the words of a *New York Times* editor who used to yell at me when I was a young journalist, 'The art of writing is the art of keeping the seat of your pants to the seat of your chair.'

I said I was too busy to go.

Jane persisted. She heads the Benevolent Society, Australia's biggest organisation of the kind once known as a charity, but now called a Not-for-Profit. 'You'll like him. He'll be good for you.'

I said too much leaving my desk was bad for me.

'Look,' she said, 'I have a hunch. Just go.'

I gave in and sent an email:

Dear Robert Theobald,

I am a friend and colleague of Jane Schwager's. I write, make films, headed up the Australian Film, Television and Radio School for a number of years, and have been on various government bodies concerned with social justice issues. I have recently been commissioned to write a book on resilience. As well as addressing individual resilience, I want to look at the kind of environments which help people and communities cope with adversity and foster resilience. If it's possible to meet with you, however briefly, I'd be very grateful.

Best wishes, Anne Deveson.

The next morning I rang Theobald to see if he had any time remaining from his tour. His voice was warm and cheerful, but he surprised me by asking a string of questions. I wondered if he was checking me out and felt mildly irritated. Later, I discovered that he often asked lots of questions — they came from an intense natural interest in other people's views and experiences. What did I mean by 'resilience'? he asked. Did I think it was merely 'bouncing back' from adversity or could it include 'moving forward'? Was I optimistic about the future or pessimistic? He said he was returning home to the United States the following day and could fit me in for twenty minutes at the end of a lunchtime talk for insurance executives.

I looked him up on the net. His record was impressive. He had published over twenty-five books on social change, written reports that were influential in the Johnson and Nixon administrations, and had been recognised as one of the world's most influential futurists. He was born in India in 1929 of British parents, studied economics at Cambridge and Harvard, worked in Paris for four years after the war with the Organisation for European Economic Co-operation, and then returned to the United States in the late 1950s, where he had lived ever since.

I couldn't help wondering what motivated him. 'Okay, okay, let's find out,' I said to the dog, who thumped her tail. (She is a Rhodesian ridgeback and her name is Bibi, which is Swahili for 'big woman of the house'.) I went to meet him, dressed in an old brown cotton dress and sandals, a gesture of rebellion against having to leave my desk, get into my car and go into town.

I arrived at one of those large inner-city hotels where the doormen look as if they're dressed for a Viennese operetta and the lobby sprouts a jungle of plastic palms. A notice-board with gilded lettering advertised the day's menu of corporate functions, and delegates were swarming at the entrances. They wore name badges and eager smiles. Conversation buzzed, plates clattered. Participants of the insurance function were already clutching drinks. Moving among them was Theobald, a tall, lively looking man with a long face and kind eyes. His crumpled linen jacket was falling off his shoulders and he wore a red tie. He said he couldn't speak with me till after his talk; meanwhile, he had asked someone to look after me during lunch.

He began his talk near the end of a steak béarnaise and just before a passionfruit mousse. The master of ceremonies, a senior insurance executive wearing a silver-blue suit and a silver-blue tie, introduced him as one of the world's leading futurists. 'One of the top ten in the *World Encyclopaedia of Futurists,*' he told us with a flourish. Everyone clapped. Robert Theobald began. He talked to us about the driving forces of our time, which were so dynamic and complex, he said, that any attempts at prediction were certain to be disastrously wrong.

'Whoever would have predicted the fall of the Berlin Wall?' he asked.

He said we were caught between two worlds, one dying and one ready to be born. The turbulence of the transformation was causing extraordinary stress. Our activities had brought us to a point where we had effectively unlimited productive and destructive power. Unless we could change the ways we thought and behaved, we would destroy ourselves.

He strolled between the tables, hands in pockets, telling stories, asking questions, wooing answers, speaking all the time with a low-key, infectious charm. The effect was curiously mesmeric, partly because Theobald was connecting with some kind of *zeitgeist* — a collective anxiety that the world was out of control — and partly because he gave the feeling he was engaging with every individual in the room.

He asked whether our emphasis on possessions gave us joy?

How did we feel about the growing gap between rich and poor? Were we willing to look beyond increases in our own wealth to the dangerous trends in poor countries of the world, where poverty and illness was worsening and anger was increasing? Free markets might produce growth, but they do not produce social equity. They may be an efficient way to decide how to do things, but they are not the best way to determine what is worth doing. Society should determine goals; the market should act as the means to reach them.

Somehow — in the immediate future — we had to find the courage and wisdom to radically change our whole way of living and being. He quoted John Maynard Keynes: 'The real difficulty lies not in developing new ideas, but in escaping from old ones.'

What he said wasn't new, it was the way he said it, together with his belief that ordinary citizens had the power to make changes, that made Theobald's talk inspiring. He wasn't afraid to use words like *love, generosity, justice*. He was a passionate man with the capacity to inspire the same kind of strong feeling in others.

'We need to shift the world onto more sustainable and resilient tracks. This can only be achieved if we re-emphasise the moral, the sacred and the spiritual over the pragmatic and the economic.' He laughed, 'I know that's not fashionable talk, especially coming from an economist.'

When he asked who was interested in being part of an email network of people wanting to contribute to change, cards landed in his up-ended Akubra hat like bridal confetti. He stuffed them in the pockets of his jacket and his trousers.

After the talk was over, Theobald found me in the middle of departing crowds. He said he hadn't eaten because he had been talking through the whole of lunch, but he should sit down and eat now because he had had oesophageal cancer two years earlier and was supposed to have regular meals. Then he seemed to ignore that statement and we settled on a large black leather sofa, just round the corner of the hotel lobby.

He mopped his face for a moment and looked tired as he apologised for having so little time. His energy seemed to regenerate when he leaned forward and began talking about resilience again.

'I think resilience is organic, not mechanical — it's part of our immune system. You might like to look at the nexus between the individual, community, nation and the world, to see how they connect.

'Look at authoritarianism — does it play a role in inhibiting resilience?

'Look at education and the absurdity of keeping adolescents in high school when their hormones are bursting out all over and we're not giving them any roles in the world outside. We isolate them from reality.' He paused and looked at me directly. 'Education is an example of the way patterns of modern societies are collapsing. It's not enough to adapt within the norms of the past. We need to discover profoundly new ways of perceiving the world in which we live.'

The allocated twenty minutes grew into two hours and still he hadn't eaten.

'How can you help?' he suddenly asked.

'Help? Help what?' I was alarmed. I hadn't come to help.

'I'm planning a major conference with the University of Canberra at the end of September, and resilience will be one of its key themes.'

Then he left, suddenly and abruptly, rising to his feet, sticking out his hand, as if to say, 'Class dismissed.' It sat oddly with his earlier warmth. Later I realised this was the pattern of most of his goodbyes — quick and unexpected, as if his energy had suddenly collapsed. As the doorman called him a taxi I reflected that being a defrocked economist must be a bold and lonely calling. He was wheeling a suitcase and clutching a plastic bag that contained an apple and a banana. He looked tired again.

'Thank you,' he said. 'Thank you, I know we'll meet again.' As he drove off, he leaned out of the window and said, 'Live with passion.'

I have, as a matter of fact, lived quite large chunks of my life with passion, sometimes disastrously. 'Live with passion,' I pondered as I made my way home. I had gone to Robert Theobald's lecture reluctantly, yet I was leaving it in a state of near euphoria.

As soon as I reached home I rang Jane to tell her something totally unexpected had occurred — one of those inexplicable sparks, connections, call it what you will, that lead two people to feel they already know each other.

Jung described this experience of meeting someone for the first time, yet feeling you have known them forever, as being like a recollection from an unknown past. Pop culture explains it differently: 'Ah sweet mystery of life at last I've found you' — so sung a whole generation of romantic tenors in my mother's heyday.

'Is he married, or with someone?' I asked Jane. (The love songs were winning out over Jung.)

'No, I don't think so,' said Jane slowly.

'Why don't you think so?'

'I'm sure he said he was divorced. Ask him.'

'Ha ha,' I said.

• • •

Later, I found Robert had reacted to our first meeting in a similar way. After he returned to the United States, he sent me an email:

> Dear Anne, I feel sorry that I haven't had time to get a note off to you since our helpful and exciting meeting. I look forward to staying in touch with you on your book on resilience. Please send me some background — I need to know more about you. Blessings and Peace, Robert.

So who was this unreconstructed idealist of the 1960s, I asked myself — and who was I? Probably also an unreconstructed idealist. And why was he signing off his emails with 'Blessings and Peace' like some West coast guru? This wasn't the kind of impression he gave in person.

But our relationship wasn't nearly at the stage of acknowledgements of love. Our initial correspondence was sedate:

> Anne, We must give people a positive sense about themselves and a feeling that life is worth living. I think my September trip will have as its theme: Resilience — Individual, Community, Organisational and Global. How much of a role is it realistic for you to play? Robert.

I hesitated. My meeting with Robert Theobald had been interesting and delightful. His view of resilience was a visionary one, sited not just in the individual but in the wider world, and I welcomed this. But while I was pleased to develop a friendship with him, I didn't want to be pulled into his work, away from mine. I also knew my tendency to take on too many projects. A familiar expression of mine was: 'One day I'll clear the decks.'

Once, an old friend and colleague — a Russian camera-man called Kara — shook his head mournfully at me and said, 'Don't wait till the ship has sunk.'

With this in mind I sent the following reply:

Happy to contribute ideas, but not help organise. Anne.

I had no idea this involvement with Robert Theobald would eventually test my resilience to its limits.

3

Everyday magic

A sea breeze blew in my face this morning, and the cat, who is ancient but refuses to acknowledge it, scampered through a few autumn leaves which lay at my feet, coppery brown. They had dropped from a Manchurian pear tree in my back garden. It should probably be growing in Manchuria. Each year it struggles in an alien coastal environment, as do my roses, which regularly fall victim to mildew and black spot. Only the white iceberg roses bloom unscathed.

'They're resilient,' a tall, stringy woman in the plant nursery told me, giving me a patronising smile.

For quite a while, every time I turned on the radio or television, I heard the term 'resilience'. Even in reference to the stockmarket. Especially in reference to the stockmarket. I was curious about the term's currency, but I was more interested in its history, both as a word and a concept. When I thought back to my childhood, I didn't remember it being around.

The earliest written use of the word — according to the *Oxford English Dictionary* — was in 1626 in a natural history book called *Sylva Sylvarum*, written by the great British scientist, Sir Francis Bacon. In 1668, H. More employed the term again: 'Strong and Peremptory Resiliency from this sordid Region of Misery and Sin,' he wrote. Two hundred years later, J. Martineau cautioned that, '[T]he heart does not always propel without resilience.'

Resilience is an old word. It comes from the Latin *re-silere*, 'to spring back'. Across a spectrum of sources, it seems to mean rebounding, springing back, recoiling — implying buoyancy and elasticity. But none of the early definitions carried any notion of gaining personal wisdom through being resilient. The range of resilient substances was eclectic: lungs, skin, metal, rubber, the human heart, the human mind, the Japanese character, the Russian rouble — and mercury, which was described as 'the Quick-silver'.

As I read about the resilient qualities of 'the Quick-silver' a memory flashed into my mind. I was sixteen years old, tall and thin with ink-stained hands, wearing a brown box-pleat tunic, torn at the bottom from where I had caught it in the door of a tram. A chemistry lesson was in session, and our science teacher — Miss Winifred Stoppard — was prancing up and down in front of us, hands clasped together, while we perched behind wooden benches littered with test tubes and bunsen burners. We were peering intently at small globules of quicksilver as they darted from one end of a glass dish to the other.

Miss Stoppard, short and stout and splendidly enthusiastic, was exhorting us in her Yorkshire accent to watch the mercury.

'Joining together, girls, then slipping apart. Like Romeo and Juliet and most young love,' said Miss Stoppard, smiling benignly at us as she tried to tuck her greying brown hair into an unruly bun. 'But girls, wait till you've left school before you try to find out about love.'

'Oh Romeo, Romeo, wherefore art thou?' we called out to each other, giggling and smirking.

Miss Stoppard lived with our English teacher, a dour frog-faced woman whose name I forget. But I'd never forget Miss Stoppard. She was one of those rare and passionate teachers who, in the middle of a lesson about the chemical properties of hydrogen sulphate, would branch off into discussions about the poetry of Walt Whitman or the importance of the suffragette movement. This time she turned the resilience of mercury into a joyful homily about the necessity of always bouncing back. 'Don't let anyone put you down, girls,' she told us. 'Use your heart by all means, but don't forget your brains.'

Another related memory: rows of pale dead frogs, on their backs, legs splayed, pinioned to dissecting dishes. Pale yellow wax. Small dark-headed dissecting pins. The smell of formaldehyde as we peered closer and attacked the frogs with our sharp little knives. 'Flick!' we went, peeling the clammy frog skin back from the cloaca, feeling vaguely apologetic.

'Look at the elasticity of the skin,' urged Miss Stoppard, beaming with pleasure, as if she were revealing some amazing new discovery. In the face of such enthusiasm it was hard not to respond. We pulled at our own skin and watched it spring back, letting our arms return to their creamy smoothness. Miss Stoppard let us yank at one of her own arms, chuckling ruefully as her skin sagged in crumpled defeat.

'O wad some Pow'r the giftie gie us, to see oursels as others see us!' she said, quoting Burns and clapping her hands together. 'Use Pond's cold cream on your face and your hands every night, girls, before you go to bed. Class dismissed.'

• • •

I was about to put the *Oxford English Dictionary* to one side when I came across an entry for 1858, from a book called *Tour Ireland*, in which its author (one S.R. Hole) wrote, 'nothing but ... the resilient spirit of roving Englishmen could have induced us to sally forth.' I laughed and toyed with the idea of emailing Mr Theobald to ask him if he had the resilient spirit of a roving Englishman — but I thought better of it.

By this time, I was receiving almost daily messages from Robert Theobald. He emailed extensively. I had obviously become part of his 'loop'. A lot of his messages were about the Canberra seminar in September. Others ranged in subject from conflict in the Middle East, the Brazilian rain forests, and water conservation, to the bombing of Kosovo and the impending dangers of Y2K. He also sent me information about the resilience of street children in Bangalore, India, with a note: 'This might provide you some leads into odd places.'

I had been to Bangalore in 1981, when I took my son Jonathan to a clinic for young people with schizophrenia, run by a bizarre woman who believed mothers were to blame for their children's illness. (She ate chocolate creams all night, insisted I played Scrabble with her, and only pronounced me a non-toxic mother after she had beaten me three times.)

Thinking about Bangalore made me remember Jonathan. Scarcely a day goes by without thinking of him — mostly happy memories. A friend once asked if living with past loss requires ongoing resilience, more perhaps than we realise. I don't know. But I do know it is possible to live with sadness in our lives. Feeling sad doesn't mean we are not resilient —

being stuck in the sadness is where there may be problems. For me, over the years, the pain of Jonathan's death has retreated and settled somewhere deep inside. I almost forget it is there. Then something will jolt my memory and the pain returns. Unexpectedly and savagely — as if this unbelievable thing that happened all those years ago needs to remind me sharply of its presence. Sometimes it comes more softly, like a cloud of gentle melancholia. The pain subsides. The cloud floats away.

A *Chitty Chitty Bang Bang* book Jonathan had as a small boy lies on top of a pile of children's books which I am exploring to see if there are any references to resilience. The books are old and much loved, some have pages missing and bindings which have come unstitched. This is a random and idiosyncratic search, based on my belief that children's books provide useful clues to the values of their day, and also because these books are full of stories about resilience — stories in which children set out on long, courageous journeys to find their way home.

I draw a blank. Plenty of fairy godmothers handing out love, fame, fortune, and even the odd obliging frog willing to turn into a prince. But no one handing out resilience. Gods and goddesses, princes and princesses, woodcutters and maidens manifesting extraordinary forms of resilience, but invariably it was their beauty, their goodness, their courage that won them the accolades, not their resilience.

The nauseatingly dainty Thumbelina, buffeted by storm and tempest, is forced to become engaged to an arrogant young toad and then to a bossy old mole, but she never gives in, never loses hope, until finally she is rescued by a swallow who flies her home to a Thumbelina prince. But does the swallow say, 'This is a just reward for your resilience'?

Certainly not. Yet the essential message is there — goodness, hope and fortitude win out.

As a child, at my school's morning prayers, we sang John Bunyan's words to the hymn, 'He who would valiant be/ 'Gainst all disaster.' I wasn't allowed to sing. I couldn't keep a tune. But at the very end, I could resist no longer. I would thrust forth my chest and bellow forth: 'There's no discouragement/Shall make him once relent/His first avowed intent/To be a pilgrim.'

In all of this the *concept* of resilience was present, but not the word. In its place we talked about perseverance, steadfastness, valour and fortitude. Perhaps ordinary flesh-and-blood mortals who dragged themselves through the centuries never thought of themselves as resilient because it was taken as a given. Life was so harsh that if you weren't resilient, you suffered the consequences. People in Western countries were also more fatalistic than they are today. Resilience was expected of people, and adversity was a challenge which brought its own rewards.

Shakespeare made this clear in *As You Like It*, when the old Duke, exiled to the forest of Arden, reflects that although the woods are freezing cold they feel safer than the painted pomp and envy of the court:

Sweet are the Uses of Adversity,
Which, like the toad, ugly and venomous,
Wears yet a precious jewel in his head;
And this our life exempt from public haunt
Finds tongues in trees, books in the running brooks,
Sermons in stones and good in everything.
I would not change it.
(Act 2, Scene 1)

A New Age equivalent would be: *Love your disaster; it's good for you.* My response is, 'No thanks, I'd rather not.'

I knew that notions of resilience were deeply embedded within the cultures in which we live, but it intrigued me that resilience had become such a fast-growing research discipline only in recent years.

I found my explanation in the story of a brilliant young American psychologist called Norman Garmezy who, some fifty years ago, began looking for one thing, and ended up finding another. Garmezy is known as the 'peerless pioneer' of resilience research. He is now in his mid-eighties, and is Emeritus Professor of Psychology at the University of Minnesota.

Towards the end of the late 1940s, Garmezy was working at the Worcester State Hospital in Massachusetts investigating aspects of schizophrenia. Those were the days before neuro-leptic medication brought at least some relief from what was a bewildering and frightening disease. I remember my first visit to a large mental hospital on the outskirts of London, where tormented-looking people — many in their pyjamas — paced up and down corridors that smelt of urine and carbolic. I was nineteen, and my colleagues at the local newspaper where I worked made crass jokes about being careful of the loonies.

Schizophrenia was then loosely categorised into two distinct groups, 'process' and 'reactive'. People with process schizophrenia tended to be chronically and severely ill. Those who had reactive schizophrenia had episodic bouts of illness, and were often well in between. But something else was different. Since childhood, people in the second group had consistently been more competent in their day-to-day life than people in the first. Garmezy wondered if this had anything to do with the way they handled stress. He decided to explore the development of childhood competence. Here he made the first of many diversions from a mainstream approach. Instead of looking for children who were failing, he set out to find those who were succeeding in spite of overwhelming odds.

The young Garmezy travelled from school to school, asking principals to help identify children who came from severely troubled homes, but who were doing so well that staff felt proud to teach them. At first, teachers were puzzled. They were more used to delivering the names of children who had failed.

The child whose story Garmezy found the most moving had no father, an alcoholic mother, and grew up pretty much on his own. He was nine years old.

'He would bring a sandwich to school each day, but there wasn't much food around, so he took two pieces of bread with nothing in between. He became known to us as "the boy with the bread sandwich". The reason that he took a bread sandwich to school was so no one would feel pity for him and no one would know about his mother.

'You know, if you get hit with a case like that you begin to think, let's take a look at children who are resilient in other kinds of stresses and circumstances. Let's find out what's making it work.'

This was the beginning of a long journey into an imprecise and fascinating science. Garmezy and Eliot Rodnick, his colleague and mentor at Duke University, became part of an international consortium of pioneering psychologists and psychiatrists who, during the 1970s, joined together in a twelve-year study to explore the resilience of children who were at risk for mental illness because their mothers suffered from schizophrenia. They believed that if they could understand how some of these children developed healthily in spite of their genetic backgrounds and their profound family difficulties, it might help them understand not only the nature of mental illness but how to help make a difference in the lives of children at risk.

Children in the group being studied were living out their childhoods in some of the most stressful situations imaginable. For anyone, watching someone you love lose their reason is painful. For children, witnessing the mental illness of a parent must at times be overwhelming. They have no control over what is happening; no time for childhood; loneliness, because it is impossible to ask friends home; sadness; anger at how their lives are being spoiled; dread of inheriting the madness.

'Mental illness steals from a family,' said one child in Mona Wasow's book, *Skipping Stone*. Wasow, who is a Professor of Social Work and has a son with schizophrenia, explores the ripple effects of mental illness on the family. 'You are not like other children and you don't want anyone else to know your secret.'

A seven-year-old in Wasow's book felt frightened during most of his childhood. He helped raise his four-year-old brother while his mother lay in bed all day, crying. When his mother attempted suicide, his father told him never to tell anyone. He survived by turning to school, friends, writing and getting drunk.

In another example a five-year-old girl prepared meals, cleaned her clothes for school and was responsible for creating some semblance of order in a chaotic household. She parented both her mentally ill parents and her three younger siblings. Looking back she said that when she was nine she

RESILIENCE

wanted to kill herself, and that as an adult, she felt like an
abused child.

For me, one newspaper story stands out as an extraordinary triumph of determination and grace. In the
Weekend Australian I read the story of Carmel Williams, who,
at the age of eight, had to take her mother to a psychiatric
hospital in Melbourne at least three times a year, travelling
on two trains and a bus.

'In my child's mind I always thought of it as a game,'
Williams said. 'My mother's fingers would clench and
unclench, her eyes would cross slightly and she would begin
to talk softly to herself. I would climb onto a chair and haul
her hospital bag down from on top of the wardrobe. Then I
would take her hand and tuck Rosa (a jointed walking doll)
between the handles of the bag and we would walk the track
to the railway station. If my timing was right, I would arrive
[at the hospital] before my mother had descended into the
nightmare of full-blown psychosis. A game, like avoiding the
cracks in the pavement.'

At school, she invented an imaginary family. 'I had a
mummy with an apron who baked things and worked in the
tuck-shop on Fridays. I had a daddy who wore a felt hat and
carried a Gladstone bag to the city every day, and I had an
ever-changing number of brothers and sisters who were all
older than I was and spoiled me.'

And then one day, when she was talking about something
one of her 'sisters' had done, an older girl grabbed her by the
arm. 'You're a little liar,' she hissed. 'You're an only child and
your mother's mad. Everyone knows that.'

Years later when she told her mother this story, they
laughed about it. 'What doesn't break you makes you strong,'
her mother said. Despite their hardships, the bond between

mother and daughter endured. Carmel Williams was thirty when her mother died in a psychiatric hospital and she still misses her terribly. 'The bad times are blurred, forgotten, the good times are remembered and savoured because she struggled so hard against her illness to have them.' Memory can be selective; without her ability to focus on the good, Carmel Williams might not have maintained her resilient outlook on life.

Children who do well in such circumstances as Williams' understand that their parent's illness is separate from their own lives and that they are not responsible for it. Having a stable, loving relationship with another adult is extremely important for such children. So is support from school and community, where they may learn the social skills necessary to reach out to others. In this way, they are able to avoid being engulfed by their parent's illness, and can seek refuge in their own interests.

By now, there have been many studies into children whose parents have schizophrenia. Outcomes of these studies are blurred because of differences in sampling, but what is constant are the extraordinary strengths these children exhibit, and the creative strategies they develop to survive. American feminist and author Gloria Steinem tells in *Ms Magazine* how she drew on her imagination to make life bearable. 'I remember longing to escape the littered, depressing, rat-infested house where I lived alone with my mother … but my ultimate protection was this: I was just passing through; a guest in the house: perhaps this wasn't my mother at all.' The fictions we create for ourselves, as with Carmel Williams' 'imaginary family', are natural strategies which protect us; they help children be resilient in times of stress and hardship.

Garmezy and his colleagues concluded that the quality of resilience played a greater role in mental health than anyone had previously suspected. In 1971 this passionate and visionary man issued a bold proposal. Up till then sociological literature had been problem oriented. Garmezy took a leap that cut across prevailing ideas and practices, suggesting that instead of trying to devise models to stop children becoming ill, it might be more useful to study the forces helping children survive and adapt. He called resilient children, the 'keepers of the dream — our best hope for learning how to use lessons of the past to help ourselves in the future.'

Throughout the 1970s, as human rights movements became involved with helping the poor and oppressed, and the world opened up to a greater awareness of environmental influences, the study of resilience expanded and became mainstream. In Western societies, the euphoria of the 1960s gave way to an increasing urgency to protect young people from the damaging effects of stressful life events and conditions. Researchers realised that if children who lived with the chaos of mental illness could reveal such resilience, there were great possibilities for others in high-risk situations.

In 1987, sixteen years after the publication of his initial research, Garmezy gave a Special Report in which he stated:

Numerous clinical case studies are housed in a broad literature that reflects children's adaptation to a variety of stressors: poverty, migration, war, the Holocaust, loss and bereavement, divorce, chronic illness, physical handicap, parental psychopathology, natural disasters and many more; these accounts offer dramatic proof of the phenomenon we wish to study.

One of the most ambitious and well-known studies of resilient children ever undertaken was begun in 1955 by Dr Emmy Werner and her colleagues, who followed the progress of over two hundred high-risk children in the island of Kauai, Hawaii, from birth to thirty-two years. These children had experienced four or more risk factors ranging from poverty to parental alcoholism. Even with such heavy handicaps, one in three of these young people grew into competent young adults who, by the age of eighteen, 'loved well, worked well, played well and expected well.' Most of the others had settled down by the time they were thirty-two, perhaps because of something that Emmy Werner and her colleague Ruth Smith call 'an innate self-righting mechanism' — the strengths that people, families, schools and communities call upon to promote health and healing. They felt that these had a stronger impact on the life course of children at risk than any potential damage in their environment might.

For a long time, the general public and the media found it hard to accept any kind of positive findings about resilience. Either they didn't believe them or, because resilience wasn't a familiar concept, they decided high-risk children who did well must be an exception. *The Washington Post* carried a story about this new field of research on March 7, 1976 with the headline, 'Trouble's a Bubble to Some Kids'. Following this came the myth of the golden child: a heroic child, who lived in the midst of despair, yet remained shining and unscathed by bad experiences. Even as late as 1995, 'Superkids of the Ghetto' appeared as the title of a book review on resilience in inner-city children, published in *Contemporary Psychology*.

The problem with this kind of approach was that it promoted the idea that not only were resilient children somehow special but that resilience was a quality given only to a few.

Another hiccup occurred when policy makers and funding bodies began thinking that if only they could discover the 'magic ingredient' that enabled people to escape being damaged by adversity, they could use it like a vaccine and perhaps develop some kind of program which everyone could learn.

On top of this, the profound bias of Western culture towards examining the negative rather than the positive was still well entrenched. Even as late as 1986, at a memorial lecture which he presented in Chicago, Garmezy wryly stated that the persistent focus of the mental health disciplines on disease processes could best be explained by philosopher Abraham Kaplan's 'law of the hammer':

> Simply put, the law's basic postulate is: 'Give a child a hammer and everything the kid sees will need pounding.' Armed with our hammer of psychopathology, everywhere we turn in our clinics and waiting rooms we perceive primarily disorders, symptoms, and their dynamics. So we pound away, even though our overarching goal is mental health, not mental disorder.

But despite this tendency, massive shifts in Western thinking were slowly gathering support. Discoveries in biology and physics were leading to a recognition that the mechanistic concepts of Descartes and Newton needed to give way to a holistic and ecological view of the world. The Cartesian split between body and mind, which had been so central to medical practice and thinking since the seventeenth century, began to be replaced by a belief that mind and body were inseparable, and that human systems — like other systems — possessed a natural drive towards health.

By the 1990s, most resilience research confirmed that resilience arises from myriad interactions within and between organisms and their environment. This recognition of the inherently dynamic nature of resilience marked a true turning point in the field of resilience research.

Scientists had therefore moved from an initial belief that resilience was a quality that some people possessed and others didn't to an awareness that resilience was an interactive process occurring between individuals and their environment. Intervention to help people develop resilience could occur at any number of places and in any number of ways.

Academic definitions of resilience then became more complex because they depended on the context of the research. Also research into resilience was still relatively new, and some languages did not yet have an equivalent word. Spanish, for example, uses the term *la defensa ante la adversidad*, 'defence in the face of adversity'. French has the word, *la resilience*, but for a long time France was somewhat scathing about resilience research, dismissing it as not only Western but worse, an Anglo-American construct.

It's true that for a long time studies of resilience were very Western in their orientation. International interest didn't begin developing until the mid to late 1980s, when a series of conferences around the world eventuated in a number of major international research projects at the Civitan International Research Center, University of Alabama, involving some thirty countries studying ways to foster resilience in children under twelve. They defined resilience as, 'the human capacity to face, overcome, and even be strengthened by experiences of adversity'. In other words, it's not enough for poor old Sisyphus to keep rolling the stone up the hill, nowadays he's expected to have a growth experience on the way.

One morning I was looking through the latest crop of Early Childhood Development research papers, when I came across an article by Ann Masten, who heads the Institute of Child Development at the University of Minnesota and was a protégé of Garmezy. She had written the following about research into resilience:

> What began as a quest to understand the extraordinary has revealed the power of the ordinary. Resilience does not come from rare and special qualities, but from the everyday magic of ordinary, normative human resources in the minds, brains, and bodies of children, in their families and relationships, and in their communities. This has profound implications for promoting competence and human capital in individuals and society.

This was a powerful statement; it gave hope, and it grounded resilience in our everyday lives. But my mind still threw up urgent questions. If we all have this everyday magic, why do so many fall off the edge? Think of mounting juvenile suicide rates, violence, drug abuse, mental illness — are there perhaps limits to resilience?

I turned back to Masten:

> Even the most basic of human adaptational systems are not invulnerable and require nurturance. All too often, children who contend with the greatest adversities do not have the protections afforded by basic resources nor

the opportunities and experiences that nurture the development of adaptive systems.

I thought back to film and radio programs I had made over the years about poverty and disadvantage, and the struggling families and bewildered children I'd met. These were people desperate to do their best but often overwhelmed by circumstance. Robert had spoken and written about this too: 'Most people, most of the time, want to develop themselves and help others develop. This is the natural order of things. It is this order that has been broken by our industrial norms which have pitted us against each other and against nature.'

Robert was due back in Sydney in the middle of April, with a schedule he described as 'ludicrous'. It took him to every State in Australia with a list of speaking engagements that made my throat feel sore. I wondered why he was driving himself so hard.

His email loop kept looping. Sometimes he sent messages at 4.30 in the morning — his time. The latest one said:

You're a wonderful person to work with. You make it all fun. Thank you.

I stopped in my tracks when I read it. I wasn't 'working with' Robert Theobald. I thought I'd made it plain. *Ideas*, I'd said. I could offer ideas.

Over on my side of the world it certainly wasn't 4.30 when I read his email, but it was early. The dog was asleep. A garbage truck rumbled past my windows, scooping up consumer detritus and banging down the empty black bins with contemptuous disregard for sleeping citizens. I was wide awake, reflecting on what I'd just absorbed and where I would go next with my research. I wanted to find out more about the human brain.

4

Shaping brains

When I was nineteen, I had a boyfriend — a medical student — who wanted to specialise in brain research. Our romance was short-lived, but we used to have passionate arguments about whether we arrived on this earth with our futures pre-ordained.

'All over, all done!' he used to insist. (His father was a real estate agent.) 'What you have is who you are.'

I could never go along with this, nor with any other reduc-tionist arguments about the relative importance of nature and nurture. It was always clear to me the two were inextricably linked and functioned reciprocally. Now I found myself wanting to go further into the amazing world of the human brain, and explore whether children's early experiences might affect their capacity for resilience later in life. The field of brain research and resilience is relatively new, so I took a stack of papers with me to *Cure* cafe, and began to read.

Early childhood experiences are supremely important, according to the scientists. The kind of input we receive as a baby influences how we operate for the rest of our lives. During the first three years of life, our brain develops to ninety per cent of its adult size and puts in place the majority of its systems and structures. At birth, the main connections of the neural circuitry are already in place; the fine wiring is completed during the next three to five years. What a baby sees, hears, touches, smells and tastes will mould the development of the brain in an extraordinary wiring and sculpting operation in which different areas of the brain are allowed different time-frames for their capacity to adapt. As a child matures, this flexibility is lost or diminished. Children whose hearing loss is picked up when they are six months of age are more likely to develop good language skills than those whose hearing loss is picked up later.

The extent of early brain plasticity is at times formidable. Children who have severe epilepsy sometimes need to have the whole left hemisphere of their brains removed to treat their fits. The left hemisphere is the site of language development, yet these children will still possess language, because new language centres will now develop on the right side of the brain.

The first scientists to discover early brain plasticity were David Hubel and Torsten Wiesel who won a Nobel Prize in 1981 for their research on visual systems and the brain. For twenty-two years they had worked together at Harvard University trying to figure out how the brain processes visual information so that a person is able to see. Hubel, who comes from Ontario in Canada, and Wiesel, from Upsala in Sweden, say they are interested in the brain for the same reason astronomers are interested in the universe. 'It is an area still largely unexplored. We are more explorers than dis-coverers,' Hubel has said.

The two men began by asking: why does a child who is born with a lens cataract not have normal vision when the cataract is removed some time later on, whereas when adults' cataracts are removed, vision is restored? Hubel and Wiesel worked first with new-born kittens, finding that if they blocked the nerve transmission from the eye to the cortex of the brain, and the block was only released in maturity, it would be too late for the cats to see. The critical time for connection had been lost. If a kitten's initial vision was blurred rather than blocked, or if their visual environment was controlled in some other way, this also had an effect. Kittens that were raised in an environment consisting of only vertical stripes were unable to recognise horizontal lines as adult cats.

From experiments like these, Hubel and Wiesel realised that how we perceive the world around us depends on the visual experiences we receive during the earliest stages of our lives.

Other animal research showed that licking, touching, mothering and socialising are all vital to resilience. If new-born rat pups are not licked by their mother in this critical early period after birth, they have less ability to cope with adult life. They don't perform well in the rat maze tests, and their cortex is only fifty per cent as thick as those that are licked — due not to a lack of nerve cells but to lack of *neuronal connections*.

The dog I had before Bibi, my current dog, was a gentle soul called Lucy who was only nine months old when she came to me, but had never been outside the kennel that bred her, and had been badly treated. She had been to several homes, but they all sent her back. She was so timid when I first brought her home that if anyone came to the house she ran cowed and shaking into the garden or tried to squeeze behind a chair. After two days like this I took her to bed with me. I figured a bit of bonding was required. It worked. But it was five years before she stopped fleeing from strangers.

So what happens to humans if they are deprived of early mothering or loving? Dramatic and tragic evidence was provided when the Ceausescu dictatorship in Romania fell in December 1989. Television and newspapers carried images of abandoned or orphaned children held captive in decrepit institutions which were under-funded and under-staffed. These children were ghost-like, wide-eyed and unloved. Some had spent their early months — or years — lying quietly in cribs for eighteen to twenty hours a day, with nothing to look at or listen to. Most didn't have enough to eat or drink.

In the year following Ceausescu's overthrow, thousands of people rushed to Romania to adopt these abandoned children. When they arrived at their new homes, a large number of the children were developmentally delayed. Many either refused solid foods or didn't know when to stop eating. They rocked back and forth; stared at their hands. They were indiscriminately friendly to strangers. They didn't know how to mix with other children.

The adopted children from Romania provided scientists with a unique opportunity to study the impact of institutionalisation on the developing brain. Electronic brain scans of some of the children showed low activity or even black holes in the active areas where interpretation of language, emotions and attention would normally occur.

Controversial neurobiologist Dr Bruce Perry, author of *Incubated in Terror*, stated publicly, 'Broken bones will heal, but a brain damaged by neglect is very hard to heal.' In his lectures, Perry shows slides of infant brains, shrunken from neglect, and states he firmly believes that just as the brain allows us to see, smell, taste, think, talk and move, it is the organ that allows us to love — or not:

> The systems in the human brain that allows us to form and maintain emotional relationships develop during infancy and the first years of life. Experiences during this early vulnerable period of life are critical to shaping the capacity to form intimate and emotionally healthy relationships.

Perry's views did not go unchallenged. Some of his colleagues were concerned that this new science of infant determinism was unduly pessimistic about children who had suffered a rough start in life. They questioned Perry's statement that 'the brain is cooked by the age of three.'

Two longitudinal studies of the Romanian children have shown a dramatic catch-up, particularly in cognitive skills. In a landmark five-year study of forty-six Romanian children who had been living with adoptive parents in Canada since 1990–91, Dr Elinor Ames of Simon Fraser University, British Columbia, found that one-third were doing very well, one-third had only a few problems, and one-third still had developmental, social and behavioural difficulties.

Ames believed that the two-thirds of children who were doing well would probably keep making good progress, but said she was worried about the other one-third. Most of them had stayed in the orphanages longer and were adopted by parents with fewer resources, or into families who took more than one orphan at the same time.

'In some cases, the parents were just overwhelmed,' Ames said. How they fared would depend on their parents' ability to seek and accept help for themselves and their children.

Similarly positive was a 1998 British study which followed one hundred and eleven children who were adopted at the age of two years or less. Michael Rutter, doyen of English resilience research, concluded that recovery from a deprived background is possible with the right level of subsequent care. Even severe deprivation doesn't necessarily lead to irreversible psychological problems. Contrary to expectations, many of the older children also fared well and had made substantial gains by the time they were six years old. However, even when their new environments were very good, there were sometimes persistent symptoms — the children had problems with close inter-personal relationships. Rutter wondered whether there was some kind of social equivalent to the blocking of vision at an early age. A critical factor seemed to be the length of time the children had been in the orphanages.

In a book called *Early Experience and the Life Path*, two emeritus professors of psychology, Ann and Alan Clarke, suggested that genetic factors might explain why some of the older children did well in cognitive tests. They were cautionary about forming judgements too soon. 'The search for effects of early experiences is a much more complex enterprise than was first realised,' the Clarkes wrote. 'Early experience represents no more than a first (and important) step on a long and complex path through life.'

That may be true — and I'm sure it is — but as I read and drank my coffee, I wondered yet again about our failure to shore up vulnerable families. My mind returned to a meeting on child abuse I had attended several years ago, and how angry I had been, asking why we kept mopping up after the damage had occurred, instead of trying to prevent it in the first place.

This issue of prevention and early intervention had frustrated me for years — going back to the Royal Commission on Human Relationships in the mid-1970s when Australians started to hear mounting evidence of child abuse. It had always existed but had rarely been publicly acknowledged. This was the first major public exposure of the extent of child abuse in Australia. Throughout my work as a commissioner, I became increasingly aware that child abuse and neglect happen at all levels of society, but that many of the root causes lie in fundamental social problems such as poverty, long-term unemployment, mental illness, rising levels of substance abuse and family violence. I could see how important it was to intervene and help vulnerable families long before difficulties reached the stage where abuse occurred or the child's development was jeopardised. Every year, small children die from assault or neglect. Others grow up in misery with deep emotional scars, often turning to drugs, crime or self-harm. In fact, child abuse and neglect is the single most important causal factor in juvenile crime, according to Australian researchers Don Weatherburn and Bronwyn Lind. The authors believe that positive parenting programs could well be the most effective way of reducing juvenile crime rates. For every thousand neglected children in New South Wales, twenty-five per cent face charges in the Children's Court. Yet most parents desperately hope the best for their children.

After hearing the Commission's evidence, I made a dramatised documentary called 'Do I Have to Kill My Child?' about a woman's desperate attempts to get help before she harmed her child. It was screened on prime-time television, then I took it round childcare centres and primary schools. When I asked my audience of young mothers if any had ever felt like the woman in the film, there was always a

RESILIENCE

silence — so absolute it had its own kind of reverberation. If I then said, 'because I have', a chorus of voices swelled in immediate relief.

What does this have to do with resilience? Plenty. Risk, stress and resilience are intertwined. Without risk we would not be talking about resilience. Sleep deprivation is a risk factor for a new mother, and indirectly for her baby, but it is also part of a process stretching back into the past and forward into the future. A baby might be unwell, or hungry, or particularly nervy. It might be a first-born, with an anxious mother who is on her own, or has a partner who gets enraged when the baby cries. Perhaps she is lonely — she has only recently moved, doesn't have any friends, her family is in another state. Or she's broke, can't afford childcare, and is worried about having to work. The impact of risk factors is cumulative and interlinked; start putting them together and you have a scenario for tragedy.

Take another scenario — a real one, which I filmed. It's the story of a man, a woman and two very young children who have newly settled in an outer suburb of Sydney. The man works in a car factory on one side of town, the woman in a pie factory on the other. Childcare is somewhere in the middle. They rise early in the morning — 5.30 a.m. and still pitch dark — wake the two small children, feed one in the car, grab bottles for the other, can't find the nappies, start fighting because of lack of sleep. In the evening they get home by seven, turn on the television, reach for the tranquillisers, open the beer, shout at the kids, and end up taking sleeping tablets before bed. In lives that teeter on the edge of such exhaustion there is little time for love, and none for play. Not a good start for those two little children. Not a good life for the parents.

Protective factors can help buffer the risk illustrated in these examples. Family, friends, kind neighbours, someone to talk to, or give two hours child-minding relief, a neighbourhood centre which can help with parenting and examine why the baby cries so much — all that ordinary, everyday stuff. Research corroborates the fact that families in neighbourhoods with higher rates of abuse have fewer available supports and smaller social networks than families in neighbourhoods where abuse occurs less frequently. Surprise, surprise.

Risk is a process and each risk has its own history and context. The same feature might be a risk factor in one situation, but a protective factor in another. A demanding baby might be at risk of parental violence in a socially isolated home, but — as I found — more likely to be heard, and thus to survive, in a refugee camp in Africa.

There is no magic formula. It has been well established by resilience researchers like Michael Rutter that each person's reaction to adverse experiences is highly individual and influenced by whatever else is happening in their lives. Furthermore, you might be resistant to one form of stress, and go to pieces with another.

One of the pioneers in the field of early childhood development has been distinguished haematologist turned social scientist, Professor Fraser Mustard. During the 1980s, he was working at the Canadian Institute for Advanced Research and headed the Early Years Task Force in Ontario, Canada. For many years, he had been concerned that children were bearing the brunt of global technological and social change. He immersed himself in a study of the nexus between social and biological influences, trying to find out what factors in a child's early years made a difference to their lives.

In 1982, he brought together scientists, economists, social workers, historians, physicists and sociologists in an effort to change the Canadian government's focus. If they wanted a dynamic and economically successful society in thirty years' time, he said, the most important thing was to provide good parenting and nutrition to children from birth to the age of five. The idea wasn't new, but his approach was.

By pushing the economic line, he ensured that politicians listened to him. He showed that good parenting, not money, is the direct driver of literacy, cognition and coping skills in adult life. Any government that backs early childhood development, he said, will see the benefits twenty years later in better citizens and less drain on taxes.

Mustard looked at the effects that upheaval had on health and behaviour. After times of great social stress, the effect was seen some decades later in chronic health problems, and in children's IQs, behaviour and social skills. Even the probability of going to jail was affected by what happened to a child in those first twelve months of life. More than forty international studies have shown that a poor start in life increases the likelihood of poor physical and mental health, a disappointing record at school, low success in the job market, and greater involvement in crime.

The most famous study in this area was one of the earliest. It began in 1962 in Ypsilanti, Michigan, as a longitudinal study of one hundred and twenty-three children from poor families who were at risk of failing in school. Five days a week, these children attended a special pre-school progam aimed at giving them maximum interaction and stimulation. The program was known as the Perry Pre-school Project. Parents were involved and teachers made weekly home visits to the families. A control group of children who didn't receive the program continued as they always had, going to whatever childcare was available or else none. The trial stopped as soon as the children started school, usually when they were six.

Ongoing assessments of these children show startling outcomes. On every scale, the children who went to the special pre-school fared infinitely better than children in the control group. There were increases in cognitive gains; improved scholastic achievement; increases in post-secondary enrolment; increases in high school graduation and employment rates. Crime and teenage pregnancies were forty per cent less. At the age of twenty-seven, only seven per cent of the women in the intervention group had mental health problems compared with forty per cent in the other group. Benefits exceeded costs sevenfold.

If these figures seem hard to believe — and they did for me — go back to the knowledge we now possess about the critical importance of early stimulation to the developing brain. Reading stories to a small baby is not only a cosy, loving pleasure, but it's driving at least five sensory pathways, all feeding into the brain, which then feeds into other control systems — even though the baby may not understand a word.

Mustard says that in our highly mobile societies where families fragment, money is not the biggest driver in pre-dicting social outcomes. Parenting is. This doesn't mean it's necessary to have a mother (or father) at home twenty-four hours a day, but parents who work, or who require help for whatever reasons, need good support systems. It is of limited value to have day-time childcare that is simply baby-sitting. Children require and deserve the very best kind of care — it can be a huge buffering influence if families are going through difficult times.

Convincing politicians and funding bodies of the importance of those early years used to be a long hard haul. Even now I have dismal memories of chairing children's and youth committees which were constantly starved of funds. Children's needs were dumped in the touchy-feely basket and weren't taken seriously until scientists stepped in with this whole new field of discovery about the developing brain. Governments in many countries of the world are now responding with a range of community-based early intervention programs. In many cases, the money is less than fabulous, but at least it's a beginning and it's certainly an improvement on the 'patch-it-up later' approach of earlier times. So is a new national research alliance for children and youth headed by Professor Fiona Stanley, which will coordinate research and lobby for improved policies and practices affecting children's lives. In Australia, the New South Wales government was the first to back early childhood programs. I think it is ironic that we had to wait for scientific evidence about the possibility of building children's performance levels and saving money before stirring ourselves to act. In the Western world we've always been high on rhetoric about children being the future of the nation — even the future of mankind — but fairly consistently we have put children at the bottom of the pile. In future, don't be impressed by politicians kissing babies. Ask what they're actually *doing* for them.

To be fair, this isn't just the province of the political scene. I think of public arguments about children being a private responsibility and not a social good; I think of new housing developments which don't allow children, and the loss of open public space where children can play; I think of parents working harder and longer hours while their children are pushed into adult-structured activities to keep them busy or help them succeed. In this downgrading of children, there is less community support and less social capital, while governments struggle to handle increasing numbers of children in crisis. Good things only happen for children when good things are provided.

I realised the critical importance of children getting the best start in life when my youngest child was born eleven and a half weeks premature. When he was delivered into my arms he was barely recognisable as a baby. He weighed less than one pound. I had scarcely stroked a finger across his crinkled red forehead before he was whisked away. His lungs weren't fully developed and he was having trouble breathing. I was not to know it would be weeks before I could hold or even touch him again. He went in one direction, I went in another. But there was another problem. I was drunk. Uproariously, hopelessly drunk. For the four preceding days, I had been on a neat alcohol drip to relax my muscles — an unorthodox Danish treatment to delay the birth. It probably saved his life. It jollied up mine.

I sobered when I was told our baby only had a five to ten per cent chance of survival. Each day the odds increased. In those days, no one other than nursing staff was allowed in the premature babies' nursery, except for an hour every day when parents could enter and look helplessly through the transparent walls of the humidicribs at these strange little beings.

'But he hasn't a chin,' I wailed. 'Do you think he'll ever have a chin?'

'He will have a chin,' promised the doctor — and he does, a most excellent chin.

My overwhelming need then was to reach out and touch this child of ours, to remind him that my blood had flowed through to his blood, that he was not alone. I tried to get him to look at me, even though I knew his vision would be blurred, but his jerky little arms and legs convulsed around his body and he turned away.

'Isn't he beaut?' said a laconic voice over my shoulder. A tall, angular woman was beaming down at this shrivelled little baby of mine. She said her name was Sister Helen and she was in charge of the premature babies' ward.

'Don't worry,' she said, 'he's a fighter, he'll survive.'

Sister Helen had never married, never had children, but she loved these premature babies as if they were her own. I watched her as she touched them, sang and talked to them, insisted on naming them if parents weren't forthcoming — perhaps fearful in case they died. She decorated their humidicribs with collages of surf boards, flowers, stars, the sun, the moon and, as they slowly grew large enough to wear a nappy, she brought in her own store of face washers, cut in two because even a face washer would have been too big.

'Gotta do better than hospital white,' she said. 'Give 'em a bit of fun. Passion purple. Hot orange. Wild red. What d'ya think your boy would like?' Mostly he wore green.

She knew it was hard for the mothers — we who had failed to deliver full-term babies, and who pumped ourselves like dairy cows day and night. If our babies were too fragile to cope with human milk, our milk went into a common pool. We sat opposite one another, feet spread apart, maternity bras dangling round our waists, as we went to work with the dreaded and painful pump. *Pump, suck, ouch* ... *pump, suck, ouch* ... big creamy breasts with large, dark brown aureoles; little breasts, white-skinned and pert; old breasts, sagging but serviceable; young breasts, tender and pink. (There is nothing like giving birth and breast-feeding to remind us we are primates, not Barbie dolls.) We provided the milk, Sister Helen provided what hospital insistence on separation denied us from giving: talking, touching and loving.

Several weeks later, I learned that the survival rate for premature babies in Sister Helen's ward was the highest in New South Wales. During the data collection, every technical and physiological measurement had almost certainly been made. I wondered how they measured love.

For millions of years, babies have been born with everything needed for deep connection with other human beings. It's that holding and loving that allows a baby to feel it has a safe base from which to start exploring the world. 'A web of connectedness' — a phrase I had used with Robert. He liked this image of our human need to make connection with one another, whatever our age.

He summed it up in an email:

Increasingly it seems that we need to rebuild at much smaller levels of neighbourhood, and develop the kind of face-to-face interactions where groups are small enough to make connection at very personal levels. It's that old adage: 'It takes a village to raise a child' — and we've lost our villages. We need to allow people to talk through a growing feeling that society needs to be more compassionate, and to take better care of the children we bring into the world.

5

A great world to be in

Mid-April, with strong winds almost blowing people off their feet. An umbrella and a man's hat had just gone flying through the air as Robert and I were walking across Sydney's Hyde Park. He had flown in from Los Angeles early that morning, and suggested meeting at the YMCA where he was staying and then going for breakfast. I had been curious to see if I would recognise him. I did. I had also been curious to see if I would still find him attractive. I did. I made a mental note to fasten seat belts and enjoy the ride.

'Why are you staying at the YMCA?' I asked.

'I'm broke,' he said cheerfully. 'I have debts to pay.'

Later, I learned he was careless about the business side of his life. Sometimes he failed to charge for his work, sometimes he charged too little; sometimes he negotiated inadequate contracts, sometimes they were good contracts which he left unsigned.

We talked some more about the Canberra seminar coming up in September and he said again, 'It's great to be involved with somebody who not only has ideas but also thinks about how they can be implemented. You're a joy. You're more than a glass half-full person; you're a glass overflowing.'

I said that the first time I heard about half-full and half-empty glasses — never mind ones that were overflowing — I was twenty and living in Paris. An American student had paid me the glass half-full compliment, and it had delighted me.

'Why were you in Paris?' Robert asked.

'I was working for a Hungarian economist on the French magazine, *Realités*, living in one room, lighting fires in a tin bidet to keep myself warm, hanging around Sartre and De Beauvoir at the *Deux Magots* cafe.'

I recognised I was showing off, so I told him a different story from my past: the story of my mother being stuck in an outside lift in Paris on the day World War Two was declared. 'It was one of those old-fashioned ones, like a bird-cage, with lots of glass.'

'Was she frightened?"

'I don't know. I was nine and more interested in whether people could see up her skirt.'

He laughed. He had two meetings that morning, followed by a lunch-time lecture and a media gathering at the end of the day. In between our conversation he stirred his coffee and forgot to drink it, put jam on his toast and failed to eat it. He reminded me of Mr Duffy in Joyce's *The Dubliners*: 'Mr Duffy lived a short distance from his body. He developed a life-style which did not require his presence.'

Before Robert and I parted, he asked if he could make a quick visit to my house sometime in the afternoon. He said he wanted to see where I lived.

Where I live is a trifle eccentric. It started life as a corner butcher's shop, then became an organic fruit and vegetable store, followed by a furniture and antique shop. When I bought it, it consisted of the shop (a large handsome room despite all that dead meat), rooms at the back and rooms upstairs, a shed, an outside dunny and one straggling banana palm. I ploughed up the concrete back yard, knocked down walls, turned the cool-room into a bathroom, and planted trees and a garden.

Then I tackled something the local council euphemistically called a 'nature strip'. Nature strips bring order to the suburbs of Australia. Every fortnight, they are mowed, watered, and their edges whipper-snipped by a gardening implement that looks and sounds like a weapon of mass destruction. My nature strip when I arrived was a patch of coarse grass, brown and sandy in summer, weed-ridden in winter. When my local council agreed to let me substitute something they called a 'pocket park', I whipped in Australian native plants, banksia, wattle, grevillia, westringia and several varieties of grasses. In the right environment they flourished — I guess that applies to us all.

I was out calling the cat early one evening when an elderly neighbour gripped me by the arm, and pointed to my 'pocket park'. 'Now listen, love, we all like bush, but this is the suburbs, right?' He walked on for a few seconds and then turned. 'You never know who might be hiding in there.'

I could use this anecdote as a morality tale and say Australia's current obsession with safety, as well as our desire to litigate at the slightest opportunity, indicates a decline in resilience. When Prince Charles in England wrote to his local MP and complained bitterly that some magnificent chestnut trees had been cut down for fear the conkers would fall on people's heads, I understood his rage.

My small 'park' on the nature strip now grows spiky grasses that can cut, leaves that are prickly and oleanders that are poisonous. A few exotics have crept in among the natives. Apart from the oleander, a frangipani sticks its plump bare arms in the air, an olive tree struggles to survive, and some orange and red nasturtiums have seeded themselves. When Robert turned up he regarded the nasturtiums with a quizzical expression. 'You're harbouring aliens,' he teased.

Inside the house, he wandered restlessly round the down-stairs rooms. He looked at books and pictures, asked for a glass of water, stroked the little cat and the large dog and told me that when he and his wife Jeanne lived in Arizona, they made their house home to an indeterminate number of cats who kept bringing in other cats, most of which were dying.

'We gave them food and love, and they recovered.'

As we talked, I began doodling on the morning newspaper.

'What's that?'

'Portrait of a resilient person.'

'It looks like an octopus.'

'It's a resilient octopus. Are you a resilient person? You must be.'

'Yes, I think I'm resilient. I have good genes,' he said boastfully.

'I have a good skeleton,' I said, equally boastfully. 'An Austrian physiotherapist in Adelaide once told me, "Goodness gracious, what a good skeleton you have."'

We were making small flirtatious forays, two steps forward, one hasty step back, retreating into the safe territory of work. My drawing of a resilient person was prompted by our musings about the qualities which might help protect people against adversity. Much of the literature threw up laundry lists of personality characteristics that would enable resilience. I did not find this particularly helpful, given that we now know our competence in the world results from complex interactions between ourselves and our environment — thus competence changes as we develop, or as the context changes.

The characteristics that help a person in one situation might well hinder them in another. For example, the resilience — and survival — of a juvenile gang member might depend on aggression, but that same aggression could be counter-productive in an employment situation later in life. A shy young woman probably wouldn't do well in a Nebraska cheer squad, but might thrive in a Buddhist retreat.

I went to Uganda at the time of Idi Amin's overthrow, and travelled in the company of the head of a major aid agency, a man with a charismatic personality, who had shown leadership, resilience and vision in his job. He was a devout Christian and had survived a major personal tragedy in his life, yet he was responsible for one of the most frightening experiences of my life. Tanzanian soldiers had poured over the borders to help liberate the country from Amin's oppression. At a road block near the Tanzanian border, a boy soldier who was clearly drunk, stopped our car and pulled us out, one by one, waving his gun. 'The charismatic leader' would not put up with being manhandled in this way, and lost his temper, shouting at the soldier, who reacted by lining us up in the boiling sun for several hours, his finger poised the whole time on the trigger of his gun. The very qualities that had served my companion well, including a somewhat autocratic personality, nearly resulted in our deaths.

• • •

Many of the early theories about resilience focused on the role of genetics. Today we know that although genes and personality are important, we are influenced by our environment from the moment of conception. Who we are, and what happens to us, helps determine how we deal with life — whether we are vulnerable to anxiety and stress; whether we are inhibited or uninhibited; how we tackle adversity; how we interact with others.

One of the most useful models for understanding child development and resilience is a bio-ecological model, developed by Professor Urie Bronfenbrenner from Cornell University. Bronfenbrenner views the child as a living system, embedded within many other systems, such as families, schools, work and the wider environment. The environment is therefore like a series of nested structures, each one exerting its own particular set of influences which, in turn, interact with each other and with the whole.

The term 'microsystem' refers to a child's immediate surroundings and includes parents, as well as close members of the family, and friends who are involved with the child's development. At this level — since all relationships are bi-directional and reciprocal — the child's biological and socially determined characteristics also influence the behaviour of adults. For example, a friendly, attentive child is more likely to evoke patient and positive reactions from parents, whereas a difficult, high-energy child might meet with restriction and punishment. Some of these personality characteristics are present from the moment of birth. People who have had more than one child often remark how different they are. One baby is fretful and agitated, another calm and serene; one snuggles, another doesn't seem to like being held and sticks a foot up the parental nose, or turns turtle and almost falls to the floor.

The second level of nested systems which have a bearing on children's development (the 'mesosystem') includes child-rearing programs, home, school, neighbourhood and community. The third level (the 'exosystem') refers to social settings that don't contain children but affect what happens to them — such as the parents' workplace, or health and welfare services. If a mother is the primary caregiver and is working somewhere that doesn't provide flexible work arrangements or paid maternity and sick leave, this will impinge upon a child's life.

The fourth level (the 'macrosystem') consists of the values, laws and customs of a particular culture. The priority that the macrosystem places on children's needs will affect the support children receive at other levels of the environment.

Within all these systems, life experiences are continually at work, and according to Colin Blakemore, Chairman of the British Association for the Advancement of Science, 'There is a mass of evidence that people can become other people despite the disposition of their genes.'

The genes that excite Blakemore are the ones that allow the human brain to respond to life's experiences by making new connections and structures. 'Experience genes' give us the capacity to learn, to remember, to develop cultural and social interactions. They are the genes that release us from the genetic constraints of our own DNA.

When I scoured the literature to see if there were any overarching characteristics that defined a resilient child (or adult), I was caught by Moira Rayner and Meg Montague's review of international literature. They identified resilience as the presence, at any given moment, of emotional maturity or 'emotional intelligence', characterised by self-esteem and self-confidence; the capacity to create and maintain friendships with peers and to gain the support of adults; a well-founded sense of trust; a sense of purpose; a set of values and beliefs that guide responses to the world; and a feeling of having some kind of 'internal locus of control'. Yet we have to look at these resilience characteristics as being dynamic, not uniformly applicable.

Resilience based on self-esteem doesn't come from telling children they are doing well, if they're not. It could do more harm than good. It's wiser to give children opportunities where they can genuinely shine, and out of that will come a real sense of self-esteem.

Cognitive competence also helps, but isn't essential. For example, many children who aren't considered intellectually very bright may nevertheless have well-developed emotional competence. They might also be better than other children at seeking help, mainly because this is a skill they have learned in order to cope with life.

Two years ago, I was escorting a friend's niece off the Palm Beach ferry so she could catch a bus to town. Margaret is in her early forties and has Down's Syndrome. Suddenly she flung herself at my feet, clasping her hands and literally beating her breast. 'I want to marry Phillip,' she announced out of the blue. 'Help me! Help me! I want to marry Phillip.'

'Who?' I asked, bewildered. I didn't know Phillip. I had never heard about a marriage.

By now, a small crowd was gathering around us. 'Help me!' Margaret repeated, drumming her feet on the wooden boards of the jetty.

'Yeah, why shouldn't she marry Phillip?' said a man with a large belly and a small fishing rod.

'Tell me about Phillip and why you love him?' asked a woman in a voice of saccharine understanding.

Margaret rose and planted her stocky legs wide apart, firmly fixed to the ground. 'Help me,' she repeated. The crowd murmured disapprovingly at my intransigence.

Margaret collapsed on the jetty again. She lay flat on her back, arms outstretched as if she were pinned to the cross. 'I'm not leaving till you tell me I can marry Phillip,' she said.

Later, I learned that Phillip — who was blind and had cerebral palsy and limited intellectual ability — didn't want to marry Margaret. He had looked alarmed and confused at the proposition when it was first put to him.

'Margaret's my friend,' he had said.

Nevertheless I was impressed by Margaret's ability to express her desires. She had a formidable sense of drama and went on to act professionally in television programs requiring someone with Down's Syndrome in the cast.

'Relational competence' it would seem, is another useful quality. It refers to the ability to recruit people who can help. People with easygoing, friendly dispositions are more likely to enlist help than those who are surly or aloof. The Search Institute, a Minneapolis-based non-profit organisation that focuses on resilience and youth, found that resilient youth had an uncanny ability to get adults to help them out. But the child who is a misfit, for whatever reason, can learn to be liked or, at least, to avoid being teased. Part of this attribute involves the ability to make and keep friends. This doesn't necessarily mean being the most popular child in the school, but being able to choose a couple of friends who will be there for the long haul.

American author Judith Rich Harris challenges the primacy of parents in her book, *The Nurture Assumption*, in which she claims that after a certain age, parents don't matter all that much; a child's peer group is much more important.

Resilience literature stresses the importance of peer relationships for learning to share, to empathise, to control impulses and to develop communication skills.

Looking back, I don't think I featured very well in this regard. My mother played plenty of games with me — Snakes and Ladders, walking in puddles whenever it rained, making honeycomb toffee, Murder in the Dark — but she left my pre-War upbringing to a traditional English nanny who reared me on maxims like: 'Patience is a virtue/ Possess it if you can/Seldom found in woman/And never found in man.'

I was kept away from other children because Nanny feared they might be rough. I didn't even have my brother for a playmate; he was at boarding school. In consequence, I was socially inept and would do anything to gain approval from adults and children alike.

I have a memory of me at the age of about five, wearing bronze dancing slippers with elastic that crossed at the front, being taken to the drawing room where my parents were having a cocktail party, and lisping in front of the guests, 'I'm so happy, I'm so happy, I'm so good.' At the same time, I was scheming how to pinch two asparagus rolls by stuffing them up my knickers.

Not long after this I went to a posh children's party, where we played Pin the Tail on the Donkey. I was about to win. Only one more child was left to play, a little girl with ringlets, dressed in pink. She was blindfolded and guided to the board. Her hand hovered. I held my breath. When it looked as if she was going to hit the precise target, I sniggered. Loudly, deliberately and with venomous intent. She shifted her hand. She lost. I won. I suppose a kindly view of such devious behaviour would be to describe it as adaptive resilience: how to get what you want, by fair means or foul.

Having a sense of belonging and meaning in life is obviously important to the development of resilience. One of the largest studies involving people recovering from alcoholism and drug addiction found that higher religious faith and spirituality were associated with increased coping skills, greater resilience to stress, an optimistic life orientation, greater perceived social support and lower levels of anxiety.

Harold Koenig, director and founder of the Center for the Study of Religion/Spirituality and Healing at Duke University in the US, goes out on a limb when he states that heathenism is a health hazard. Koenig says there is not only a connection between religion and longevity but also between religion and general good health, lowered chance of drug abuse, alcoholism, depression and suicide. Not only did religion provide a greater sense of hope, but often it also provided a supportive community. According to the *Medical Journal of Australia* the number of articles presenting original research on the relationship between spirituality and health has increased six-fold over the past decade. Researchers have found that greater participation in religious activities is associated with better health outcomes.

My main concern about these findings is that most of the studies of spirituality and health have examined adherence to religious beliefs and practices, rather than a more broadly defined idea of spirituality. Having a sense of connectedness and meaning in life gives us resilience, but this connectedness can come in many different ways, not only from the blueprint of a particular religious institution. We can draw resilience simply from a profound wonder at the beauty and mystery of life, and from the way in which everything is connected to everything else. Remember those lines of the mystical poet, Francis Thompson:

All things by immortal power near or far,
Hiddenly to each other linked are
That thou canst not stir a flower
Without the troubling of a star.

People who have survived terrible accidents often talk about their zest for life, their joy in living. It shines out of them. Australian world-class cross-country skier, Janine Shepherd, was critically injured in a terrible road accident during the period leading up to the 1988 Winter Olympics in Calgary. When she was asked why some survive such terrible accidents and others go under, she said, 'When it comes down to it, I think it's that fighting spirit, that will to live. A certain belief that it's a great world to be in, no matter what happens.'

She thinks it is possible to change negative attitudes, and make a positive decision to switch to optimism. 'Because I was an athlete I always had a powerful body. Since the accident my power isn't physical any more. It is emotional and mental. I have learnt to use my mind to create the person that I want to be — a person who can do anything they want to do.'

Life is not necessarily a matter of holding good cards, but of being helped to play a poor hand well. Those children who draw a genetic short straw and are born with something like Huntington's Chorea or cystic fibrosis might process a luminous resilience of spirit which comes from their own temperament — and, perhaps, an exceptionally loving family.

I think of a friend of mine, Jacob Baldwin, quick-thinking, audacious, a persistent optimist. He was born in China, three months premature, and had such severe cerebral palsy that he spent the next twenty-two years of his life in an institution which his doctors told him he would never leave. When he told his school headmistress he wanted to be a physiologist, she said, in a benevolent tone, 'You can't do that, Jacob, you're a spastic.'

He says his mother and adoring Russian grandmother always believed that his life had a reason. They saw his cerebral palsy as a key to unlocking his mind and his heart. He eventually left the institution, became a prime mover in the International Year of Disabled Persons (1981) and Australia's first Rehabilitation Counsellor with a classified disability. He circled Australia in a motorised wheelchair to raise money for cerebral palsy, a journey that took four years and was filmed for Australian television. To promote the film he went bungy-jumping and drove the first wheelchair to cross the Sydney Harbour Bridge in peak-hour traffic. He is now happily married, lives in Byron Bay, and runs his own successful training business — the Australian Company of Ethical Network Trainers.

When I last met him, he was wearing a black Akubra hat and driving a wheelchair with red streamers flying from the back. He still has to control his spasms and sometimes his speech is hard to understand, but all this is overshadowed by his enormous vitality. 'To me, resilience is the ability to tap into hope. I've never viewed myself as disabled. Different, yes. Able to achieve things in an unusual way, yes. But I've never looked in a mirror and said, "You're disabled."'

One of the giants in childhood development, researcher, psychologist and author Martin Seligman, challenges the pessimistic beliefs that pervade Western society when he says, 'The remarkable attitude of resilience need not be a mystery. It is not inborn. It can be learned.'

After brooding for years about human aberrance and anxiety, Seligman made a scholarly about-face into the study of human strengths and positive emotions. He claims that not only can children learn to alter their attitude, but adults too can make a choice. He tells the story of how, shortly after taking over the presidency of the American Psychological Association, he was weeding in his garden when his five-year-old daughter Nicki began singing and tossing the weeds in the air. He lost his temper.

She looked at him in exasperation. 'Daddy, do you remember before I was five? From when I was three to five, I was a whinger. I whinged every day. When I turned five, I decided not to whinge anymore. It was the hardest thing I've ever done. And if I can stop whingeing, you can stop being such a grouch.'

Seligman said this spurred his desire to change his life. 'I had spent 50 years mostly enduring wet weather in my soul, and the last 10 years being a nimbus cloud in a household full of sunshine. I resolved to be different.'

He maintains that as adults we are free to change. Our parents do not frog-march us at the age of six into being guilty thirty-year-olds. We aren't forced to become alcoholics even if our biological parents are alcoholics. 'We are not prisoners of our past. How we were raised — by authoritarians, or permissive parents; how we were fed — on demand or according to schedules, on breast or on bottle; even our mother's death, or our parents' divorce, exert, at most, small influences on what we are like as adults.'

Whether it's as easy as that is an interesting point of

debate. Australians have one famous example of mid-life change of heart: former Australian Prime Minister, Malcolm Fraser, who, in his later years, seems to have mellowed and grown wise beyond seeming belief.

At one level, what Seligman offers is exciting. We are not stuck with ourselves as we are. We can change. Nor are we hemmed in by lists of virtues we don't possess. If we can learn to tackle negativity in our lives and be optimistic, we can also learn to be resilient. But I have reservations — no, call them observations. Some people suffer from such terrible, black depressions that it will take more than learned optimism to make them feel well. And whatever our age, environmental influences will always impinge upon our wellbeing and our lives.

When I was in despair about Jonathan one day — he had just absconded from hospital for the third time — a psychiatrist offered me therapy to deal with my deep-seated childhood unhappiness — his view, not mine.

'Stop my son from running away,' I said tartly.

For me now, the heartland of understanding resilience resides in a statement by eminent English psychiatrist, Michael Rutter. He said that resilient people are formed by more than just their genes or their temperament. Rather, it is the way they engage and respond to situations in life.

By now, I realised engagement with others was one of Robert's strengths — his passion, humour, curiosity and intense interest in other people. When I joined him at a media gathering above an inner-city pub, he was urging people to get together in small groups and talk about the kind of future they wanted. Someone demurred: 'You can't make changes just by making places for people to have conversations. What's that all about?'

Robert nodded. 'People are sick of griping and groaning,' he said. 'They want to talk about where they could be going. Not about how they're stuck.'

'Yes, but the world is full of people talking. All talk and little action,' I said.

'It's only when people change their thinking that action follows.'

'Sometimes you need to act before you change the way you think.'

'You need both approaches,' he said calmly. 'As I've grown older, I've recognised that the way I live is far more critical than the actions I take. Fundamental change in thinking isn't triggered intellectually. It's more emotional than that.'

So here was this tall, gangly man with the large Akubra hat and the mission to wake people to the need for change. A wide and sweeping vision set against the backdrop of crises: technological crises, ecological crises, moral crises, social crises. It would be easy to descend into psychic numbness. But Robert didn't.

On the drive back to the YMCA, I asked, 'Don't you get tired?'

He sounded surprised. 'No, not often. My work seems to give me energy rather than take it away. Will you write the foreword for my next book?' he asked suddenly. 'It's called *Yes, We Do Have Future Choices*. Do you like the title?'

Long ago, I recognised I'm not good on titles — ever since I made a film on discrimination called, 'They Smell Different', which sounded fine until it appeared on the television screen as 'They Smell Different with Anne Deveson'.

I said that the current fashion was for snappy titles, like 'Rape', 'Arson', 'Mayhem', 'Blood'.

He laughed. 'My title says what I mean: It's not too late for us to have choices. But we'd better hurry up about it.'

He was due back in a week, and would spend one night in Sydney before flying home to the United States. I asked him to dinner with some friends. The following day, he came to lunch before leaving for the airport. Light was shining through my kitchen window as I looked at this man who would be flying off any minute to start another round of lectures in the United States. He radiated energy and explained that each speech charged him up again — and no, he wasn't trying to be a guru. 'Gurus make a lot of money,' he said ruefully.

'Do you honestly think you can change enough people's ideas and actions to make a difference?'

He hesitated. 'Sometimes I think we're heading into trouble very fast. But I daren't stay with that kind of thought.' He got up from the table. 'People are wiser than we give them credit for.'

I reflected that he was himself a good example of resilience. Quite apart from the huge pace of his work, he'd had enough setbacks in the last three years to defeat most people. He and his wife, Jeanne, had divorced after forty years of marriage. The Canadian Broadcasting Company cancelled, at the last minute, the prestigious Massey lectures he was supposed to deliver. By the time he was diagnosed with oesophageal cancer — a cancer with a poor prognosis — he had no marriage, no money, no home and his work had collapsed. When old friends and colleagues, Bob Stilger and his wife Susan, suggested they look after him during his illness — or that they 'adopt' him into their family — he accepted, and went to live with them in Spokane.

When the taxi cab arrived, he hugged me and was gone, advising me out of the taxi window not to forget the bamboo steamer was under the sofa where he had found it the night before. From Sydney he was going to South Australia, then Western Australia. We would not meet again until September, five months away. As I watched him drive away, it struck me that our friendship was falling into the category of G.I.

'Geographically impossible,' was what we used to say at school.

6

families — we all have 'em

'I have no family,' said one of my children when he was eleven. He threw a tennis ball in the air and caught it. Then he threw it at the dog who chased it. He was acting casual but looked distressed. It was clearly no use saying, 'But you have family all over the world.' The fact that they were all over the world was part of the problem. So was our recent move from Sydney to Adelaide.

A kind relative, with whom I share one of those tortuous relationships several times removed, organised an assorted collection of family for us to meet when we made a special visit to Tasmania. She gathered everyone together in her enormous dining room in Hobart: aunts and uncles, cousins and second cousins, nephews and nieces. Roast lamb and three vegetables followed by trifle and cream. Family silver. Family jokes.

'Why did the chicken cross the road?'

'I dunno. Why did the chicken cross the road?'

'Because it saw a Kentucky fried. Get it?' A seven-year-old

boy cousin, his eyes shining, rocked with laughter from side to side.

On our flight back to Sydney, my son ate my peanuts as well as his, and said politely, 'I'm sorry, I don't mean to be difficult, but it still doesn't feel like family. I might never see them again.'

Clearly in his mind, family needed to be more accessible than a plane trip away across the Tasman sea. He felt his tribe was too dispersed for comfort.

The influence of family is one of the dominant themes in resilience literature. Families can be joyful and nurturing, the place where a child learns love and locates themselves in the world. Or families can be prisons of brutality and neglect, eroding a child's natural resilience, sometimes even destroying their ability to survive.

Much of the resilience literature presents proscriptive images of family life which are enough to make me head for the nearest chocolate bar or a swig of stiff gin. An online bulletin from Ohio State University summarises seventy-seven research sources in its recommendation of home environment factors which will help a child develop resilience. It is an intimidating list. Families apparently need to be caring, kind, supportive, temperate, affectionate, content; they need access to large numbers of alternative caregivers; they need to go to church, exercise wise and kindly discipline, develop their own set of values, have positive and high expectations but not be competitive or class-conscious; they need to establish daily routines, encourage hobbies, supervise daily chores, have ties with school and community, provide nourishing simple food, keep fit, and live in a house that is clean, neat and free of clutter. In times of duress the whole family will turn to God, think positively and look towards the future.

Hallelujah.

There's nothing *wrong* in any of that — except can any family live up to such impossibly high standards? It also fails to acknowledge the child part of the dynamic — expressed so brilliantly by Peter Ustinov's line in the book *Dear Me*: 'Parents are the bones upon which children sharpen their teeth.' I know I am taking an aggregate summary of the research so perhaps I am being a little unfair, but any advice which ignores the glorious, and at times inglorious, chaos of family life probably does more harm than good. Andrew Fuller's humorous and wise book, *Raising Real People, Creating a Resilient Family*, focuses on adolescence, and acknowledges that 'being the parent of an adolescent is more like being a correspondent at the front line in a dirty and shifting war.'

I know of only one family who seemed to achieve text-book perfection — a kind, loving family, who found themselves in the kind of trouble they could not have anticipated in their wildest dreams. The father was the editor of a geographical magazine, a mild man who wore russet hand-woven ties. The mother, once an academic, looked like Virginia Woolf and stayed contentedly at home. The parents and their five children lived a life of robust but simple pleasures in an English country house set in English pastures green. One day, the headmistress where the children went to school summoned the unsuspecting parents and informed them she was devastated to learn from their eldest daughter, Polly, of the crises in their home. She realised how hard it was for Matthew — my friend — to cope with his drinking prob-lems. She understood why Emma — his wife — had run to the bed of another man. She accepted that in these circumstances, Polly might find it hard to do her schoolwork and need to take up smoking — unfortunately in the school grounds.

The parents — my friends — were aghast. All this was news to them. When Polly was confronted, she confessed she had fabricated every word. 'Lighten up,' she said. 'We're all so jolly *boring*, I decided it was time to put some drama in our lives.'

There used to be an assumption that if you came from a 'dysfunctional' family (such a loaded word) you were doomed. But to some extent aren't all families dysfunctional in their own way? Maybe not all the time, but they can certainly wobble out of control with remarkable speed.

Middle-class families and middle-class therapists struggle with tensions between ideal and reality. My hobby as a child was stealing plants. My father went to church because he loved to sing, but he so embarrassed the rest of us that we refused to accompany him. When I was nineteen and suffering from my first broken heart, I quit university and went to bed where I ate and ate and ate. Finally my mother had the wit to tell me to 'work for a man with an interesting job'. I wanted an interesting job, so I rose from my bed of depression and despair. In Sydney, one of those bronzed West coast American therapists won over his audience when he confessed to mounting hysteria at the 'green slime' which oozed from the bedroom of his adolescent son.

In other words, the majority of us have lives of messy volatility, interspersed with periods of calm. We hang in the best way we can, and if we have any sense, enjoy as much as possible on the way.

Poor families are more vulnerable than middle-class families, not because they have less capacity to be resilient, but because they are likely to face more adversity in their lives. For quite a while, resilience researchers tended to focus on the big things that went wrong in people's lives — major traumas like war and death. But it is a cumulation of adversities — poverty, overcrowded homes, overcrowded schools, alcoholism or drug abuse, unemployment, sickness, separated families — that does the most harm and can damage the natural resistance of a child. A child is a living system, embedded within many other systems.

I remember a particularly hard time, after the war, when my family returned from Australia to England. My father was depressed and unemployed, debts mounted, the electricity was cut, we couldn't pay my school fees, my mother became ill, and I began truanting from school. Yet we were protected by middle-class expectations and a middle-class confidence that this wouldn't last for ever, and nor did it.

One factor relating to resilience stands out above everything else — children need a secure base from which to explore the world. Resilient children are said to be 'securely attached' children, whose most important need is to grow up with one or more adults who are there for the long haul. People who love and believe in them and will provide *consistent* emotional support are immensely important — ideally, parents play this role, but good relationships with other relatives or close family friends can also make a big difference in a child's life.

What happens if that security isn't there? What happens if a parent dies or walks out, or a safe home becomes unsafe? Risks are always present in our lives. If we escape them, it doesn't mean we are resilient. It means we are lucky. These are the times when protective factors need to kick in, either for the children, or for the parents who are under siege. When my seventeen-year-old son Jonathan developed schizophrenia, we had just come to live in a strange city and had few friends. Pure survival instincts saw me change from being someone who never asked for help to someone who asked for it wherever and whenever possible. A plumber came to mend my blocked drain and ended up sleeping on the sofa that night because Jonathan was psychotic and I was scared. A woman who had come to help me clean the house accompanied me to the magistrate's court when my son was arrested for stealing five bottles of Coke. Later, his probation officer extended her bounds of duty to become a family friend — a bridge between us and the chaos in my son's life.

One of the most important competencies we can give our children is this ability to link into their neighbourhoods and communities. Without a sense of connectedness, life can become fragile.

Emmy Werner's famous research in Hawaii, which followed two hundred high-risk children's progress from birth to the age of thirty-two, found the informal relationships worked best, not the formal ones. Grandparents, uncles, aunts, friends and teachers were the ones who brought resilience into young people's lives. Werner has suggested that programs should work towards strengthening informal ties rather than introducing additional layers of bureaucracy into the delivery of services for vulnerable children and their families.

There was a time in my adolescence when I assumed an air of superiority about family life. I used to infuriate my mother by reciting Ogden Nash: *One would be in less danger / From the wiles of the stranger / If one's own kin and kith / Were more fun to be with.* Now I am grown up I realise my family was a rare and eccentric lot. It included a grandfather who performed magic tricks, and an inventor uncle known as 'the Baron', whose inventions included one of the first monoplanes to fly the Atlantic, edible crockery which was marketed at the Ideal

Homes Exhibition, the first collapsible bicycle, and cars that ran on water. I had a veritable circus of relations who provided endless fascination. But they also provided something more.

Aunt Kate was the youngest of my great aunts, and belonged to my mother's side. Of all my relatives, she is the one I remember most. I write about her at some length because she falls into that category of important adults in my life, although at the time, I did not realise this.

She was a small woman with a determined chin, bright eyes, dark hair piled high on her head and held by a tortoise-shell comb, and a trim figure that looked as if it had been packaged into her tight-fitting black or dark red dresses. Small buttons ran from her neck to her waist, lots of beads and a lorgnette hung round her neck, and a roll-your-own cigarette was always somewhere near at hand. The cigarette was daring, but then lots of things about Aunt Kate were daring.

In her youth she had worked on my great-grandfather's newspaper in the north of England, then she had run away to live with Cyril, a shadowy figure who had been a businessman with a rolled umbrella and a bowler hat until he decided to become a professional gambler. When I asked her why she hadn't married Cyril, she said brusquely, 'He was already married — use your head, girl!'

As soon as Cyril embarked on his gambling career, Aunt Kate insisted he set her up in her own apartment in Hove, on the south coast of England where she was still living when I used to visit her as a schoolgirl. It had a dark red front door and three steep, stone steps which used to worry my mother in case Aunt Kate fell and injured herself. (Aunt Kate would snap that she would do no such thing. She was only seventy-five and well able to look after herself, thank you.)

Her apartment was an Aladdin's cave of books and papers,

beads and feathers, heavy velvet drapes, jewel boxes, political tracts on the growth of unionism and communism, photograph albums, and her Tarot cards wrapped in orange silk which she forbade me to touch because she said I might weaken their magic. It was a glorious hotch-potch of memorabilia, steeped in the smell of musk and cigars, and belonging to a small, determined soul who said that what she did with her life was her business and no one else's.

After tea and plum cake, she would take me walking along the Hove or Brighton sea fronts where retired couples braced themselves against chilly winds. Seagulls shrieked and whirled over our heads; Brighton pier stretched into the cold grey Atlantic sea. Old women with their stockings in wrinkles round their knees would emerge from dingy bed-sitters, hunting for a shilling for the gas meter or a tot of gin. Aunt Kate walked so quickly I was usually dragging behind — I had that ennui of adolescence — and she would snap at me to 'Hurry up, speak up, and put your shoulders back or you'll develop curvature of the spine.' Were she alive today, she'd still be telling me the same thing.

Every walk Aunt Kate and I enjoyed together always became an adventure. On Brighton pier we would put pennies into a large chrome machine where a life-sized model of someone called Madame Lola winked as she dispensed advice for the love-lorn on a printed card.

'Next week you will meet the love of your life. Take care, he is not the reliable kind.'

'I've already met *him*,' snapped Great Aunt Kate, putting a second penny into the machine for me.

'You are too passionate for your own good. Do not be led astray.'

I blushed. Aunt Kate tucked her arm in mine and led me away, remarking, 'Make sure you're well provided for.'

Sometimes we would stop to buy pink and white Brighton rock which she cheerfully said would rot my teeth, or we'd walk to an area known as The Lanes, where we'd fossick for old books and explore antique shops which sold everything from ruby-red glass to Victorian pistols. If the outing had pleased her, Aunt Kate would conclude the afternoon by reading my tea leaves in a cup of fine bone china, decorated with yellow peacocks and blue roses.

One holiday, when my mother and I knocked on her door, Aunt Kate greeted us with the news that Cyril had dropped dead at a casino in Monte Carlo, leaving her with nothing but his pin-striped suit and red spotted bow tie, returned in a beautifully wrapped box, compliments of the casino. (She never received his underpants — a fact that irritated her, as she was a woman of parsimonious bent.)

My mother asked what she was going to do, knowing almost certainly that Cyril had died penniless, and suggested she come and live with us in London.

'Certainly not!' said my aunt. She would become a professional clairvoyant and hold seances. She had been to so many, she knew exactly what to do. Furthermore, her American Indian spiritual guide would help her. She transferred her tarot cards from orange to purple silk, and bought herself a crystal ball. Her guide, who was called something like Big Bull, spoke to her clients with a disconcerting Yorkshire accent. (Big Bull also tippled sherry. I found rows of bottles under Cyril's desk where my aunt would sit in her role as clairvoyant.) Heaven help any clients who walked out her front door without leaving money in the bronze Indian bowl she kept conspicuously by her side. Stuffy relatives said Aunt Kate had gone nuts. My mother said she was resilient.

Why did I like her, even though she had such a sharp

tongue? She liked me, and that's always a good start. She gave me her time and was interested in what I had to say. Her honesty was important, as was her ability to turn boring walks into magical adventures, full of surprise. Her independence even outmatched my mother's.

As we grow older we shape our own mythologies. For a long time I submerged the realities of my own family life in a story which had me growing up somewhere in the country, with the secure mother and father, the house with the scrubbed wooden table, the loaf of home-made bread, the pot of home-made soup. Over the years I tried to recreate that same scenario for my husband and our three children, and then later just for me and the children, and finally just for me and for my friends. One day, after we had been hearing Royal Commission evidence about people with broken family lives, I found myself reflecting on my luck in having such a stable and ordinary childhood.

But then the truth came to me — I had never enjoyed any such thing. Until I was nine, I lived in an English household consisting of a nanny, a cook, a maid and my mother, who was often absent. She was a fashion designer who flew around the world. My father was a rubber planter in Malaya who came home every three years. My brother was at an English boarding school. During my childhood I lived through two wars, one with Germany and one with Japan; I was wrenched out of my English upbringing to escape the German war, only to encounter the Japanese invasion of Malaya. I then spent five years as a refugee in Australia. I went to nine different schools in three countries and lived in fifteen different houses. My mother did make home-made bread — in Australia — which rose and spilled over onto the table, and I made home-made bread that was so tough I cracked a tooth.

The point about this story is not that my early life was bad
— it was far more stable than the lives of millions of others
at that time of war and dislocation. But I had obviously felt
the need to transmute a life of constant upheaval into one of
conventional stability. At one level, I knew it was fantasy, but
it was a level I didn't bother to visit. I had wrapped myself
inside a comforting dream. Still, when I look back I realise
that all the changes I experienced during my childhood
required adaptive responses if I was going to get the best out
of life. I had plenty of minor crises on the way, and I wasn't
always happy, but I have no doubt that the challenges helped
develop my resilience.

By the 1950s I was married and trying to break into
news-broadcasting at a time when women on radio were
corralled into talking about cooking and fashion. By
the 1960s I had three children. By the 1970s I was
storming the ramparts of patriarchy with feminist colleagues and friends. In those three decades, huge social
changes had begun to challenge traditional notions of
what constituted a family and family life. Some people
believed change was long overdue and that the family, in
whatever shape or form, was an oppressive institution and
should be abolished (how they proposed doing this, I have
yet to discover). 'They fuck you up, your mum and dad,'
wrote the celebrated English poet, Philip Larkin, waging
verbal war.

Inexorably, the so-called nuclear family, predicated on the
institution of marriage, was giving way to broader arrangements where people lived together out of love or friendship.
By the twenty-first century, families in Western societies had
exploded the nuclear family concept: there is now more
blending, more divorce, more single parents, more same sex

couples, more working couples, more defacto couples and more groups of people who share rent, housekeeping bills and argue whose turn it is for dustbin night. Diversity dominates.

It may sound unbelievable but little more than twenty-five years ago, when I was a member of the Royal Commission into Human Relationships, the notion of people living together in so many different ways was considered by many to be an outrage, a threat to the morality and stability of society. Even today, purveyors of the mantra of 'family values' write letters to the paper, arguing that the family has been destroyed. They talk about those 'good old days behind the picket fence', ignoring the fact that the 'good old days' also harboured violence, alcoholism, child abuse and a repressive moral code which treated women and children as chattels.

Some of those problems are still with us, some have almost disappeared, some are new. In her discussion paper, *New Families for Changing Times*, Pamela Kinnear points out that social change often rights the wrongs of yesterday, but in doing so it usually ushers in a new set of problems for us to solve. We have yet to grapple with the impact of parental break-up on children's lives, although most research shows it is not the actual break-up which is damaging. It is if the loss or separation brings about fighting or poor parenting. Conversely, disturbed relationships or poor parenting carry a risk even when no loss or separation is involved.

Just as there is a tendency to view the family as a panacea for all evils, there is an equal tendency to blame the family when things go wrong. Families are forever vulnerable to forces that reflect the values and systems of the wider world. For example, take that horrible expression, 'quality time'. Most young, working couples and their children don't get enough of it — life's an ongoing rush in an aggressive labour market that extracts ever-longer working hours from its employees.

Yet families have existed as far back as our knowledge takes us, across cultures and across time. In spite of their imperfections and sometimes dangers, we don't seem to have found a better way of bringing up children. American author and philosopher, Thomas Moore, talks about the family as 'a sometimes comforting, sometimes devastating house of life and memory.'

One of the most emotional issues in modern Australia was the removal — during a large part of the twentieth century — of Aboriginal children from their parents. For a long time there was a view that Aboriginal mothers would soon forget their children. James Isdell, who was appointed travelling 'protector' for the north of Western Australia in 1907 wrote:

> The half-caste is intellectually above the Aborigines, and it is the duty of the State that they be given a chance to lead a better life than their mothers. I would not hesitate for one minute to separate any half-caste from its aboriginal mother, no matter how frantic her momentary grief might be at the time. They soon forget their offspring.

Today, when we listen to the accounts of men and women who were taken from their families as children, many of us are moved to tears. What happened assaulted one of the closest of human bonds — the bonds of family. What then occurred showed the resilience and endurance of family — of parents who never forgot and of children who never gave up hope. Maria Tomlins was born at Mount Doreen, a cattle station west of Alice Springs, where her mother, aunty and grandmother used to look after the station goats. She was seven when she was taken away:

I remember that day very clearly. O yes, very, very clearly. It was just me and my brother Ted and my two cousins Jackie and Tommy Cusack. We were all playing and a man come in the truck and he said he was taking us for a ride. So we all got in. We thought it was fun. We thought we were just going for a ride.

The ride lasted through Maria Tomlins' childhood and her youth, in and out of institutions, her name changed, separated from her mother, her brother, her grandmother, her aunt, her cousins. After the war, when Aborigines still had no freedom of movement, she was sent to the town of Alice Springs. One morning, she was doing the ironing when a friend pointed out a group of people on the other side of the fence:

'They're looking in here,' said the friend. 'They're calling out to you but your name's not Laura, eh? They're calling you.'

I couldn't believe it … All those years when I was walking anywhere in the streets I was looking at all the black faces, looking for that familiar face I had planted in my mind all those years. That face of my mother. And then I went over and I saw that face. I couldn't believe it. She just grabbed me and she's … she held on to me. She was crying and hitting herself. My grandmother and aunty was also there, hanging on, crying. We just cried. Sat down like that and cried and cried … All those years she came — fourteen years — not only her, but my aunty and my grandmother — they were all coming, sitting there looking for me … It's over four hundred kilometres from Mount Doreen to Alice.

When Maria Tomlins had her own children, she worked so that she could keep them herself and so that nobody could take them away. 'That was the biggest fear I had.'

I tried to imagine the anguish of Maria Tomlins' mother when her two children disappeared — and the anguish of all those Aboriginal mothers who lost their children but who, somehow or other, never gave up hope.

I put down the book which contained Tomlins' story and felt a mixture of melancholia and wonder at how my investigation of resilience kept returning to a central theme: the power of hope. Outside, rain was chucking down on this late autumnal day and I wondered if it was raining for Robert, who by now was in Western Australia at a place called Bridgetown.

18.5.99
Dear Anne, I am in the middle of the old-forest controversy here in WA, wondering how I am going to pull the pieces together. People from both 'sides' are feeling bruised, and it will be important to give everyone a chance to speak. Keep going with your reading on resilience, it's one of the core skills we will need in the future. Our systems are so brittle and overstressed — human systems and ecological ones — and we need opportunities, time and space for regeneration. I am feeling tired, but bearing up. Thank you for making everything such fun, love Robert.

20.5.99
Dear Robert, As you know, I'm now in Adelaide where I gave my speech about mental illness last night and tomorrow will be off to Kangaroo Island to stay with a

friend. Thanks for trying to change your ticket so you could stop off here on your way back to America. Sorry it wasn't possible. Have a safe journey home and a good homecoming. If I say it's been great working with you, it sounds like a finale, and I do not anticipate that. Thank you for your generous words, love Anne.

20.5.99
Dear Anne, No finales, please! I look forward to many more years of friendship. I've never had an email from a place called Kangaroo Island. Please send me one, love Robert.

21.5.99
Dear Robert, I am on Kangaroo Island looking out across sand dunes and a choppy grey sea. I have flu and when I cough I sound like the penguins — more news later, Anne.

21.5.99
Dear Anne, I hope that the flu gets better soon. I am relatively good at soothing fevered brows. Much experience with Jeanne. Do you like to be left alone or supported when you're ill? Apart from my cancer two years ago, I am in good health and can expect to live a long time, love Robert.

I read this last sentence several times. Was it a declaration of worthiness, letting me know he was sound of mind and limb? When you barely know one another and are wary about making assumptions, correspondence can be a tricky business. It's easy to read too much between the lines.

22.5.99
Dear Robert, Sometime I would like you to stand still long enough to get to know you, love Anne.

23.5.99
Dear Anne, How about my ten-day holiday break in October, hopefully on the Great Barrier Reef? Love Robert.

24.5.99
Dear Robert, Excellent. I'll bring the shark repellent, Anne.

90

7

It takes a community

It had rained for days; sometimes it seemed like weeks. Water spilled through cracks in my window-frames, cascaded down drain pipes, swirled in angry torrents along the street and eventually poured under my front door. I started getting out towels and lifting rugs, books and papers on to tables and chairs. I had taken off my shoes and was standing in a river of muddy grey water when my neighbours arrived to offer their help. Mine is a corner property that lies lower than any of the other buildings, so its potential for flooding was well known. People brought buckets and we attempted some kind of sandbagging to help stem the flow.

On one of my stereo speakers, which someone had stood on a chair, I noticed a soggy pile of research papers on resilience. They happened to be the ones that dealt with community. My neighbours laughed when I explained I was just about to write the section on resilience and community — and I thought that had people not helped, had I been on my own facing this disaster, I might very well have been crying, not laughing.

'Community' is an all-encompassing word which features frequently in the writings on resilience. It can describe a group of Australian people practising permaculture in the hinterland of northern New South Wales, a gang of street children in Bombay, a religious order in Italy, or a Connecticut housing estate with high walls, armed guards and women in pink denim shorts jogging with their cocker spaniel dogs. Then there are the cyber communities, using the internet to work together on a common cause.

It's not easy to say what it is that pulls people together to form communities — deep historical connections, cultural ties, a sense of shared adversity, common interests. Nowadays the reasons are many and varied. But in Victorian times, the word community was often reserved for 'communities of the poor', whose welfare and morals were the philan-thropic concern of groups of middle-class women.

Throughout a large part of the twentieth century charitable organisations continued to feed the poor. It was only in the 1960s and 1970s with the rise of human rights movements that the voices of an underclass began to be heard. Grass-roots activities and the funding of community development projects became a feature of Australian life.

By the mid- to late-1990s, governments felt the cost of broad-based universal welfare programs were increasing at unsustainable rates, and the concept of 'mutual obligation' became the new face of social welfare in most countries in the Western world. Paralleling this shift to mutual obligation was a growing sense that traditional welfare — which focused on individuals and treated them as passive receivers of care — was outmoded and needed to be replaced by a social capital approach incorporating mutual obligations and reciprocal responsibilities. Major non-government organisations, religious institutions, big business and government began joining together as government contracted out its work, and communities were exhorted to become social entrepreneurs.

This new approach is not without controversy. Critics ask who it leaves to walk with the poor, to advocate on their behalf and identify structural problems that cause poverty and inequality? Are the best interests of people at heart, or is this really about governments off-loading responsibility?

Jane Schwager, the friend who introduced me to Robert, heads up the oldest and one of the largest non-government organisations in Australia, the Benevolent Society. She says firmly that the new approach is all about building resilience into communities and individuals by identifying problems and then solving them with identified strengths. It is not about the corporatisation of welfare, and there must always be a safety net.

In far north Queensland, Aboriginal leader Noel Pearson is also seeking an economic model for his people, in place of a welfare one. Ninety-three per cent of Aboriginal people in Cape York are on welfare, and Pearson talks about an 'industry in Aboriginal dysfunction'. He believes there is a direct connection between passive welfare dependence and the outrageous social problems that now confront most Aboriginal communities. 'Dependency and passivity are a scourge which must be avoided at all costs,' he says, and goes on:

> The right to self-determination is ultimately the right to take responsibility. Our traditional economy was a real economy and demanded responsibility (you don't work, you starve). The white fella market economy is real (you don't work, you don't get paid).

After we became citizens with equal rights and equal pay, we lost our place in the real economy. What is the exception among white fellas — almost complete dependence on cash handouts from the government — is the rule for us. There is no responsibility and reciprocity built into our present artificial economy, which is based on passive welfare (money for nothing).

Passive welfare has undermined Aboriginal Law — our traditional values and relationships ... Passive welfare and grog and drugs are finally tearing our society apart ...

We have to be as forthright and unequivocal about our responsibilities as we are about our rights — otherwise our society will fall apart while we are still fighting for our rights.

We do not have a right to passive welfare — indeed we can no longer accept it. We have a right to a real economy. We have a right to build a real economy.

As a consequence of Noel Pearson's leadership, a group of philanthropic and corporate leaders have come together, dedicated to pursuing a bold new indigenous agenda. Indigenous Enterprise Partnerships involves building partnerships with philanthropic, indigenous, government, corporate and community organisations, to assist indigenous people to break out of welfare dependency and participate in a real economy. Decision making remains with indigenous people. Forty businesses are already in incubation — from establishing a Cape York Credit Union to buying trawlers to join the local fishing industry. In an enterprise known as 'Boys from the Bush Program', boys (and occasionally girls) who are juvenile offenders or are at risk of offending are already running a business harvesting, bottling and marketing eucalyptus oil.

During this time they are given intensive counselling. The non-reoffending rate is almost ninety per cent.

Parallels exist here in situations of many young people who find themselves trapped in environments from which there seems no escape. Reports from the New South Wales Youth Drug Court reveal the shattering circumstances of many young people's lives:

> *Client one*: father killed in industrial accident when
> boy was two, brother addicted to drugs, left
> school early;
> *Client two*: left school in year 9 after having attended
> 23 schools, broken family, father in jail;
> *Client three*: disrupted schooling, father died of heroin
> overdose when client was ten, stepfather murdered when
> boy was fourteen.

On and on they go, every case its own tragedy. The cards are stacked against such children rising above their circumstances of their own accord. This is where properly resourced communities can help.

Fostering resilient communities is a process and not a program. Essential to it is a sense of optimism and hope. New initiatives encourage communities to identify their problems and advise on best solutions, with support coming from government, business and non-profit organisations. Programs include everything from sport and leisure activities for disadvantaged youth to homework programs helping Arabic-speaking young people improve their literacy and numeracy. The message is: start slowly and be prepared for setbacks; give second chances; look for practical solutions and innovative partnerships; recognise that change takes time.

Stories of hope and success are essential to understand how resilience can emerge out of disaster, and how it is only by working together that progress can be made.

THE STORY OF CLAYMORE

Claymore Estate was one of five enormous public housing estates established in the late 1970s in the Campbelltown area, fifty kilometres southwest of Sydney. It began with heady optimism — an escape from city slums, it provided job opportunities in new light industries in the area, clean air and townhouses configured along the lines of the garden city of Radburn in New Jersey, USA.

But instead of a planning masterpiece, the estate became an urban nightmare, plagued by crime, poverty and tragedy. Brian Murnane, executive director of a local community housing estate, said that Claymore was an obvious recipe for disaster. The bureaucrats were focusing on bricks and mortar, not people. Four thousand desperately poor people found themselves concentrated all together. John Mant, author of a major review of Australian government agencies in the 1990s, said public housing should be scattered throughout the private sector. It was wrong to put numbers of people with multiple problems in one place, as occurred in Claymore — it was bad sociology and bad planning.

By the end of 1995, the Claymore community was stressed and frightened. Almost half of households were single-parent families, many on incomes of less than twelve thousand dollars a year. Nearly half the population was younger than fifteen. Massive economic restructuring, plus cycles of boom or bust, had decimated initial prospects for work. Unemployment ran at fifty-two per cent, more than six times the national average. Public transport was infrequent, there were no public amenities like cinemas, sporting clubs, cafes, restaurants. Houses were vandalised. Mail was routinely stolen. Streets were unsafe. Muggings and high-speed car chases occurred every day.

One street was worse than any other. Proctor Way was scrawled with graffiti and littered with tyres, car engines, broken bottles and syringes. Many residents were too frightened to step out of their houses. By the end of 1995, twenty-five houses in Proctor Way were boarded up; nobody would move in. Claymore shopping centre, with its barbed wire and steel grille, looked like a concentration camp (or a refugee camp); the school looked like a prison. The community reserve was eerily empty — a dumping ground for rubbish.

Then a tragedy occurred. A house in Proctor Way was burned to the ground. Six people escaped, but five died — including three small children. In the same year, in a nearby street, a mother had ended the lives of her eleven-year-old son and ten-year-old daughter by putting sleeping pills in their Milo and drowning them in the bath. In 1992, a man had taken to his seventeen-year-old daughter with a meat cleaver.

The turnaround came when, in desperation, the Department of Housing turned part of Proctor Way over to Argyle Community Housing, a local initiative managed by Brian Murnane, with a brief to lease and manage twenty-five houses on a trial basis. Murnane, an engineer by training, had worked with alcoholics and homeless men and set up a women's refuge before he directed his energies into housing.

First, he moved into the house next to the one that had just burned down. Residents regarded him with suspicion. When he asked what they wanted to improve their street and they told him a street light and removal of rubbish, he organised both these requests. Other people in the area then wanted their rubbish removed. They joined him in working parties to help clean up the mess, then went on to remove the graffiti.

Tuisila Mack, a Samoan chief and father of six, was another resident of Proctor Way. He was an ex-schoolteacher, and bus and taxi driver, who retired in 1993 and came to Campbelltown when his eight-year-old grandson drowned and he and his family needed to move away.

Tuisila was concerned by the rising number of robberies and assaults in Claymore. He asked to set up street patrols. This was no Rambo-style vigilante group, but fifteen Samoans who walked the street in pairs, armed with torches, beginning and ending each patrol with singing. Their aim was to deter, rather than intervene. Disturbances were immediately reported to the police so members of the street patrol would still be seen as part of the community — 'us' rather than 'them'. Police records in one year showed a thirty per cent drop in crime.

Tuisila's next request was to start a vegie garden in the abandoned reserve. A working bee cleared the land of car wrecks, mattresses and old furniture. Then vegies were planted — taro, sweet potatoes, bananas, sugar cane, tomatoes, pumpkins, cucumbers. Now the reserve looks like a tropical garden, and islanders, asians and caucasians all hoe and rake together. The garden hasn't eliminated poverty, nor given paid employment, but it has given hope, a belief that something better is possible than the violence of the past. Hope is the key to the resilience of the Claymore community.

New initiatives are now regularly started in Claymore. As well as the community vegetable garden, there are realistic plans for a community park, a community tool library and an employment cooperative which will also teach a range of leadership skills, including financial management. Then there's something known as the Gumnut Service, which offers a one-stop shop for people in need of help — housing advice, domestic violence counselling, police assistance, parenting advice, as well as a centre for women's health, an Aboriginal women's space, art workshops and a laundromat/cafe.

It took a terrible tragedy before the Claymore community was willing to look at their own despair; then they needed the leadership of people like Brian Murnane and Tuisila Mack, and later the support of organisations like the Benevolent Society. The story is ongoing, and problems still exist, but Claymore today is no longer a place of apathy and despair. The community has discovered the capacity to nurture and look after itself — to grow gardens where there once were dumpsites.

THE STORY OF BEN

This story is about the courage of a sixteen-year-old homeless boy, and a school which became his community and provided him with the chance to make something of his life.

It all began one cold grey morning in Melbourne. I was making a film about homelessness and met a group of pinch-faced children sleeping on park benches and huddled in doorways. They were slow and miserable in those early hours, shivering in skimpy clothes, but by afternoon they had revved up into speedy deals, mainly drugs and prostitution. Later a social worker took me to visit a boy who had also previously been homeless. He had run away from a father who beat him up and sexually abused him; however, instead of taking to the streets, he kept turning up at school, where he would doss down behind school buildings, hoping he wouldn't be found. School friends kept him going for a while, and then he came to the attention of one of the teachers, who set in action a program that enabled Ben to continue at school. He was too scared to live with another family, so public housing provided a one-bedroom flat, a social worker was detailed to visit him once a week, and the school became his family and his community.

When I visited Ben in his flat, I found a gangly boy with prominent ears and the sharp tenderness of youth. He offered me a cup of tea and when he poured the hot water onto a shared tea-bag, he stirred the brew carefully, flashing me an awkward smile. The room was neat except for his school books which were strewn around the floor. When I asked cautiously about his family, he stared down at his reddened knuckles, saying he couldn't see them anymore: 'My Dad was bad, you know, real bad.'

He said he found it tough doing his homework on his own and having no one to talk to. He didn't invite any friends home because he felt like a freak with no family around, and besides he had nothing to offer anyone — it was hard enough buying his own food. He was scared sometimes and had nightmares his father would find him.

Something of the small child lingered in him. He missed his mum but didn't dare see her in case his dad found out and bashed her up. Sometimes he cried himself to sleep at night. His social worker visited only once a week because of an over-crowded case load; when she came, she brought him chocolate biscuits and there was an obvious rapport between the two. But was this enough to keep the boy at school?

Ben grinned. He said he liked school — it was safe and he liked learning even if he wasn't very good. He 'had Fossy, see' — Mr Foster, a teacher who was cool with the kids and took an interest in him. 'He's nice to me,' he said in some wonderment. 'Comes early sometimes. Gives me a hand an' that. Helps with my work.'

I told Ben I thought he was terrific, and he looked down at the table and scratched at it with a knife. 'I go to school cause it's the only way I'll get outa all that shit that happened an' that at home. I wanna make somethin' of my life. Dunno what. But somethin'.'

I don't know what ingredients made this boy different from the others. I don't know what made him decide he'd not give in. Personality? He was quite shy. Determination? Almost certainly. Being in the right place at the right time — at a school which had a program for homeless students? Yes. Having a teacher who liked him and was willing to help? Absolutely. What about his parents? He'd been able to separate out his mother from his father, and to recognise that while it would be dangerous to contact his father again, his mother was important to him. Was his success due to having some sense of purpose? Yes. Even though his choices meant being lonely and at times afraid, he had made a clear decision that one day he'd make something of his life. I felt that he was making something of it already, but he shook his head.

'One day,' he said.

THE STORY OF RWANDA

I went to Rwanda just after the 1994 genocide in which up to one million people were killed. From there I travelled to Zaire to film the refugees who had fled Rwanda after the liberation. Many of them were the militia who had committed the killings. Others were their victims — people whose families had been slaughtered. A million men, women and children, thrown together on a desolate patch of black rock. No trees, no water and a volcano shooting orange flames into the air, covering everything in coarse black ash, making it hard to breathe.

People everywhere sick and dying, dead, sleeping, defecating, pushing and shoving for food, hitting one another. People in every conceivable state of distress. An exhausted aid worker stumbled down the hill carrying a child in her arms, not realising she was being filmed, not realising the child was dead, calling out to no one, yet everyone — this was the end of the world. Wagons from aid agencies criss-crossed the ground, their pennants flying like crusader flags. There were lorries laden with corpses, and boy soldiers armed with Kalashnikovs. No roads, no tracks and, in the acrid smog, it was difficult to spot our destination somewhere ahead of us, a World Vision camp for children whose parents had been slaughtered, mostly in front of their eyes, or whose parents had disappeared.

When we reached the camp, children came tumbling out to greet us, some still with machete wounds on their heads and bodies. What bastards did this, I thought, and why didn't the international community prevent it, as it could have done? A small boy wearing a yellow t-shirt, branded with the Kentucky Fried logo, clung to my legs. Other children were pulling us down to play, or frolicking in red and yellow plastic baths, wriggling like little fishes and shrieking with delight as young schoolgirls, probably aged about twelve or thirteen, rubbed oil into their skins, cuddled and tickled them.

I laughed, and then I remembered the horrors down below and turned to the man standing next to me, a grey-haired German paediatrician who had left his practice in Munich to come to Rwanda and help.

'My God, how can these children even smile, let alone play?'

He nodded, as if he were used to answering this question. He said that in the beginning they didn't play. They stared and rocked. Some put fingers in their ears to block out memories of horrific sounds. Just behind me a nine-year-old boy still rocked and howled, his fingers in his ears. When another child came near him, he made as if to break his arm.

'These children need to be held,' said the doctor. 'To know that not all adults do them harm. The older girls asked to help — this way they know their lives are still of value. They make a family, and together we are a community.'

Experts in different disciplines — volunteers — had flown in from all over the world to help these children. They were working with Rwandans, training them if necessary, monitoring the children's health and, most importantly, setting up programs for trauma recovery. Getting the children to write, draw and act out their experiences, making sure they didn't stay locked within themselves.

The German doctor picked up one of the little boys and hugged him, disregarding the water that dripped down his clothes. 'These children are resilient,' said the doctor. 'You will see.'

Why did I believe him, this courteous middle-aged man

who spoke with such quiet confidence? I'm not sure, though I have thought about it since, particularly whenever I remember the horrors I had seen in Rwanda. But inside this camp, with its barricades of green canvas, its children playing, came a thrust of clean bright energy, as if trampled blades of grass were springing back towards the light. The laughter of children, the splash of water, the shrieks of delight transcended the horrors surrounding us.

Out of horror can still come moments of joy. Out of sadness can come memories which are rich and true. This was certainly true of my own experience. What would Robert feel about it? I thought. I knew his seventieth birthday was approaching soon, and I wondered how he was faring. Was he sad about this coming birthday — especially as he must have expected to spend it with Jeanne, his former wife. I sat down and wrote him another email from Kangaroo Island.

3.6.99
Dear Robert, Perhaps because I am still unwell and therefore a little light-headed, I began thinking of your birthday and how you must have expected you would celebrate this time with Jeanne. I hope you are able to remember all the good times you spent together. I don't believe you can say a relationship has failed just because it has ended. I hope you don't think I'm being presumptuous in any way. These are just reflections. The longer I live, the less I know, except to be aware that most people's lives will traverse an extraordinary range of experiences, and that with the help of love we can usually muddle through most, even if they aren't always resolved

the way we would like. With love from the Penguin of Kangaroo Island.

3.6.99
Not presumptuous at all, oh Penguin, I have reached the point where I realise that Jeanne and I are more effective apart than together. I'm not really reconciled to this because I thought this was a lifetime bond and I was a one-woman man. But given that things have changed and that the change must be lived with, I committed myself to remembering the good times and I hope that she will get to the point where she does this also. My situation is so dramatically different from eighteen months ago that I vainly attempt to keep up with it. Thanks for feeling free to send your thoughts. Love, Robert.

8

Violence

In 1945, American author and celebrated war correspondent, Martha Gelhorn, wrote this account of survivors of the Nazi concentration camp of Dachau: 'Behind the barbed wire and the electric fence, the skeletons sat in the sun and searched themselves for lice. They have no age and no faces; they all look alike and like nothing you will ever see if you are lucky.'

Gelhorn knew better than most that our record as human beings is not a pretty one. Our depravities seem to get worse, not better — or perhaps we have just become more skilled. So how do people cope in the context of extreme cruelty? What happens to their resilience when they lose everything they care for? How do they manage, the hundreds and thousands who are jailed without trial and without hope because of their political beliefs, their religion or where they come from? What of the millions who languish in refugee camps, including camps in Australia, my own country? People endure in extremes that makes us hold our breath in pity and disbelief.

In 1979, I went to Uganda immediately after the overthrow of the brutal dictator President Idi Dada Amin. One of the people I interviewed was a Ugandan bishop, Jerome, who one day had unwittingly parked his car next to the President's at a civic function. Jerome was arrested the next day and charged with plotting to assassinate Amin. His wife and children fled, and he did not know where they were or even if they were alive.

Jerome had been sentenced to death, and held underground in Amin's State Research Bureau — a euphemism for slaughterhouse. Once, he had been a tall, young and vigorous man. Now his black clothes flapped from a wasted body. His eyes were red-rimmed from three months living in the dark. His handkerchief was spotted with blood from frequent coughing attacks. The State Research Bureau was a pretty, pale-pink building which looked like a modest suburban motel. Bloated bodies still lay in a courtyard where white roses bloomed. A sign by the entrance read: 'Secret! When you come here, what you see here, what you hear here, when you leave here, leave them here, secret.'

Killings happened every night, Amin getting drunk as he watched the grotesque spectacle he had devised. Each man had to kill the man in front of him by bashing out his brains with a sledgehammer, on and on down the line. Women's throats were cut. Children were strangled. The dungeons were in darkness except for a spotlight trained on the killings.

We stood in the cellar where the killings occurred. People's clothes and possessions were scattered around us on the dank and slimy floor. Walls and floor were stained with blood. Jerome said that night after night he was forced to take his place in the 'killing line'. Always at the very end, he would be pulled away.

'Would you have killed the man in front?' I asked.

He looked tormented. 'I don't know,' he said after a while. His voice was so quiet I could hardly hear him. 'I never found out. I used to wish I was dead so I had no more to hear the screams. I felt shame that I lived and others died.'

He reached out for my hand. 'I tried to keep my humanity, and every day I prayed for a heart that did not want revenge.'

'But it is humanity that has perpetrated these horrors.'

'It is humanity that is sick in its soul. And that's what they want to happen to you. To obliterate your soul and then to kill you. "Where is God?" I used to cry aloud.'

When people are tortured, they suffer damage to the basic structure of the self. Psychiatrist and trauma expert Judith Herman explains how traumatised people lose their trust in themselves, in other people and in God. The identity that they have formed prior to the trauma is irrevocably destroyed. 'The conflict between the will to deny horrible events and the will to proclaim them aloud is the central dialectic of psychological trauma. When the truth is finally recognised, survivors can begin their recovery.'

Herman says survivors need to have affirmation and protection; they need friends and family, and to feel political movements are behind them, helping to give them voice.

This moral support is an essential part of recovery. When a group of East Timorese men and women, who had endured years of imprisonment and violence from Indonesian soldiers, attended a workshop in Dili for survivors of torture, they listened transfixed to the text of the United Nations' 1987 Convention Against Torture. For the first time they learned that the people who tortured them were indeed considered criminals by the outside world. At this realisation they broke into broad smiles and gave thumbs-up signals.

Viet Nguyen-Gilham, the psychotherapist at the workshop (which was run by the International Catholic Migrations Commission) works from a model of strength and resilience. She says that all the rhetoric of 'building a new nation' has prevented people going back to their sufferings during those twenty-four years of Indonesian occupation. 'People have been taught to forget the past and to forgive, and the result is their feelings are frozen. Unless you can revisit the past, you can't write a new chapter.'

People do survive and they do so by many means — hope, luck, adaptability, a reconnection with life and with family and friends, a realisation that there is still some kind of morality in the world.

Some of the most moving accounts of resilience in the face of prolonged and horrific suffering have come from the writings of Primo Levi. Levi was a young Italian chemist when he was arrested as a member of the anti-fascist resistance movement during World War Two. He wrote to bear witness, and to speak, by proxy, for the *sommersi* — those who were submerged, annihilated, blotted out of existence. In his writings he uses the word 'civilised' time and again, as if this is the last light that remains and must not be extinguished:

Nothing belongs to us any more; they have taken away our clothes, our shoes, even our hair; if we speak, they will not listen to us, and if they listen, they will not understand. They will even take away our name: and if we want to keep it, we will have to find in ourselves the strength to do so, to manage somehow so that behind the name something of us, of us as we were, still remains.

Levi says his survival came partly from an ability to maintain a detached curiosity — he tried to regard the camp as a gigantic biological and social experiment — while at the same time salvaging a humane moral vision from mankind at its worst.

Thomas Laqueur, writing in the *London Review of Books* in September 2002, felt that Levi's survival lay deep in his knowledge that to struggle against failure and error is the human condition. 'Even epochal and unprecedented crimes, his life seemed to say, can be assimilated into a secular, humane reasoned world view.'

This is a significant comment. To be resilient in the midst of such horror requires a moral view of the world that refuses to be distorted or annihilated. It also requires someone with an open mind. Early in his imprisonment, Primo Levi comes upon one of his friends, fifty-year-old ex-sergeant Steinlauf of the Austro-Hungarian army, grimly washing in icy water, scrubbing his neck and shoulders with little success because he has no soap. He demands severely why Levi does not wash. Levi thinks, 'Why should I wash? We are all about to die.' But Steinlauf convinces him otherwise. Washing, even in filthy water, is an instrument of moral survival:

> Precisely because the Lager was a great machine to reduce us to beasts, we must not become beasts; that even in this place one can survive, and therefore one must want to survive, to tell the story, to bear witness; and that to survive we must force ourselves to save at least the skeleton, the scaffolding, the form of civilisation.

On one occasion, civilisation for Levi comes from an unexpected memory of Dante's *Canto of Ulysses*. He was on soup duty with another prisoner, Jean, a young student from Alsace who was given the post of Pikolo, messenger–clerk for one of the prisoner huts. The heavy soup pot hung from a pole across their shoulders and the sun was already high when Levi was moved by some irresistible impulse to start clumsily translating Dante to his young companion.

'Here, listen, Pikolo, open your ears and your mind, you have to understand, for my sake.'

The effect of this recitation for Levi was as if he also was hearing it for the first time: 'like the blast of a trumpet, like the voice of God. For a moment I forget who I am and where I am …'

Then Levi forgets at least twelve lines and says he would give the day's soup to know how to connect the last fragment to the end of the canto: '… I close my eyes, I bite my fingers — but it is no use, the rest is silence.'

Thirty years later, Levi returned to the depth and truth of this particular moment in his last book, *The Drowned and the Saved*. He said that culture was useful to him and perhaps it saved him:

Where I wrote, 'I would give today's soup to know how to retrieve the forgotten passage', I had neither lied nor exaggerated. I really would have given bread and soup — that is blood — to save from nothingness these memories … They made it possible for me to re-establish a link with the past, saving it from oblivion and reinforcing my identity. They convinced me that my mind, though besieged by everyday necessities, had not ceased to function. They elevated me in my own eyes and those of my interlocutor. They granted me a respite … in short, a way to find myself.

In Auschwitz, the forgotten poem became literally priceless: in that place, at that instant, the very survival of Levi's humanity was dependent on it.

Levi always claimed he wasn't a fully fledged intellectual during his internment, but his curiosity and his willingness to learn helped save him. He says he came to realise that physical labour could bring fulfilment:

I almost never had the time to devote to death; I had many other things to keep me busy — find a bit of bread, avoid exhausting work, patch my shoes, steal a broom, or interpret the signs and faces around me. The aims of life are the best defence against death: and not only in the Lager.

Yet of Levi's own contingent of ninety-six healthy Italian men, selected for labour on their entry into the camp, more than half had died within two months. Why? Levi tried to explain it:

They are overcome before they can adapt themselves, they are beaten by time; they do not begin to learn German, to disentangle the infernal knot of laws and prohibitions until their bodies are already in decay… and then it is too late. Their dissolution of their old sense of self, their shame at this dissolution, the guilt when the passion to survive swamps every other feeling. But in the end, survival is not a matter of moral strength but of pure blind luck.

Sometimes — in fact often — survival must have been just a matter of good luck, just as death was a matter of bad luck. In between good luck and bad luck are other possibilities — seizing an opportunity, expecting to survive, hanging on to hope, taking risks. The ones who believed nothing would change were often the first to let go. Hope may be fleeting, it may be lost and refound, but with hope came the strength to carry on.

'A person with hope between her or his teeth,' wrote English author and scholar, John Berger, 'is a brother or sister who commands respect.' Maria Pilar was twenty-one when she was kidnapped by secret police in Pinochet's Chile in 1973. She was put into an isolation cell where she could hear screams, day and night; she was taken with dogs to see her friend being tortured; then she herself was stripped naked, gagged and blindfolded, had electric shocks applied to her genitals and breasts, was insulted, beaten and humiliated. Finally, after more shocks, she passed out in a pool of urine, excrement and terror. And then one day she found hope in the middle of her despair in the form of a letter. She received a message from an Amnesty International Group, telling her that she wasn't alone, that they had taken up her case and were campaigning for her release.

'This meant so much to me, it gave me so much hope.'

Later, she was moved into an overcrowded prison with one toilet for one hundred women where she waited for more interrogations and for her trial. She says that even though she was with 'common criminals', she was able to talk with other women. 'I was given warmth and care. I felt human again.'

Friendships were crucial — even if they were short-lived, even if people died. They enabled Maria Pilar to tolerate deprivation and immense hardship.

Friendships were also critical to the twenty-two thousand Australian prisoners of war in Japanese camps during World War Two. The story of those prisoners of war and their resilience under conditions of great cruelty and deprivation has been vividly told by broadcaster Tim Bowden in a series for the Australian Broadcasting Corporation, *Prisoners of War, Australians under Nippon*, based on original interviews with survivors. In his book, based on the same interviews, Hank Nelson writes that compared with soldiers from other armies, the Australians were egalitarian among themselves, 'and refreshingly casual and curious in their meetings with local peoples.' Many were young country boys when they enlisted. They had lived through the economic depression of the 1930s, and had served their apprenticeships in survival. A man who had swung a pick day after day in Australia was confident of his capacity to work long after other prisoners in the camp had dropped with exhaustion.

The Australians' hardiness and ingenuity at finding solutions stood them in good stead when they were working on the infamous Burma–Thailand railway. When a Japanese officer transmitted the instructions of Imperial General Headquarters to the prisoners working on the railway, he said — in stark terms — 'Nippon very sorry, many men must die.' Here was the brutal reality: many men did die — from starvation, disease, exhaustion and cruelty.

An account of their working conditions shows the capacity of prisoners to adapt and cope with conditions so horrific they are almost impossible for us to imagine:

The ground turned to mud, your clothes rotted away, your boots, if you had any boots at that stage, rotted off. The six-foot latrine pits which we had dug filled up with water and in no time the whole camp area was crawling with maggots. In the cemetery, the graves filled up with water and the bodies came to the top. But none of this affected the progress of the railway.

Mateship was another important factor in the men's survival. The Australians took pride in their ability to keep each other going with friendship, generosity, encouragement and affectionate abuse — their own particular way of expressing love.

There is a tenderness in the accounts we hear and read, a tribute to the power of mateship and how this peculiarly Australian characteristic helped so many to survive, nourishing the spirit as well as the body. Needless to say, if one man was sick, the others would look after him:

When we'd get back and have some tucker we'd go and see how Mick is, how Curly is, how Bluey is and wake him up and say, 'How're you going, Bluey.' Prop him up and make sure his bed sores are all right and do what you could. You couldn't do bloody much, just make sure he had water, get him talking, get him interested.

When a prisoner was deteriorating more quickly than the rest of his group, a mate might sell something or steal eggs to help sustain his ailing companion. '[I]f the bloke wouldn't eat you'd say, "If you aren't going to eat that I'm going to ram it down your neck."'

Some were kept alive through innate optimism and a bloody-minded determination to survive: 'Well, I had a wife and a little girl. And the will to live. I said, "I'm not dying in this bloody place, and that's all there is to it."' Another observed, 'I hated their guts, and I wanted to get home. Perhaps I was a determined, irritable, cranky sort of bugger, and the more they did to me, the more it made me spark a bit. I never believed we wouldn't win.'

One night, listening to tapes of the broadcasts, I realised I had tears in my eyes when I heard one man describe in a laid-back, laconic way how a belief that his life would not end in the camps kept him going:

> At the back of my mind I could visualise myself as an old bloke somewhere. Whether this was seeing into the future or not I don't know. But I'd just imagine myself as an old bloke, and I thought if I'm going to be an old bloke I'll have to see this lot out.

Many didn't see this lot out. By the end of the war, one in three Australian prisoners had died — over seven thousand men. Mateship played as big a role in death as it did in life. In Australia, the majority of people still die in a hospital bed. If the doctors are quick enough, the relatives might be there, but often a person dies alone. Australian soldiers who were prisoners of the Japanese died in 'an aura of love and brotherhood', surrounded by their mates in a manner that helped both the living and the dying. Stan Arneil, whose father died of war wounds in 1938, describes the closeness of the bonding:

> You died with your head in the lap of a mate, with somebody holding your hand, with somebody with a hand on your forehead, saying a little prayer, and people actually sorry to see you die. That's a bond which you just cannot obtain now. Any of the people who were there became closer to their friends than to their family.

Friendships have helped people survive situations of extreme horror. In Auschwitz, Primo Levi found friendships fostered hope, and hope in turn fostered survival. A sense of common unity could mean the difference between despair and hope. Some prisoners were able to band together:

> Next to us there is a group of Greeks, those admirable and terrible Jews of Salonika, tenacious, thieving, wise, ferocious and united, so determined to live, such pitiless opponents in the struggle for life; those Greeks who have conquered in the kitchens and in the yards, and whom even the Germans respect and the Poles fear.

Levi told how the Greek prisoners used to sing and beat their feet in time and grow drunk on songs; or sing and circle, shoulder to shoulder, stamping out the dances of their homeland. He wrote that their 'aversion to gratuitous brutality, their amazing consciousness of the survival of at least a potential human dignity made of the Greeks the most coherent national nucleus in Lager and, in this respect, the most civilised.'

To survive a place whose sole purpose was to obliterate the memory of its victims one has to want to survive. Levi's aim was to bear witness. He found himself, like the ancient mariner in Coleridge's famous poem, unable to find peace until his story was told. Almost certainly he had no idea when he wrote his first book that its message would resonate around the world — literature can speak out of vast silences, and touch people across their loneliness and despair.

Some way into writing this book, I came across the work of the great Turkish poet, Nazim Hikmet. It was a passionate and wonderful piece of writing from a man who was imprisoned for most of his life, yet whose protest never ceased, and whose sensitivity and passion for life remained undimmed.

Nazim Hikmet was an unusually tall man who was known affectionately as 'the tree with the blue eyes'. He wrote about the universal nature of love and beauty, even though he was denied any recourse to them. Half his life's work was penned behind Turkish prison bars. Words came through the space, rose into the sky, crossed mountains, opened doors.

In 1949, he wrote a poem which blazed with defiance, illustrating that defiance, as well as acceptance, is a way of finding resilience when little else is left:

'Some Advice to Those who Will Serve Time in Prison'
If, instead of being hanged by the neck
  you're thrown inside
  for not giving up hope …
It might not be a pleasure exactly,
But it's your solemn duty
  to live one more day
    to spite the enemy …

Hikmet said you can endure imprisonment 'as long as the jewel on the left side of your chest doesn't lose its lustre.'

Primo Levi found personal peace and a way back to society not through the social activity of talking but the private one of writing. 'By writing I found peace for a while and felt myself become a man again, a person like everyone else, neither debased nor a saint: one of those people who form a family and look to the future rather than the past.'

Levi supposedly suicided in 1987 — he was found dead at the foot of the stairwell of his apartment in Turin. His death dismayed and shocked those who had seen him as a synonym for survival. The truth is no one can be certain how or why Primo Levi died. In his latter years, he suffered at times from deep depression but, even if his death were suicide as a consequence of that depression, it does not detract from his courage and resilience, nor from the terrible yet magnificent testimony his writings gave to the world. His work told of the capacity of the human spirit to rise above the demoralisation and humiliation of the concentration camps; it told the story of those whom Levi always said were the true witnesses, those who saw the Gorgon and did not survive, the 'submerged'.

In writing about the shame of the camps, Levi also wrote about the shame of the world — of those who, faced by the crimes of others or their own, turned their backs so as not to see it and not feel touched by it.

Each time I read Primo Levi I am in awe of both the man and of what he stands for. His resilience was not once tempered by expressions of hatred and revenge. In the after-word to *If This is a Man*, Levi writes that he refuses to give in to the temptation to hate. 'I believe in reason and in discussion as supreme instruments of progress, and therefore I repress hatred even within myself. I prefer justice ... The judges are my readers.'

But what role does forgiveness play in achieving ultimate reconciliation? Levi is able to abstain from 'explicit judgement' but he is not able to give an 'indiscriminate pardon'. He is only able to forgive if there has been true recognition and condemnation of the crimes that were committed, and a determination to uproot them from individual and collective conscience. 'Only in this case am I, a non-Christian, prepared to follow the Jewish and Christian precept of forgiving my enemy, because an enemy who sees the error of his ways ceases to be an enemy.'

In the writings of Primo Levi a number of important issues are raised in connection with resilience. One is that holding on to hatred binds victim and persecutor together and prevents the person who has been wronged from moving on. A second is that letting go of hatred and a desire for revenge does not necessarily open the way for complete forgiveness — not unless there has been true apology. An apology that is not honest is not honourable.

Only a few days after my son died, I spent a few days in a Buddhist watt in bush outside Sydney. I was struggling not just with the grief of Jonathan's death but with anger, because I felt the health care system had let him down. I did not tell all this to the Abbot, I said I had grief and anger over the death of a child. 'That is very hard,' he said gently, acknowledging my pain. Then he looked up into the great expanse of clear blue sky which stretched above us, and opened up both his arms, 'It is a part of life, a part of a whole.' I smelled that sharp sweet tang of the bush, and watched a small ant make its way through the sand, just past my foot. I felt liberated as if the pain and anger had begun floating away into the enormity of life around me.

Stephanie Dowrick, in her book *Forgiveness and other Acts of Love*, writes with great insight into this hardest of all virtues to achieve, and points out that to grope our way towards forgiveness, we may need momentarily to circumvent the rational mind, or transcend it. Being locked in anger, even if it is submerged, eats away at the body's natural resilience, chokes the flow of energy and love.

Much anguish has occurred in Australia about Prime Minister John Howard's refusal to acknowledge collective responsibility for the historical wrongs committed against Aboriginal people, and to apologise on behalf of the Australian people. Why should we be implicated in apologies, he says, so long after the initial deeds occurred, and when our generation had no hand in committing them?

Australians are implicated because Aboriginal people are our fellow citizens and we do have a collective responsibility to acknowledge that terrible injustices occurred. Former prime minister, Paul Keating, expressed it clearly and simply in his Redfern speech of 1992: 'We took the traditional lands, committed the murders, took the children.'

An apology does not lead to an expungement of past wrongs, but through acknowledgement of those wrongs, it provides a basis for healing.

Unless Australians have the grace and humility to give that apology, I do not believe my country can ever be fully healed. There will be a fault-line in our national psyche, deeper and older than any other fault-lines, challenging and weakening our collective morality and our collective capacity for resilience.

9

The problem is the problem

Negativity fills the mind with doubt, and makes resilience near impossible. Simon Champ should know. He has been an activist in mental health reform for twenty years, from the time he was diagnosed with schizophrenia when still at university.

He pours us both a beer. 'If we're always told what we *can't* do, how will we ever know what we can do? Remember when I said that to the Human Rights Enquiry into Mental Illness?'

I nod. We are sitting in the garden of my house late one afternoon, reminiscing. The vines on the back fence are almost bare, and it will soon be time to prune the roses. A snail moves slowly over the brick paving, leaving a glistening trail, and I wish it would disappear. Salt shrivels snails — effective, but I don't like using it because the combination of snail and salt makes a nasty hissing noise, and I can't help feeling sorry for the snail.

Simon laughs. 'Get a snail trap,' he says.

We are old friends. I look into his laughing eyes, and think of the journeys we have made together. The first time we met was in 1985 at a packed public meeting in Sydney to launch the first Schizophrenia Fellowship in New South Wales. I was chairing the meeting, and Simon was sitting near the front. I noticed him because there was something impressively staunch about him.

'Large, you mean,' says Simon cheerfully, adjusting the wide red braces which have become his trademark. 'I'm quite thin now compared to then.'

'Staunch,' I repeat, unperturbed.

At that meeting, no one with schizophrenia had spoken. Then Simon stood up, just as heavy rain started beating down on the iron roof of the Teachers' Federation where the meeting was held, making it hard to hear.

'I am Simon Champ and I have schizophrenia,' he said in a low voice. He repeated himself. This time his voice was louder.

Such a declaration would be quite commonplace today, especially at a mental health meeting but, in those days, its impact was dramatic. Simon is a modest man and I have to remind him of this now.

'You went on to say that a century ago you might well have lived out your whole life in an asylum like Bedlam, with people paying a penny to see the loony.'

'Did I say that? Nowadays it'd be twenty dollars, and cheap at the price.'

Simon is one of the most respected leaders in the mental health movement in Australia. He and I were both founding members of the Schizophrenia Fellowship in New South Wales; he served for five years on the National Community Advisory Group on Mental Health and on the Mental Health Council of Australia. He is a director of the national mental health organisation, Sane Australia, and was inaugural chair of the Australian Mental Heath Consumer Network. I tell him I still feel awkward with that word *consumer* — it reminds me of Big Macs. He says being a consumer means being an active participant in health services, rather than a passive recipient.

When Simon talks or lectures, in Australia and abroad, he often gets standing ovations. He is a natural speaker, clever and funny. But the pressure of public speaking can set off another psychotic episode for him. In the past, this meant experiencing the kind of paranoia in which he feared he was being poisoned, or spied upon, or about to be harmed in some unknown way. Nowadays, because he has learned to manage his illness, he is more likely to experience a generalised sense of heightened anxiety. He also knows that should the paranoia return — for example, if he begins to think he is being poisoned — he can take a reality check with one of his friends. He has had an ongoing struggle, over twenty years, to maintain balance and sanity in his life.

'I used to spend many years looking for positives in what happened to me, because it's very important to salvage meaning from schizophrenia. It is not a beautiful experience for most people. Nor is it a mystical experience. Life would have been much better if I hadn't had it. I'm forty, and I don't have a regular job, I live in a public-housing flat, I don't have a girlfriend, I don't have children. People who romanticise the experience of mental illness don't live through the paranoia and the daily delusions. Most people do not grow through experiencing schizophrenia. They grow through how they choose to live with it.'

When Simon was first told he had schizophrenia, he went

to the library at Sydney University where what he read about his condition was so depressing he thought about killing himself: 'Instead I decided to treat my life as an experiment — to find out what schizophrenia meant to me. I don't fight my schizophrenia. Rather than seeing it as an enemy, I see it as a teacher. It informs my life.

'Because of the experiences I've had and because I've tried to change things for others, my life has become very rich. I was able to turn my disability into something that worked for me. I've also been blessed by the fact my illness wasn't worse. I don't want to kill myself, I enjoy my life, I have a loving family — my parents and my two brothers. I have my education, and my nature, if you like.

'Resilience is a combination of all those factors, a psychological motivation towards finding a balance in life in spite of what's happened. You structure your life so you minimise your illness and stop relapses.'

Simon has degrees in fine arts and painting, but he finds it hard to reduce the amount of time he still gives to mental illness, even though he tries hard to keep faith with his art.

I ask him where his resilience comes from and he thinks for a moment before he answers, 'Friends. Natural inquisitiveness. The consumer movement which gives me friends, a sense of hope, and practical information in dealing with my illness. And my art.'

'What about your art?'

'It's like a meditation. I take stuff into my consciousness, and filter it through my art. It's a way of learning about myself and processing the world. I'm a closet gum tree painter,' he says, looking at my garden and chuckling. 'Postmodernism is all very well, but deep down I just want to paint a gum tree.'

Not long after this meeting, Simon had another breakdown. It lasted for three weeks, during which time he had to withdraw and keep his life as calm as possible. Then he was up again and off to an international Psychiatric Research Conference in Oxford, England, where he was giving a major address on consumer reflections on mental health research.

'This last breakdown was a shocker. It was really frightening. But I came out of it okay and I'm trying to think of it as a refresher course, a reminder of schizophrenia, and what it's like.

'I'm not really sure there will be a cure and that's why it's so important that we research what helps people learn to live with their illness. Western notions of psychiatry are too limited and confining. It's important we embrace not just the individual, but their family, their community and their spiritual beliefs. Spirituality is the process of making meaning out of life. It's fundamental to resilience and recovery. Yet our increasing emphasis on biochemistry in mental illness means the spiritual understandings of people are given less importance — even though they are the key to what gives them courage and the motivation to find a better way to live with their illness.'

Simon Champ's life challenges that strongly entrenched culture of negativity that Garmezy first talked about in the early 1970s, when he appealed to society to start looking at how people became resilient rather than why they failed.

A community psychiatrist friend of mine, Alan Rosen, has written that mental health professionals have colluded in a systematic colonising of the mentally ill by becoming their politically anointed custodians or foster families, 'for their own good'. 'In the process we've inadvertently broken their spirits and disempowered them and their families. What we think people need and what they need are very different. We might think residentials [residential care], they might want a home; we might think medication, they might think paid work.'

The growth of advocacy groups and consumer movements have challenged this kind of paternalism. Only about fifteen years ago, members of organisations concerned with mental illness sometimes used to argue that people who were mentally ill couldn't become board members in case the strain of participating made them ill. Yet it was vitally important that their voices were heard when policy decisions were made which might deeply affect their lives.

Overt and incipient negativity permeates many aspects of our lives. We still talk about the youth problem, the single parent problem, the migrant problem, the Aboriginal problem, the old age problem, the problems of people with disabilities. We study a woeful list of problems, but rarely those who have overcome them, or learned to cope with them, like Simon.

So why has this happened, I wondered, why has Western culture such a profound bias towards examining the negative — even in America with its culture of optimism? Is it because such an approach allows a welfare industry to develop around it — an industry of helping the helpless? When compassion turns to pity, people are generally rendered ineffective and powerless.

Alan Rosen's use of the word 'colonising' is interesting. Dominant cultures colonise weaker ones, sapping their natural resilience. As Simon Champ said, if people are always told they are inferior or in some way incompetent, this is how they may behave. For many years I made films in Africa where the media images which dominate show people engulfed by war and famine, eager recipients of international aid. We have developed a type of voyeurism in the way we look at Africa: the starving child, the dying infant, the emaciated mother. These are the images that bring in money, and they spring from a media-controlled view of relief. Most other aspects of life in Africa — which after all is a huge continent — are ignored. Developing countries are rarely shown helping themselves, as they effectively do — programs to try and combat AIDS in countries like Uganda are inspirational. If we showed images of what these people actually do with the meagre aid we give them, we might be inspired to give more, instead of feeling that trying to help is hopeless.

Myths are powerful, particularly when it comes to damaging the human psyche. In 1998, I came across a paper by American researcher Sylvia Rockwell which identified four myths that prevent the fostering of resilience. These were:

— the myth of predetermination, which says that people will never be able to escape the cycles of violence, poverty or failure which have haunted the lives of their parents;
— the myth of irreparable damage, which holds that some children can be so damaged by their experiences, they have no hope for the future;
— the myth of identity, which labels and dismisses people who are ill, or at-risk, rather than constantly engaging in a talent search, defining people in terms of their strengths;

— the myth that ultimately it doesn't matter, which states that whatever is done or not done makes little difference to the final outcome.

My friend, Krissy, confounded the myth of predetermination — that people cannot escape the cycles of violence, poverty or failure experienced by their parents. I met Krissy outside a King's Cross cafe in Sydney in 1983 when I was making an ABC documentary series about the changing role of women. She came walking towards me, swinging a large red plastic bag and teetering on high-heeled, pointy-toed shoes. Her hair was multi-coloured — green, red, purple — and heavily greased and spiked. She wore tasselled, black leather trousers and a leopard-print blouse. When we sat down in the cafe I thought for a moment that someone had given her two enormous black eyes. Then I saw it was make-up.

'Give you a shock, did I?' she said cheerfully. 'It's me way of rebellin' an' that. It's why I'm a punk. It's not a fashion, but a political statement. I feel how I look.'

She said people thought of her as a dirty, rotten, scum-dog of the earth, a rebel. I said I thought she was being a bit hard on herself and she laughed and reached for a doughnut.

'My image is also a guard,' she said. 'It keeps people away.'

In the film series we were looking for a young woman who had broken away from the kind of life her mother had experienced. Krissy's mother had worked, brought up seven children and been regularly beaten up by her father.

'Her black eyes were real,' said Krissy sadly, munching on a doughnut and looking suddenly vulnerable, like a small child wearing her mother's make-up. 'I mean the men who are like that, who have wives to beat up, beat you physically and mentally because they beat up your confidence — to make you stay. Some people are beaten down so much they're trapped. And it all stays the same, normality in abnormality.'

The big shiny coffee machine at the entrance to the cafe was belching forth steam and Krissy said Yes, she'd have another coffee. She kicked off her shoes. Outside there was a sudden deluge of rain, and water cascaded down the big, blue street umbrellas.

'See, I love my mother a lot,' said Krissy. 'She's the backbone of the family, as far as supporting us all. And working and breeding us all. And she got us away from our rotten old man, so it means a lot just to have that, to say your mother did that for you.

'She's basically given me the will to do as I want, knowing it doesn't matter how desperate things are, you've always got the choice to leave or make a change. Anything bad I erase from my memory because I've got so much future to put in. I don't blame my present on my past.'

At twelve, Krissy wrote and illustrated her first book, *Henry the Elephant*, and it was followed by several more. At sixteen, she made the decision that her life would be different from her mother's. At seventeen, she joined the Movement Against Uranium Mining because she wanted to save the world. She stuck up posters, joined a sleep-in protest in Melbourne city square, wrote her own protest pamphlets and was sacked for producing them with office supplies from the firm she worked for. Then she found a job in the classical studies department of Melbourne's Monash University — 'ancient Greek and ancient Latin, very classy'. Later she tried to buy a tank to use in anti-mining protests at Katherine, in the north of Australia, but when she didn't raise enough money she went to Brisbane and joined anti-uranium protests there. She did a cartwheel in front of the police and was locked up for being drunk and disorderly — despite the fact that she didn't drink.

When Krissy moved to Sydney she found work in a government office (where she wore sober clothes) and joined a band called *Animal, Vegetable, Mineral* which she said was 'primitive and off-beat'. She joined a credit union, paid off her debts and set about finishing her latest book, *Don't Follow the Leader*, a futuristic story about workers and bosses. Krissy has written several books now, all of them with a strong political focus on the oppression of the working class.

Being involved in the film we were making gave Krissy control over how her life was portrayed. It was her story and she decided how she wanted to tell it. When she saw the rushes, she said she was gobsmacked with delight. For the first time she saw herself as intelligent, articulate and strong — my reactions the first time I had met her. She had never had any confidence in her own creative work but after the film was completed, she took a portfolio of her work to the University of Technology, Sydney and was accepted. I am not saying the film changed Krissy's life. I am saying her own intelligence, her guts and her resilience were almost certainly going to pull her through. She was right: her life would not be the same as her mother's.

Jake's story challenged the Rockwell myth of irreparable damage — the idea that some children can be so damaged by their experiences they have no hope for the future.

I had known Jake since he was a young boy — a quiet, dark-haired child with a wide, humorous mouth and a quirky view of the world. His parents were separated and he was brought up in South Australia by an intensely loving, middle-class mother, who watched with increasing alarm as he began disappearing in clouds of marijuana smoke once he had started high school.

The next few years followed a pattern well-known to those who are familiar with young people and drug abuse: Jake began dropping in and out of school, and consistently under-achieving; he moved to Sydney where he worked in various food bars; he experienced a psychotic episode which frightened him, and subsequently sought treatment from a psychiatrist whom he really liked and trusted. He enrolled at university, and things looked promising for him. But he again began using drugs heavily and drifted back to Sydney, where his slide downhill accelerated. When he came to visit me one day, he looked ill and raddled. He was unwashed, chain-smoked and had a nasty cough. He said he was engaging in unprotected homosexual sex and pimping to raise money for his drugs. I felt sick.

He told me not to worry. When he was fifteen, he had taken a whole packet of antihistamines. 'I had an idea they wouldn't kill me, but if they did, I wouldn't be around to know about it and so that was okay. I remember waking up a few times, heart fluttering, room too dark, and thinking, "Now you've done it, you've gone too far." But I was okay.'

'Use condoms, go and get an AIDS test, and go back to your psychiatrist,' I said, feeling desperate. He was only nineteen.

The next news I had about Jake was from his mother, who rang to say she had persuaded him to come home for 'rest and rehabilitation.' Or 'chicken and chocolate cake,' as we called it. She was determined to stop Jake drifting back to Sydney and had persuaded him to accompany her to

America to visit her family. He went, but then insisted on leaving her and chancing it on his own in New York.

This time, I felt even sicker. If life in Sydney had nearly killed him, how would he possibly fare in a city like New York? Yet, despite my fears, New York proved to be a turning point for Jake — one of those moments when a sudden shift in environment jolts a person out of destructive patterns of behaviour.

Two years later, I was in New York and arranged to meet Jake in Greenwich Village. His mother had said he was doing well — working as a production assistant at a documentary film company and living in Brooklyn with his girlfriend, an artist, who worked for the same firm. Even so, I was apprehensive.

We met at an old-fashioned New York diner in the unfashionable part of the Village — one of those cavernous, dark wood places with fixed wooden seats and benches, and mostly male customers tucking into huge plates of steak and chips. Nothing fancy about this joint. Jake looked well. He gave me a wide smile. We hugged. He said, 'Don't look at my fingers — I still smoke.' And almost immediately he plunged into an account of how he'd managed to straighten up his life. As I'd suspected, he said moving to New York was important, a geographical escape.

'I was worried that I would continue to use needles if I stayed in Australia. The problem is that if you know where to get heroin, then it's very tempting. However, I never got into it too heavily in Sydney. I used it very carefully and rarely. I preferred speed. I used it for about three months. Short-run, but enough to make me feel like a junkie. The stuff isn't really even addictive compared to cigarettes or dope. Just one of those force-of-habit addictions.'

He took a large bite of his hamburger. 'I don't know what made me so confident I could pull back at any time. Maybe delusions of grandeur! Everyone says they can stop whenever they want. And theoretically it's true. But in practice, it's another thing. To really want to make a change in your life involves an enormous amount of courage, but it can also happen on a whim. I had wanted to push rebellion as far as I could, but I always knew I was in control.'

I pulled a face and said that many people who claimed they were in control were now ashes in the wind, so what saved him?

He laughed and pushed the remains of his chips around his plate. 'Well, I said I wasn't going to do it for ever. There had to be a time to stop. The people I admired and respected didn't behave the way I did. Also, I began to feel older. To realise I was missing opportunities that would not come again. If I was to do the things I wanted to do, then I had to act soon, because I wasn't proud of what I'd done already.'

I sighed and felt a terrible anxiety for him. He responded immediately, even though I had not spoken.

'You're right. I still feel like I'm turning the corner, Anne. I still feel like I could suddenly turn into a junkie. Bang! Pop! you know. I still get angry at things that are outside my control.'

I leant back on my diner bench, exhausted, vague memories of Jonathan rising to the surface.

'It's okay,' he said. 'I'm getting there.' He said the turning point in his life came when he had his first psychotic breakdown in Sydney at the age of nineteen. His psychiatrist lent him a book called *Adaptation to Life*, by George Vaillant.

Jake said that when he read Vaillant's book, it was the beginning of a long, slow journey to realise how he had shaped the destructive patterns of his life, and how he could change them.

'I think it was the first time I understood we are all on even ground and it's how we respond to what happens around us that separates us from our peers. I realised I had a choice. Ken Nunn, my shrink, gave me a lot of confidence, especially when he said he thought I saw the world all too clearly — because it was the world that scared me. If you're intent on fucking up, you can pretty much guarantee you'll succeed. But if you attempt to make it, well there is no certainty that you will.'

'So was it easier to fail than to try and succeed, whatever that means?'

'Yes, I don't think the Vaillant book gave me an instant cure — it doesn't work like that. Look at all that time in Sydney when I was prostituting and you nearly freaked right out. Sometimes it takes years to filter through that, before you can actually begin to change your life. Put it this way, I think the most resilient thing I am doing now is actually trying to live a decent life. I'll settle for what I get or make, and be happy with that.'

It had been a long conversation in this diner in Greenwich Village with this young man I once feared would end up dead. It was such a normal, ordinary setting: glass-topped tables, narrow benches. The hamburger was excellent, the chips were good, the coffee had revived me, and Jake was alive and well and safe. I felt absurdly like shouting out to everyone in the cafe, 'God's in his heaven, all's right with the world.'

When we left, Jake said with a grin, 'I'll even pay the bill.'

• • •

The third Rockwell myth, the myth of identity, cautions us not to label and dismiss people who are ill or at-risk, but to define people in terms of what they *can* do.

One of the most moving examples of the benefits of this approach comes from the story of a forty-four year old man called David — the son of a friend of mine, Mona Wasow, who is a leading authority on mental illness in the United States. David has had a particularly virulent form of schizophrenia — similar to Jonathan's — since late childhood, and his mother does not believe the illness itself has abated over the decades. The newer medications cause fewer side affects than previous ones, but in David's case, they are not otherwise more helpful. Nevertheless, there is a dramatic difference between the David of twenty-five years ago and the David of today.

Mona Wasow sent me an article she had written about the changes in David's life, hoping it might be helpful in the writing of this book:

In the old days, David's life consisted of sitting and staring into space, chain-smoking, walking a lot, listening to his beloved folk music, and coming home once a week for dinner. Today he still smokes and walks a lot, but he also works at a restaurant an hour a day, gets himself to a clubhouse for lunch every day, and has learned to ride the buses so that he can get to his music and pottery lessons every week. On his weekly visits home, he often helps me prepare dinner, cracks a few jokes, and plays some live music with the rest of us.

David's changes came about when professionals and family members began to focus on his considerable strengths instead of his illness. In the old days, the emphasis in his treatment was on his illness and on improving his 'abysmal daily living skills', which is how his mother described them — helping him learn to ride the bus, take a shower, make eye contact with people, and so on.

The David I remembered was a big, tall, bearded man who walked with his eyes cast down, was too fearful to venture outside on his own, and did not like to take showers. David's living skills were indeed abysmal — and with good reason, for, as Mona wrote, 'Where should David go on the bus? For whom should he shower? With whom should he make eye contact — with those fearful strangers on the street who he knows want no contact with him whatsoever?'

A few years ago, at a regular half-yearly treatment meeting, one of his social workers was reporting on David's considerable deficits, when the psychiatrist said, 'I don't want to hear all that again. That's his illness, and we haven't been able to change that for years. Tell me about his strengths. We would do better to work with those.'

David comes from a musical and artistic family. His mother remembered hearing him pick out parts of a Bach fugue on his guitar — 'which is pretty good for a guy who never had a music lesson.' A friend recalled his interest in a neighbourhood pottery studio, and with David's timid consent, pottery and guitar lessons became the focus of a new treatment plan. After his first guitar lesson, the teacher recognised he was unusually talented and told him so.

'Now that was worth taking a shower for,' wrote his mother. 'Maybe the music teacher would say that again … Learn to ride the bus to get to the pottery studio. You bet. Even make a little eye contact with the friendly pottery teacher who laughed with pleasure at David's newly created ceramic bear sitting in a canoe. The $215 he made in a pottery sale a year later produced even more eye contact. Now that he had the experience of pleasant interactions with a few people other than family and professionals, he dared to take on a job at a restaurant. He has never missed a day.'

Mona says that once a conscious effort was put into developing her son's strengths, the turnabout in his behaviour and sense of wellbeing was dramatic. David's life now has some meaning for him, and playing music provides a way for him to join his family members on an equal footing.

In May 2000, Mona's university department threw her a retirement party and family and friends came to sing for her. 'In the past, David would have been sitting miserably in the corner of the room, head bowed, out of it. This time he was up there in the front row, playing his harmonica with the rest of my motley crew, and we all cried with joy.'

The fourth Rockwell myth — that ultimately, it doesn't matter — tells us that whatever is done or not done makes little difference to the final outcome. Upholders of this misanthropic view fail to recognise that final outcomes aren't always as important as present happiness. My son's seven years of schizophrenia was a harsh period, but threaded through the miseries were moments of joy — one, in particular, stands out for me.

I had flown to Sydney to be with Jonathan one New Year's Eve during a period when he lived mainly in refuges or on the streets. He lolloped towards me in the dusk, wearing a bowler hat, pin-striped trousers hitched up by a piece of string, and a long black overcoat. His feet were bare. Safety pins in long chains dangled from his ears. He wore a daisy in his buttonhole and was giggling.

'Happy new year, ear, 'ere 'ere,' he said, and kicked an empty soft drink can so it rolled down the alley way, clinking loudly in the darkness.

'Where are we going?' he said, 'A darnce, a dance, a prance, somewhere posh, oh my gosh?'

We caught a bus to the lighthouse at Watson's Bay where people were already gathering to celebrate the New Year. This was an eccentric crowd: two old women dancing ring-a-rosie, a Japanese bridal party, some young bloods drinking champagne, old men with beer guts, children and families. A warm breeze, the lights of Sydney, fish and chips, beer, and this boy, my son, with his long black overcoat and his bowler hat and poor sore feet. We danced, around and around the lighthouse we danced, like a Fellini film. 'Home is where the heart is,' I say, 'and be damned if that's a cliché.'

'Chichi,' says Jonathan, 'give me your heart, Anne, and I'll give you mine.'

I sat at dusk in my garden, remembering Jonathan and his bare feet, thinking about the effect of negativity on the human spirit. A mosquito buzzed around my head and I tried to flap it away. I thought of Robert, and how one of his greatest strengths was his optimism — the spirit of possibility he was able to engender in others, even those who disagreed with him. I had just received an email from British Columbia where he was engaging in a series of forestry debates.

22.8.99

Hi Anne, I am looking out at a mountain across a lake with a glacier on the top. Deer and bears come into the garden but I have not seen any. Looking out at the beauty it's difficult to see what the environmental furore is about, but I know the issues all too clearly. However, it's clear from listening to people at the meetings here that the environmentalists are just as locked into their rhetoric as the loggers. The trouble comes when oppositional groups are committed to fighting those whose views differ from their own. From their perspective, the world is divided into good guys and bad guys. Scoring occurs as the good guys win and the bad guys lose. There is often total symmetry in the process. Both sides see each other as evil and destructive and are unwilling to talk.

Yet it is only through this listening process that we can create new understandings. If we are to have any hope of bringing about the kinds of changes that are required to prevent massive breakdown in the near future, we must learn to work together across current institutional and organisational boundaries. I am convinced we can only achieve these changes if we commit to spiritual values, and to honesty, responsibility, humility and love. We're at a point in history where we need to be gentle with each other and value each others' efforts to create a better world. Few who get up in the morning are wanting to make the world worse. Take care, love Robert.

10

Values — what happened?

Is it really true, as Robert wrote, that few of us actually want to make the world worse? I pondered that possibility early the following day as rain lashed against the window panes and wind rattled every door in the house. I had woken up wondering whether tyrants like Idi Amin and Pol Pot opened their eyes at the dawn of each day from dreams of childhood innocence — or did they wake up already planning to dispatch thousands of citizens to torture or death?

Do bad leaders only flourish in cultures whose values and circumstances permit malignant influences to grow? Most Westerners are increasingly hesitant about the concept of a God-given moral law, written on the tablets of eternity. Given that we entered the twentieth century believing we had grown out of our war-like past, much of that century was an unpleasant surprise in terms of large-scale killing and cruelty. I think that, gradually and reluctantly, this horrible truth has led to a shift towards looking at the demons within, and to acknowledging responsibility for the actions that shape or destroy our lives. Satan is no longer such a convenient scapegoat.

Our values help determine the way we live our lives, the governments we choose to elect, the laws our society makes. These in turn affect our health and wellbeing and, particularly, the health and wellbeing of our children. I was back in Urie Bronfenbrenner's bioecological systems theory, thinking about the rings of influence and support which affect our children.

If a society does not value its children, money will not flow to support those children. Already we know that millions of children are needlessly dying or are at risk because they are not protected by the 'everyday magic of ordinary, normative human resources'— to use the eloquent words of Ann Masten, head of the Institute of Child Development at the University of Minnesota.

Yet when decisions are made about how governments should spend our money, or what kind of laws should underpin issues such as euthanasia, or how we should treat refugees, where are the ethical debates? Why do we consistently avoid talking about values, ethics or morality — the big forces in our lives which influence all others?

At conferences, delegates will often become glassy-eyed if anyone strays to value-based ground. Everything has to be evidence-based. Traditional values, evolved with the greater good in mind, seem to have passed their use-by date, to be replaced by values that fit more comfortably with ideas of growth and consumption. Matters that would largely have been the subject of religious or moral discourse are now determined by adversarial courts of law.

This was becoming too complex a thought process for

pre-breakfast consumption, so I decided to go for a walk. The rain was still chucking down outside, and the dog hates the rain, but she grudgingly eased herself out the door. As we picked our way through the puddles I recalled a Drug Summit I attended in Canberra in 1985. It was a high-profile public event, convened by Prime Minister Bob Hawke, with the aim of seeking solutions to mounting concerns about drug use and abuse, particularly among the young.

Participants were divided into three streams: legal, medical and social. I was asked to chair the social group, and found myself with a hanging judge, two young men who were heroin addicts, several politicians of varied hue, a fundamentalist minister who thought all people with addictions should be jailed, and another minister who worked with homeless street people and decided the whole summit was 'rigged'. The latter sat on a window-sill looking like Humpty-Dumpty and refused to take part.

In the end, the only way to achieve cohesion was to pull our discussion back to the unanimous agreement that none of us wanted the death and suffering caused by drug abuse. From that position we were able to move forward — painfully — to acknowledge that sources of the drug problem, like those of many other problems, went to the heart of our society — its values, its culture and its economy. It seemed to me that to ignore this was to tinker around on the surface and achieve little.

At the plenary session, when we delivered our report, which asked people to look beyond the short-term, we were met with stony faces. When political elections are held every three years, as they are in Australia, it is hard to persuade governments to take a long-term view. Ministers are impatient to get tangible proposals that will put rungs on their electoral ladders. A long-term focus on prevention does not fit short-term requirements for political action — particularly when the public require immediate responses to immediate problems.

Several years after I'd attended this Drug Summit, Richard Eckersley, who is a Fellow at the National Centre for Epidemiology and Population Health in Canberra, began writing a series of hard-hitting papers in which he argued that broad cultural shifts in Western societies, and the shifts in values associated with them, were having a major impact on the wellbeing of Australian young people. He referred to rising suicide, drug abuse and crime rates, as well as an increasing sense of social detachment and alienation among the young.

Eckersley referred to surveys that suggested a deep tension between people's professed values and the lifestyle promoted by modern Western societies. 'Many were concerned about the greed, excess and materialism they believed drove society, underlay social ills and threatened their children's future. They yearned for a better balance in their lives.'

Eckersley believed that a range of economic, social and technological changes had combined and interacted to create a society that was increasingly hostile to our wellbeing, especially young people's wellbeing because of their greater social and psychological vulnerability.

He identified some of the immediate changes as increased family conflict and breakdown, youth unemployment, poverty, education pressures, media influence and pessimism about humanity's future. Together, these factors were denting the natural resilience and buoyancy of youth. Eckersley also warned that superficial measures to combat these problems would never fully succeed.

Over ten years later, by all the social indices, Eckersley was correct. We are still losing the war against drugs; crime remains a serious social problem; the epidemic of youth suicide continues; children are still being abused and are falling through the cracks of government care; and one in five Australian teenagers experiences significant mental health problems.

These are similar to problems Professor Fiona Stanley identified when she said that children and adolescents were experiencing significant psychosis, schizophrenia, depression, and anxiety — and that the rates for these conditions were rising in Australia just as they were in every country in the Western world.

All the evidence suggests these difficulties are not confined to the socially disadvantaged and marginalised in our society. Eckersley states that such problems are a product of being young in the last decades of the twentieth century. A recent study of Australian university undergraduates found that almost two-thirds admitted to suicidal ideation (thoughts) or behaviours in the past twelve months, ranging from 'life isn't worth living', to more extreme reactions, such as 'I want to kill myself. I wish my life would end.'

An equally disturbing picture emerges for adults. Rates of mental illness, depression and anxiety are rising in every country in the Western world. Psychologist and author Martin Seligman points to the paradox of societies like Australia and the United States which have never been richer, yet have unprecedented epidemics of depression. He is quick to point out that this is not a biological phenomenon. 'There hasn't been a change in our hormones or our genes. The ozone layer, our nutrition, does not account for this phenomenon.'

The other worrying trend is that the average age for the

onset of depression is getting younger. A couple of generations ago, first bouts of depression were likely to happen at about thirty-four or thirty-five years of age. Now, the mean age is fourteen years.

Stories like these are echoed around the world. A sobering lesson from Europe arrives in a book by criminologist David Smith and psychiatrist Michael Rutter, which points out that general increases in living standards, and the reduction of social inequities in the European community since World War Two have not been paralleled by reductions in disorders of youth. Suicide rates, rates of depression, drug and alcohol problems have risen — even in a country as socially committed as Sweden, which provides free pre- and post-natal care for children, paid parental leave, excellent education and housing. In Stockholm, twenty-eight per cent of urban families are presently considered at risk because of chronic alcoholism and parental psychopathology.

So why is this happening? I asked, and immediately remembered a story told by eminent scholar and psychologist, Abraham Maslow, in the 1970s. He was recalling the frontispiece of a book on abnormal psychology: the lower half of the frontispiece showed a picture of a line of babies, pink, sweet, innocent and lovable. Above that was a picture of passengers on a subway train, glum, grey, sullen and sour. The caption underneath said, very simply, 'What happened?'

Part of what happened is personal and specific: family violence, alcoholism, family break-up, conflict, abuse and neglect, increased mobility leading to the scattering of family members, fear of failure, the unpredictable nature of modern life, the problems of achieving trusting relationships with caring adults outside the immediate home. These problems are usually dealt with singly — few services have the time or resources to take a holistic view of an individual. We live in a quick-fix society.

One in forty Australian schoolchildren is being medicated for an emotional or a behavioural problem — a thirteen-fold increase over the past decade. A quarter of these drugs are taken for behavioural problems. Remedial classes, better schools and support at home might be the answer.

'We have been so used to "fixing things",' wrote Robert in a pamphlet he had sent me called *The Healing Century*, 'that this is often the only approach we consider. We fix our hyperactive children with Ritalin, our depression with Prozac, our lack of self-worth with alcohol and drugs. We fix our social problems with legislation ... and we fix our health problems with drugs which cause resistance in the next generation of germs and viruses: this is causing an increasingly recognised threat to our ability to deal with past and future diseases.'

I hadn't heard from Robert for several days and was beginning to worry about him. Earlier he had written that he was feeling exceptionally tired and had discovered he was anaemic. The last email I'd received had been at the beginning of his journey through British Columbia. Another one arrived that night:

21.8.99
I came through the mountains by bus yesterday and got a better sense of the vegetation. British Columbia is heavily wooded and it's difficult for an outsider to make sense of the forest debate which I'm meant to help clarify today. I can probably only do so by enlarging the framework.

Robert used the term 'enlarging the framework' to indicate a need to explore the broader pervasive influences which help define our lives — even if we also need bandaids to fix our immediate ills. When psychologist Martin Seligman began looking at underlying causes for depression, he turned to children's books. This amused and reassured me. It was the same approach I had taken some time previously, thumbing through my children's books to see how resilience was portrayed. Seligman found that two generations earlier, children's books were all about doing well in the world through hard work and the desire to help others. He cited titles like *The Little Engine that Could*. Today's primers are increasingly about individual self-esteem — Seligman related this to the fact that our society was hurtling down the path of rampant individualism.

Dr Margaret Somerville, founding director of the McGill Centre for Medicine, Ethics and Law in Canada wonders whether our intense individualism has come about through society's failure — in a secular democracy — to provide an adequate cultural framework of values, hope, purpose and belonging. She believes we have lost our sense of mystery, and must act to protect the human spirit — 'that deeply intuitive sense of connectedness to the world and the universe in which we live.'

As we cannot live fully human lives without having a sense of connectedness, an absence of this hits at the heart of resilience. Fashionable expressions of today include words like rootlessness, anomie, meaninglessness, existential boredom, emptiness, estrangement, alienation. Other factors that must surely impinge on our sense of wellbeing are a heightened sense of insecurity and fear that we have begun to destroy our own nest.

In England, the two British researchers David Smith and

Michael Rutter also believe that shifts in moral concepts and values are among the causes of increased psychosocial disorder. They, too, note the shift towards individualism, the increasing emphasis on self-realisation and fulfilment and the consequent rise of our expectations. I wondered if maybe 'The Little Engine that Could' engendered despair in 'The Little Engines that Couldn't' — expectations of success are a feature of contemporary life which can damage all those young people who fail to 'succeed'. One answer is to help them win in some other way.

Overarching Western life is a market approach to values which increasingly measures human worth in monetary terms. The pursuit of the public good has been replaced by the pursuit of individual self-interest. Most people don't appear to believe that life is getting better, despite being richer. Social decay and environmental degradation dominate visions of the future. People have not become happier by becoming richer. Only in the poorest countries of the world is income a good measure of wellbeing.

Many young people are not comfortable with these broad changes in social values, nor are they inspired by materialistic views of a world where everything is valued primarily in economic terms.

Eckersley remembers reading an old saying in a Jewish prayer book which warned about the sacrifice of the moral to the economic, and about our failure to ensure that the things that matter most are not at the mercy of the things that matter least.

I asked myself, What does matter most to people? Is it not our personal relationships and the meaning we make of our lives? Wealth is largely irrelevant to health and happiness — although poverty does limit opportunities.

It seemed to me that my reading and beliefs about values and resilience linked in strongly with Robert's work. Consistently, he said that we had a choice. We could continue to direct growth towards increasing personal wealth and consumption, which would ultimately lead to breakdown. Or we could direct our resources towards restoring and protecting our environment, strengthening our social relationships and equipping young people with the skills and resilience to navigate their way through life.

'I am much more concerned with human values. Our need to focus on quality of life issues, rather than ever-greater consumption of goods.'

One of the most moving stories about the need for deep connectedness in our lives is told by Buddhist philosopher and deep ecologist, Joanna Macy, who was invited to run a workshop in an area south of Chernobyl after the Russian nuclear reactor disaster of 1986, where radioactive fallout had killed or poisoned every living thing for a radius of many kilometres. Scientists had tried to prevent radioactive material from falling on Moscow. Instead, it fell on a forested area, in which a thriving community of people lived whose livelihood came from the trees. Some months later, because of radioactivity, workmen destroyed their houses and built them concrete houses instead. Then they cut down all the trees.

When Macy met the community in their village hall, she saw a giant photographic mural of the forests, stretching from one wall to another. This image was all they had left.

Everyone in the community was angry. They were angry at the tumours which were already growing inside their children; angry at being cut off from their connection with the land; angry that their livelihood had been destroyed. They directed the full force of their anger at Macy. That night, when she reflected on her day's experiences, she realised how important it was that she bear witness to the anger and grief of this community, and acknowledge the terrible loss and sadness that had entered their lives.

Macy says that deep ecology work taps into the power of our interconnectedness with one another. 'It is essential that we develop our inner resources. We have to learn to look at things as they are, painful and overwhelming as that may be, for no healing can begin until we are fully present to our world, until we can learn to sustain the gaze.'

Macy's is a powerful story. Of all the levels of resilience I have so far explored, the need she identified — our need for deep connection — is the strongest of all. Without this, children fail to thrive, families become emotionally impoverished, communities grow vulnerable. Without a sense of connection, societies are fearful and move to control and dominate each other and the environments in which they live.

'These are big issues we need to discuss,' said Robert in an email which he sent in September, just before he returned to Australia for his twelve-week tour:

Increasingly it seems that if we are going to do good work, it will be by allowing people to talk about their experiences and their concerns. Power elites believe in maximum economic growth, international competitiveness — all those things — with small regard for the impact of maximised growth either on the world's resources or on the psyches of the people. The rest of us (though we seldom articulate it) want a higher quality of life, healthier relationships and a more compassionate society. They want maximum productivity. We want a life that makes sense.

11

The briefest joy

Robert returned to Australia in September for a twelve-week stay which would include the three-day conference in Canberra and our holiday in Queensland that we'd arranged earlier. When I met him at Sydney airport I was shocked by his gaunt frame and the greyness of his face.

'Are you all right?' I asked, driving home from the airport. It had been raining and the roads were skiddy.

'Not as energetic as I'd wish,' he said. 'Perhaps I'm just tired.'

'You must be. Revising two books during your summer break wasn't much of a rest.'

'I'm used to that sort of thing, but usually I recover more quickly.'

He stayed at my house for two nights before he went ahead to Canberra to check arrangements for the conference. I was to follow. Except for that brief first meeting in March six months earlier, and a couple of rushed car trips across Sydney in May, this was the first time we had ever been alone together. We circled each other with all the gaucheness of youth. On the second day, before Robert flew to Canberra to prepare for the conference, we went for a walk on the cliff top and he said he looked forward to having time to get to know each other, but it would have to wait till his first spell of work was over. Then he said, abruptly, 'What's a *bure*?'

'A Fijian hut, tourist-style.'

'How many rooms?'

'One. Does that bother you?'

'No,' he said in a throw-away manner, 'No, I'm sure we can manage to share a room.'

'It has six beds,' I said in some irritation. I hadn't organised the holiday — he had asked Julie Walker, his tour coordinator, to make the arrangements after consultation with me, and one-room *bures* were all that had been available. This had also somewhat alarmed me. We had achieved the promise of intimacy on email that mightn't necessarily unfold in real life.

Our path had taken a downward turn, the sand was slippery and the dog was hanging back, when Robert said, 'And then when we get there we can talk about sex.'

I looked round, bemused. 'What are you trying to tell me, Robert?'

'Well, some people like sex, and some people don't and for some people it isn't important.'

'Uh-huh,' I said. Two joggers were pushing past me, the dog had now decided to shit, this wasn't a good time or space to have a conversation about sex. I took a deep breath. 'It'll be fine.'

I went back and read one of my favourite Dorothy Parker poems:

Oh, life is a glorious cycle of song,
A medley of extemporanea;
And love is a thing that can never go wrong;
And I am Marie of Romania.

There was an ever-increasing urgency about Robert now, as if he had all but abandoned his body. He made some small pretence at eating, slept little and would be at his computer well before the sun rose. He appeared driven, as if he feared for the future and yet, because he was an intelligent man, he must have known that all the talking he did, to all the audiences, could only shift a few small grains of sand. Yet he still had an unshakeable belief that, together, people had the potential to choose wiser, gentler and less destructive ways to live.

The conference, which was held at the University of Canberra, was one of those open-space gatherings, one-page papers, plenty of time for discussion, the usual shortcomings and disappointments, but also a sense of possibility, of hope. From Canberra, Robert began a nine-week tour of Australia — a tour which led Deirdre Macken of the *Australian Financial Review* to write, 'the most extraordinary aspect is that it is taking him from the most powerful in the country to the least powerful, from the richest companies to the poorest towns, from ballrooms full of suits to picnics with the poor. Theobald has been invited to address almost every major interest group in the country.' She believed that much of his appeal lay in his belief that a more humanist future was possible, and likened his tour to both the financial roadshows of the 1980s and the crusades of the Middle Ages. Then she added, 'This tour touts neither script or scripture but ideas for the future, centred on values, ecological integrity, equality in communities, better decision-making and quality of living.' She said that although too often thought of as a guru, Robert resisted the call to preach or even find answers — these, he said, lay within the community. Janet Holmes à Court, in an introduction to one of Robert's new Australian books, *Visions and Pathways for the 21st Century*, wrote that his strength lay in being able to mesh the larger global shifts with the smallest, most pragmatic steps that a person, a company or a country town might take to achieve their goals.

In Rockhampton, for instance, he urged groups to consider the things they like about their Queensland city. 'The zoo is still free: is that of value to you?' he challenged his audience. 'You are entitled as a community to decide if that is what is important. You don't have to do it another way, the way the economists would.'

The issue of overload was frequently brought up by his audience. 'Downsizing institutions and overloading the remaining people doesn't necessarily work. Tired people don't make good truck drivers and they don't make good policy.'

Each time Robert telephoned, his voice sounded more tired. He was to break his tour in Adelaide, where I was to join him in a community consultation program before we flew north for our holiday.

Julie had made the bookings some time back and had chosen well. Long Island was a small island just off the Whitsunday coast in Queensland. A boat trip, clear green water, seagulls, gentle breezes. Another boat trip on a much smaller boat, curved white sandy beaches, oleanders, frangipani, hibiscus, fourteen *bures* set around the sandy sweep of Palm Bay, and a variety of small boats pulled up on the shore. This particular resort was built just after World War Two and had remained undeveloped, which meant it was low-key and old-fashioned. No television or telephones, but hammocks on the verandahs, wallabies and bush turkeys venturing up to the verandah steps. The *bures* were spare but comfortable, and there were the six beds. Great sulphur-crested cockatoos arched through the sky. Curlews and pelicans drifted through the water. I stepped off our verandah onto the sand and four paces later my feet were in the water.

Love is a kind of divine madness, said Plato. Was this how I felt? Yes. If you're going to fall in love with someone there's no point in being half-hearted about it. And just as love brings strength to resilience, so can resilience bring strength to love. In fact, I'd take it further and say that in all relationships, some kind of resilience is essential. Maybe in its early stages a relationship requires a different kind of resilience, more concerned with riding out all those challenges new love brings, from the ridiculous to the enormous. We start out seeking perfection, without recognising that perfection is a bore, that it is only through accommodation and good humour that we learn more about ourselves and each other. Yet how many times do we expend our energies trying to change people as soon as we feel we've 'caught' them — like my friend who worried because her new lover persisted in training his few strands of hair across his shining bald head. Should she put photographs of good-looking bald men on the refrigerator to show him she thought bald was sexy, or should she become Delilah, and snip off his hair in the middle of the night? (She snipped.)

I thought of that age-old lament, woman to man, 'Speak to me, touch me, be gentle with me' — but it seemed to me that men and women often still spoke different languages, and in our frustration we neglected to listen and translate into our own words.

'I love you,' I used to say to a passionate but emotionally inarticulate man.

'Likewise,' he would mutter in embarrassment.

'We have to talk about Our Relationship,' I would continue, until 'Our Relationship' was almost all we talked about — it developed a weight and a presence of its own which had little to do with us: the two people sitting opposite one another, angrily dissecting their unreal expectations. Sometimes, in our concern to 'get it right', we analyse love into extinction.

Now, with Robert, I hadn't done any analysis. I hadn't drawn up any lists of pros and cons. Except with a few close friends, I hadn't even talked about what was happening. I trusted myself. I trusted Robert. I looked at him now in the darkness, so neatly folded, so still as he slept. This was a warm-hearted, brilliant and creative man who challenged the way people thought about the world and about their abilities to make a difference. A big man in every sense of the word. A few years earlier, I would have watched and measured every move forward we made, determined that I wouldn't be patronised or dominated. But since then I had learned that relationships do not have to be a battle ground, but can be a place of mutual pleasure and trust. In her book, *The Orchard*, Drusilla Modjeska wrote that it takes time to come into one's own life, 'to know one's strengths and capacities, to develop the flexibility that allows not the domination of others or ourselves, but a mutuality that trusts those we love with the truth about ourselves.'

For four days we lived in joy. We talked, slept, made love, swam, read, played Scrabble, behaved like adolescents in a world reborn. It is hard to write about those times of silent intimacy, the closeness we had that needed no words. In the late afternoons we took to walking up a sandy track to a small half-moon of beach on the other side of the island. This was a beach of pebbles, dark grey and cream, red and pale yellow, pebbles that crunched beneath our feet while seaweed coiled itself around our ankles in fronds of green. This was where we shared tales of our former lives. Half the fun of falling in love is having a willing audience for stories that by now have bored the pants off most of our friends. Self-disclosures — avoiding the damaging bits or occasionally throwing them in our partner's lap: 'Here, see if this turns you off.'

Robert told me briefly about the time he spent in India, where he was born and where he returned during the war years. He had been evacuated from England to India about the same time that my family sailed from England to Malaya. We had both returned to England in the same month and the same year. Coincidences like this make it tempting to play synchronicity games. I am wary of these and think of all the absurdities they can give rise to: 'Fancy that, he likes raspberries. D'you hear, he likes raspberries. Same as me. Isn't that *extraordinary*. What's that? Hitler liked raspberries?'

Robert's father was a director of a firm called Binny's that managed cotton mills in Madras and Bangalore and a ship repair workshop in Madras harbour. His grandfather was the Reverend Canon Pulleine, Rector of Ripley, a village near Harrogate in Yorkshire where Robert often spent his holidays when he was at his school in England. He said he felt close to his father, who loved India and bothered to learn as much as he could about its culture and history.

I told Robert about my life in Australia and, as I did so, I realised for the first time how I had changed from being a somewhat pathetic child, easily victimised, through to an adolescent of rat-cunning and silent rebellion, to finally emerge in my last years at school as a reasonably honest, competent and honourable young woman. (I was even well liked.) Up till then, I hadn't quite thought of my transformation in those terms.

Robert and I had walked back from the pebbly beach and were sitting outside on our verandah, playing 'I remember'. A bush turkey came inquisitively up to the steps — I could just make out its shape in the darkening blue light — but when I stretched out a hand it scuttled away again.

'I remember … "Poms Go Home!",' I told Robert. 'That was the graffiti we saw on suburban walls in Perth, during the war.' We had moved from the country back to Perth, to find that British migrants were by no means universally welcome in Australia after the fall of Singapore in World War Two.

'Was that because of all those young Australian soldiers who were sent to Singapore at the last minute, straight into the arms of the Japanese?'

'Yes,' I said, emptying a pocketful of pebbles I had brought back with me. 'I think Australians decided a bit of come-uppance wouldn't do us Brits any harm.'

Robert picked up a flat smooth pebble and skimmed it across the surface of the water. It was a long throw. 'And what about you?'

'We copped it. Looking back it was all pretty harmless stuff — like mimicking our accents — but I just remember this strong feeling of being "other". So we children banded together and started talking with such broad Australian accents that not even Australians could understand.'

He laughed. A large bird flew low overhead, white against the gathering dark, and I wondered if it was a pelican. I told

Robert how I used my wits to survive. In exchange for peace and protection from schoolmates, I did their homework and wrote letters for them — scurrilous and amorous, a penny a sheet. A social science researcher might say I was exhibiting 'adaptive resilience'.

Robert laughed. 'I'd say you've been exhibiting it ever since.'

The most devious part of my story was yet to come. We had moved to Perth with the two families we'd lived with in the country — all of us in a two-bedroom house with a big closed-in verandah where the children slept. It was a noisy and fractious household because our mothers were barely coping. Halfway through our first year in Perth, we kids became accomplished thieves. We had decided we were sick of being poor. Other kids had fridges, not a smelly old ice-box like ours. Other kids had hot water that came from a tap, not from a chip-heater. Other kids slept in bedrooms, not on verandahs. Other kids didn't wear hand-me-downs, like the dress made from an old pair of curtains which my mother sewed for my first school dance, or the sandals made from felt inner-soles, tied together with coloured tape. 'Roman sandals,' my mother had said hopefully. They fell apart the first time I danced.

Then I had had this ingenious idea — a way to end our poverty. Every night, carrying a torch and a couple of trowels, we wheeled our old bicycle, with its wicker basket, to the nearest municipal buildings where we dug up plants from the surrounding flower beds. We wrapped the plants in damp newspaper and sold them the following day, either on street corners or to shops a safe distance from where we lived. Occasionally, we also raided private gardens, particularly if some colourful plant took our fancy. We also answered advertisements for free pets 'needing a good home', tied ribbons round their necks, and sold them from door to door.

I have no idea how much money we made, probably not very much, but it seemed a fortune each week as we divvied up our spoils. We would always buy something for our mothers, convincing them we had worked after school for the money. Once we saved up enough to buy them a bottle of gin because we decided they deserved a treat — my frail Aunt Doreen's tropical illness was worse, my French god-mother Yette was still grieving over the death of her husband, and my forty-four year old mother was exhausted from looking after us and a tiny baby, with no husband to help her.

Our days as plant thieves came to an end one afternoon when an elderly woman, white-haired and frail, spotted us tugging at her Christmas bush, and invited us in to choose whatever plants we wanted without having to steal them. Then she gave us lemon cordial and biscuits. Shame over-came us, and we made no further expeditions but graduated to less hazardous ways of earning money — paper and chemist shop deliveries.

Looking back, I think we had few qualms about our stealing. In fact when it came to municipal flower beds, we didn't see it as stealing, merely levelling what seemed to be an unjust score. It's easy for young people to go astray.

'You were lucky,' said Robert. 'If you'd been caught and been an Aboriginal child you'd have ended up in an institution.'

I nodded. He was right. 'Go on,' he said. 'Tell me more.' He sounded tired. I stretched my legs and suggested it was time for dinner.

'I feel a bit sick,' he said apologetically. 'You go without me. No, I don't want anything brought back.'

• • •

I never finished telling him my story. On the fifth day, Robert's energy left him and he found it hard even to walk to the shoreline where the water broke in gentle, blue curves. Mostly he lay curled up on the bed, feeling nauseous and exhausted.

He agreed to ring Ryan, his doctor in America, but first he made notes about his symptoms. It was a formidable list — so many points of pain held at bay by a man who lived in his head not his body, and ordered his world through a formidable will.

It may seem strange, or even naive, to say I hadn't thought about Robert's illness recurring. For once, I had been living in the present, day by glorious day. But Robert's pain was now in ascendancy, thrusting itself into our consciousness in ways that could no longer be denied.

'Are you frightened it might be cancer again?' I asked. I was standing by the open door with the sun warming my back. Inside, the room was in shadow.

'It's possible,' he said. 'Except I had an all-clear before I left home. And I'm very strong.'

That was true. Robert had made a rapid recovery from his first episode of cancer, refusing both chemotherapy and radiation after his surgery, saying he did not want to violate his body. When his doctor told him that cancer could violate his body even more, he said he had no time for treatment, he needed to be back at work.

When we arrived home in Sydney, Georgia, my daughter, met us at Sydney airport and there were tears in her eyes when she saw how ill Robert looked. But he had to keep going — the tour was not over, and Tasmania was next on his itinerary. In Hobart, he made time for a visit to a young woman doctor who listened to his medical history and said, 'If you were my father, I'd tell you to fly straight home.' He struggled through his Tasmanian engagements but by the time he returned to Sydney he felt so terrible he agreed to cancel the rest of his engagements in Australia and fly to America the following day. On that last evening in Australia he insisted on talking about how we would put our lives together. Maybe half our time in America and half in Australia.

I nodded. 'Yes,' I said, 'yes, that would work well.'

When I think back to us at this time, I am reminded of an olive tree I saw on the Island of Santorini in Greece, growing out of a fissure high on a cliff. It clung tenaciously to the dazzling white rock, challenging nature, which threatened to send it tumbling into the blue of the Aegean sea.

12

Shadows of illness

I needed to communicate with Bob Stilger — Robert's oldest friend and colleague, who had worked with him on social change programs for nearly thirty years. Bob and his wife, Susan Virnig, had looked after Robert two years earlier when he was first diagnosed with oesophageal cancer. They were part of Robert's original 'Healing Circle', a small group of people he had brought together to support him during his illness. Some didn't know each other; some Robert barely knew himself. He was more or less a stranger in Spokane where he'd come to live with Bob and Susan, and realised he quickly needed to make friends. He chose people he liked and trusted, whom he sensed would help him get well. But the Healing Circle continued meeting long after Robert had recovered, coming together for two hours every week to listen to each other's concerns, and to deepen their capacity for intimate friendship. I was yet to realise how important they would be in my life.

3.10.99
Dear Bob, I put Robert on the plane yesterday — he's very weak, appetite gone, and lost masses of weight — but humour still firing. I guess it could be total exhaustion and collapse after such a gruelling schedule, or it could be cancer again which is everyone's fear, most of all his I think. We had some close and lovely times. It's great that he has such a terrific friendship with you and with others in the healing circle, thanks for making me an honorary member. Membership deeply appreciated. Love Anne.

3.10.99
Hi Anne, Wonderful to hear from you. Robert just called earlier from the Seattle airport, we'll pick him up in Spokane in a couple of hours and take him home to bed. He sounded pretty pooped. Please don't hesitate about calling me anytime, night or day … You're not an honorary member — an incorporated member! Fully part of the circle. I am so very glad that you and he had this time together, and hope there will be many more opportunities. Love Bob.

Waiting was hard. Through the white rice-paper blinds of my room, I could see the shadows of people walking by in the street. I felt as if I were suspended between two worlds. One was outside, where I could hear laughing and talking. The other was inside, where I waited for news about Robert in growing apprehension.

I hadn't felt like this since the years of Jonathan's illness when the phone would ring and I would learn from strange voices that Jonathan was in jail, or missing, or in hospital after an overdose, or found living in a cave. The worst calls came in the middle of the night, and they were usually from Jonathan himself. He would say he was holed up in a phone box and three standover men were waiting outside to gun him down, or strangle him, or take him hostage. He would be weeping, pleading with me to come and rescue him, and I would never know if these were his psychotic delusions or reality. By that stage nothing surprised me anymore. But my heart would still pound and the hairs on my arms would stand on end. Even now, phone calls that wake me from sleep can send me into panic.

The first phone call about Robert came very early in the morning. It was Bob.

'Anne, he's arrived safely. Looks like shit, but he's tucked up now in a hospital bed. We'll keep you posted.'

Phone calls and messages became the measure of my existence; everything else seemed irrelevant. The next day, Robert rang at about two in the afternoon. His voice was unexpectedly strong.

'Do you want the good news or the bad news?' He chuckled. 'That's a silly question. Let me tell you the good news first. I'm in hospital, still doing tests, but feeling better. The bad news, the cancer has returned, but they think — with luck — I'll have six months to live. It can be a good six months.'

In one way I had expected this but, even so, such a finite sentence came as a shock. I wondered what he was thinking and how he felt. In hindsight, he had almost certainly been living with this possibility for quite some time, storing it away in the back of his mind, letting it out occasionally and then dismissing it to stay focused on the present. 'Oh dear,' I think I said or, 'I'm sorry, so very sorry.' The truth is I have no idea what I said except at some stage I asked if he was in pain.

'It's not very comfortable, it's the fluid in my lung and heart cavity that's causing the pain and they're going to drain that, maybe later this afternoon.'

'I'm coming over. As soon as I can.'

'Wait, I need to get out of hospital first. To go home and make things comfortable for you.'

'I don't need to have things comfortable, I need to be with you.'

'You will, you will. I think a friend can lend us somewhere quiet by the water in Hawaii, where it's warm because I need to be warm, and we can have those six months there together.'

After we had said goodbye, I sat on the floor and cried. The dog came and licked my face, and I pulled her down beside me. I felt there was nothing I could do.

'Read Seneca,' a scholarly friend advised.

'Why?' I was curious. 'How's he going to help?'

'He was a Stoic,' said my friend, 'and well-schooled in accepting disaster.'

So I read Seneca and how he had comforted his family and followers when a centurion had arrived at his village outside Rome with an order from the mad Emperor Nero that he should kill himself. Seneca had been a loyal and wise tutor to the young Emperor, but Nero was paranoid, and had already fed various faithful senators to the lions and crocodiles, as well as murdering his mother, his sister and his half-brother.

All Seneca's family fell about weeping when they heard the news, but the old man received the order with courage and dignity, saying they had always known Nero was cruel. He used his philosophical teachings to help him accept the reality of his situation with tranquillity: 'That which you cannot reform it is best to endure,' he said.

I am more likely to challenge a difficult situation than to accept it — such is my temperament — and yet I could see there was no point in my railing against circumstances I could not change. I had learned that lesson with Jonathan, but I still found it hard. Acceptance was certainly a part of being resilient.

'It is in our spontaneous acceptance of necessity that we find our distinctive freedom,' writes Alain de Botton in *The Consolations of Philosophy*. De Botton quotes a Senecan *Praemeditatio*, which includes these lines:

> *We live in the middle of things which have all been destined*
> *to die.*
> *Mortal have you been born, to mortals have you given birth.*
> *Reckon on everything, expect everything.*

I sighed. After all, we weren't dealing with the impending death of a young man, but of someone who had lived a robust three score years and ten. As for the sadness, sad things happen to everyone, I told myself sternly.

The palm tree which grows outside my back door groaned and swayed in the wind, scattering its seeds in small orange bullets which showered down on me as I stepped outside. Dead palm fronds hung above me, too tall for me to reach. I pulled out the ladder and leant it against the tree-trunk, grey and wrinkled like an elephant's foot. My mind was flying everywhere. If I worked in the garden, pulled up weeds, pulled down palm fronds, I would ground myself. Wasn't this what I had done at other times when my resilience was put to the test? Test? What test? What was I thinking? I had used this expression before, when I first started writing this book. It made resilience sound like some challenge to be passed or failed, as if only the strong were resilient. Yet I knew there were times when my own resilience flagged. I have little resilience in the face of physical discomfort — put me in a blizzard and I might well give up the struggle.

I am also a sprinter, not a long-distance runner. I do not believe I could have coped with a situation that required my ongoing resilience and endurance: for instance, looking after a severely intellectually disabled child who then became a severely disabled and demanding adult. When I read about an elderly couple, Ethel (seventy) and her husband Joe (seventy-eight) who had done just that, for fifty-four years, I was so impressed by their story, I rang them up.

Ethel and Joe's daughter, Diane, was born feet first and crying like a kitten. She didn't sound like other babies, and they knew something was wrong. First, they learned she had cerebral palsy; later, that she also suffered from *cri-du-chat* (cry of the cat) syndrome, caused by a rare chromosomal abnormality. Diane, who is now fifty-three makes mewing noises but cannot talk. She cannot stand. She cannot walk. Her mother, Ethel, boiled her daughter's nappies for forty-nine years, until disposables became available. Diane can no longer sit up because of her arthritis and Ethel cannot get down to the floor because of hers. Ethel has a dodgy heart valve, high blood pressure, scoliosis, a goitre, bad legs, diabetes and is half deaf. She has also had a stroke, and had five heart by-passes. Joe, a survivor of diverticulitis (an infection in his intestine), says:

> Our house is a happy house. When people ask Ethel if she would do the same again — marrying so young and

having Diane — she always says she would. I mean, look at our other daughters. They all married young. They've all still got the same husband, they all own their own home, they all come to see us often. And Diane's good. We feel we've been lucky.

A photograph of Ethel and Joe shows them sitting side by side and hand in hand. Joe wears shorts and a blue singlet; Ethel, a blue-and-white print dress. They have generous, smiling faces and they look as if they are forged of one piece, solid and strong. I don't know where or how they found their resilience and they probably don't know either. They would say they had no alternative.

People who have read my book, *Tell Me I'm Here*, about my son Jonathan's battle with schizophrenia often ask me, 'How did you cope?' There were times I didn't cope.

One late afternoon, after a run of disasters with Jonathan, I came home to find he had trashed the house from one end to the other and strewn most of our belongings in the street. I stood among the broken glass and china, raising my arms to the heavens, wailing that the gods were punishing me and our woes would never end. I was aware my behaviour was melodramatic, but after a succession of blows I felt like Prometheus in Greek mythology, chained to a rock, bound to perpetual torture. For an hour, nothing would assuage me. How did I recover? I rang our doctor and he came — not with sedatives, but with a large straw broom. I rang a woman I'd met the day before whose son also had schizophrenia. She arrived bearing a bottle of grog, surveyed the wreckage and said cheerfully, 'Oh well, at least you taught him to do a thorough job!'

I have thought about the damage of cumulative stress in

my own life. First, Jonathan became ill. Then his father, my former husband, developed cancer and died. Then my new relationship in Adelaide — the one where we would all live happily ever after — began disappearing up the chimney stack. My two younger children, who were trying so valiantly to cope with their brother's illness, desperately needed my love and attention but I had little left to give. Then Jonathan's illness grew even wilder, with spells in prison, three months lost in India without shoes, money or passport and, when he returned, 'command voices' — part of his psychosis — telling him to kill me. 'Don't kill Mum,' he wrote on the walls of the house in which he was squatting.

We survived in a haphazard kind of way, lurching from one disaster to another. I can't speak for my other two children, now grown up, except to say they have my profoundest love and admiration. For me, there were times when I think I simply clung to whatever life-raft came my way. Once, I leaned against the door of my bedroom in Adelaide, thinking, 'The longer I lean against this door, the less of life I have to endure.' I still remember those words with a discomforting clarity. At the time, they shocked me. I wasn't a person given to depression, but I felt hollow, all my energy gone.

I found two clever psychotherapists who ran group sessions at a time when it was fashionable to share bean bags and psychic wounds, and that helped challenge my need to seem perfect even if I was falling apart. I learned to ask for help. I learned to seek out friends. I cherished my humour.

In America in 1985, five years into Jonathan's illness, I began researching my book about schizophrenia, and attended an international symposium on Psychotherapy and Schizophrenia at Yale University. There I heard Dr Theodore Lidz, one of the grandfathers of psychotherapy, thundering from the lectern that parents were generally the cause of the illness. Mothers were particularly to blame. We were toxic. We were also noxious. This man was given to hyperbole.

I knew what he said was wrong. And yet I felt shame and wanted to hide. This feeling lingered until, in New York, I met Ros Rosnan, then a leader in the National Alliance for the Mentally Ill in the United States. She was a large, handsome Jewish woman, with dark rings under her eyes, and a warm and generous heart. She looked at me for a moment — tears running down my cheeks — then held out her arms.

'Pig's arse honey, the guy's an idiot. You gotta laugh. My son has said to me, "You shit, I'm going to murder you." And I've said, "Anything else troubling you?"'

I laughed. It helped.

And Jonathan? For seven years he fought his illness with rebellion, anger and his own wild love. And then one day it all became too much. When I cradled him in my arms, with the late afternoon sun streaming through the window, he said, 'It's too hard. I'm too sick. I have no more energy.' And I knew he had decided he would rather die and I could not stop him.

The next day, Robert's voice was much weaker. He said he was having more tests.

'I'm coming.'

'I think I need you to wait, and I also need you to think very carefully about what you're doing. I've never done this kind of thing before so I don't know what I'll be like. I might get rough and I'm afraid I won't be lovable. It's a tough thing you'll be taking on.'

'You can be totally crotchety whenever you want.'

'And you can tick me off whenever you want.'

'I'm coming.'

'Wait.'

By the third day his voice was extremely weak. 'Okay, things are getting rougher. I can't talk for long. But I'm making arrangements to get you a separate bed put in my study, and that can become your study so you have a place to get away from me when you need to, especially as you won't know anyone. You'll need your own space.'

He took a breath.

'I want this to be a time that gives you joyful memories as well as sad. We have to move from being in courtship to being in a relationship, and I need to unpack what has been happening to me, to be clear about it by the time you arrive. In the meantime I want you to finish the outline for your book on resilience and send it to me. I may sound woozy but I can still think a bit, even though I don't have the energy to fight my way out of a paper bag, even a wet one.'

Strange word, 'courtship'. Old-fashioned but vaguely pleasing. 'Courting' carries a certain gravitas as well as delight. A friendship with intent. It brings to mind peacocks and turtle doves, diamonds and rubies, roses and more roses; Robert and I courted with pebbles washed smooth by the ocean, and a white and yellow feather from a parrot swooping low through the trees.

On the fourth day of phone calls, Robert's voice was so weak that I did most of the talking. I told him that while I was away, my son Joshua would mind the house and my dog and the ancient cat which, as Robert knew, had long outlived its nine lives.

'Like me,' he chuckled. 'You ought to tell Josh it's not his fault if the cat dies while you're away … I want to get out of hospital and go home so I can make it good for you.' He paused. 'I wanted things to be wonderful for you and now they can't.'

'We'll make it wonderful in its own strange way.'

'I've put on two stone, I'm frightened you won't know me. It's the fluid, all that damned fluid round my lungs and my heart.'

I felt as if the wind were writing a story which I neither chose nor liked. It blew through my house in gale force as I tried to keep my feet on the ground. When I sat at my desk to write about resilience it all seemed meaningless.

7.10.99

Dear Bob, I wish I could say I am as calm inside as I am possibly sounding on the outside. I alternate between feeling as if I am caught in the middle of a storm, and then manage to walk by the sea and find some kind of peace and acceptance. How are all of you coping, especially you, Bob, with your very deep closeness to Robert? Much love, Anne.

12.10.99

Hi Anne, I am out of town, and on my way to bed. Tonight I am exhausted, but mostly doing pretty well. Being held by grief and joy, joy and grief. Much more to say but it has to wait. Love, Bob.

14.10.99

Dear Bob, I have to let go of fear and anxiety. Maybe you have. I haven't and I have realised it is cramping and exhausting. I'm working on it. Although, paradoxically, it's not something you can work on, is it? It's something that happens. I have never considered Robert and I as a one-way situation — I feel I am receiving every bit as much as I am giving. I am glad I've joined up with all of you. Love, Anne.

Just when you've found a bloke he goes and karks it. I bought homeopathic Rescue Remedy from the neighbourhood health-food cafe, *Cure*. Rescue Remedy is ten dollars a bottle; Grief Remedy, also ten dollars a bottle. Put five drops under your tongue. Robert has said he has 320 alternative therapies banked up on his email, sent from all over the world by people wanting desperately to help. Bees' honey, camel dung, smoke sticks, 'take the juice of a ripe pear and the gizzard of a lizard'.

'I need to concentrate on getting my pain under control, pain is so exhausting,' Robert said.

So what does resilience mean in the face of pain? Does it mean working through that pain, and trying to transform it? One thing is certain: pain will weave its way through our lives from infancy to old age. Pain of so many different hues, physical pain, emotional pain, chronic pain, sharp, all-consuming pain which pulls us down in its undertow. Pain can be a reminder of a cherished wound. A glimpse of a tall, fair-haired young man padding barefoot down the street and the pain of my son's death unexpectedly floods through me.

Colette, in her last and most beautiful book, *The Blue Lantern*, chose to write an account of her final years when, although she was eighty, crippled with arthritis and largely confined to her room, she maintained a capacity to find beauty and delight in the smallest of experiences: the shape and curve of her blue lantern, a seed pod which expelled a delicate silvery follicle, the sound of children playing in the square. She even found fascination in her pain — 'pain ever young and active, instigator of astonishment, of anger … the pain that enjoys an occasional respite but does not want my life to end: happily I have pain.'

'Don't make a fuss, you'll disturb the male patients,' said the matron at a Men's Fever Hospital in Malaya (Malaysia) when my mother gave birth to me. And so she suffered the agony of a breach birth with no anaesthetic but only an injunction to grin and bear it.

How many injunctions to bear pain do we receive throughout our lives, starting with childhood: 'no pain, no gain'; 'cheer up, it'll soon be better'; 'stop crying, you'll empty the ocean'; 'good soldiers never cry'.

Jenny Diski, writing in the *London Review of Books* in September 1999, tells of an Israeli Defence Force lieutenant who had one leg blown off by an exploding shell during the Yom Kippur War. He was deeply distressed and tearful. When someone asked him about his pain, he said, 'The pain is nothing, but who is going to marry me now?'

Diski reviews a book called *Pain: The Science of Suffering*, by Patrick Wall and describes a study of pain which looked at the experiences of patients in a hospital emergency room. Professional staff assessed the urgency of their complaints as if there were such things as objective and appropriate levels of pain. Staff thought that forty per cent of patients were making 'a terrible fuss', nearly forty per cent were understating their pain, and twenty per cent gave 'an appropriate answer'. Wall puts the blame firmly on the philosopher Descartes for our tendency to separate physical and mental pain.

'Good old Descartes,' said my friend Jane, who was in the kitchen, opening a bottle of red wine as I was telling her the latest news about Robert. The wine made a comforting gurgling sound as she poured it into two glasses. She had dropped in on her way home from work — never under-estimate the value of friendship in surviving difficult times.

'You look sad,' she said, holding out a hand.

'I am sad.'

'Did you ever read *The Tibetan Book of Living and Dying*?'

'Yes, I did read *The Tibetan Book of Living and Dying*,' I said crossly.

'You have to let him go, you have to accept he is dying, you have to accept we are all dying.'

'Yes, but not so fucking soon.'

Resilience is learning how to absorb sadness and how to live with it. At first, shock cushions sadness. Fear can come next, anger, outrage, pity, denial and ultimately, hopefully, acceptance. There's no 'right' order. At the moment I was a mixture of angry and sad. Acceptance was the last thing that felt possible for me.

Robert had insisted on arranging my air ticket but, when it arrived one morning, I saw that I was to travel in ten days time and return to Sydney six months later. I recoiled from the significance of that return date. Did that mean someone anticipated that by then Robert would be dead?

I rang Jane and said in a thrust of black humour, 'I've changed my mind, I'll say, "Thank you Robert for your ticket, I'm off to Rio de Janeiro in the morning."'

'Make sure you travel first class,' said my equally black-humoured friend.

7 a.m.

'This is Robert. I am still alive and kicking, my body may be on the way out but my brain is still firing, there are a few synapses left and I want to tell you how much I love you. And I have no intention of accepting the bum's rush. I am going to get this thing beaten and some nutrition into me so I can get out of here, and we can have some good times together —'

'I don't want you —'

'Shut up, don't you join the people who talk me down! Anne, I'm sorry. Was that very rude? But I want you to know you are working *with* the grain of the wood.'

'I talked to you through the night, telling you to hang in.'

'Well, there you are, that must have made all the difference! In the middle of the night I decided I wasn't going to have the bum's rush.'

'Didn't you always feel that?'

'No, there was a time a few days ago when I just felt so tired that I thought I would let it all go, but then I thought of you and I said no. We have to get this thing worked out together. Has your novel gone to the publisher yet? Good, I told you you'd feel better. I can even crack a few jokes.' He paused. 'I am worried for you about memories of Jonathan, that it will all come back again and make it twice as hard.'

'It might come back again, but I don't think it'll make it harder. In a way it might even help because I know how to come close and how to let go. It's okay. I'm not scared.'

'Thank you, that's helpful for me to know that. And my friends. You'll like my friends. I have wonderful friends, my mother would have approved! You need to be able to say whatever you want to them and they to you.'

When I rang the following day and spoke to Susan Virnig, Bob Stilger's wife, I said, 'I need to be vulnerable. I must warn you I'm a weeper.'

'So are we,' she said. 'When he went for a cat scan and came back, he said, "What did you talk about?" and we said we mostly wept.'

I put down the telephone. My book and my life were clearly merging. I felt somehow caught inside my own writing, observing myself observing, wondering how it would end. I picked up a magazine article and read, 'Death and love can change your life.' I stared at the words.

13

Freedom

The irony of my situation had not escaped me — that here I was, writing a book about resilience, and at the same time having once again to draw deeply on my own capacity to endure. Most days I would go for a walk on the cliff top and gaze down at the sea. Again and again it crashed on the rocks, each time heaving back to renew its strength.

One weekend I was accompanied on my walk by a good friend who had helped me when Jonathan died. Bibi, my dog, bounded ahead of us, her tail held high, her head down, not because she was battling the wind but because she had all the scents of the sea in her nostrils, plus the smell of other dogs and delicious hamburger wrappings and stinking old barbecue bones. A small boy was flying a kite. Correction. His father was flying the kite, a huge red and blue fantasy, while the child looked bored and kicked the ground. Tom and I watched for a while and then continued our walk.

'Are you all right?' he said, putting his arm around me. I was grateful for his concern. Sometimes people avoid difficult subjects out of tact, but most of us, deep down, want an acknowledgement of our pain. And a loving arm.

'Yes,' I said, 'I'm all right.' As I spoke, a memory of my mother slipped into my mind. Perhaps 'slipped' is the wrong word — my mother always announced her presence. I recall one occasion when our drunken Polish landlord had just smashed his way into the bathroom at twelve o'clock one Saturday lunchtime, while my mother was sitting in a chipped enamel bath, in about three inches of rusty brown water. The landlord was waving a riding crop at her, and swearing lustily.

Tom's eyes sparkled. He likes a good story. 'Did he swear in Polish?'

'Of course he swore in Polish.'

'And what did your mother do?'

'She rose, naked and majestic, and pointed at the door. "How dare you," she said, in a voice that would have scared Medusa. "Leave my house. *At once!*" As it was his house, and the rent was overdue, I expected him to swear again, or fall into the bath, or hit my mother with his whip — he was very drunk — but no, he beat a hasty retreat, shouting over his shoulder, "Fuck you Madame!" I watched him stagger up the garden path. When he yanked at the iron gate it fell off its hinges. Everything fell off its hinges in that house. Our life was falling off its hinges.'

Tom laughed. By now we were sitting on the grass, with the dog panting at our feet. 'But I don't understand,' said Tom. 'How old were you, where were you, and why was life falling apart?'

'I was sixteen,' I said, patting the dog who obligingly thumped her tail.

'Go on,' said Tom.

My story took me back to the fall of Singapore. My

father had been working in the Colonial Service in Malaya, and sent for us from England when war broke out. Then my parents organised for my brother and I to go to boarding school in Australia because they feared the Japanese invasion. My mother stayed on with my father, but then managed to escape on one of the last planes to leave from Singapore. My father remained and joined the Police Rescue Squad. Singapore dockside was ablaze when he pulled a sailor out of a burning building, saving his life. A few hours later, he bumped into the same man — debris, bombs, gunfire everywhere — and the man grabbed him and gasped, ''Ere guv, we got a boat, gunna make a getaway, wanna come?'

The boat was a small launch the navy had somehow failed to scuttle. Eight or nine men got it going again. Spluttering, stopping and starting, lurching forward as Japanese planes strafed the water, it inched its way out of the harbour towards the open sea. They made it to the Dutch East Indies (Indonesia) which had not yet fallen to the Japanese. From there they hitched rides in Dutch army lorries heading south and climbed aboard one of the last cargo boats to leave Cilacap. Six boats were blown up in front of their eyes. Their boat escaped.

By the time my father arrived in Australia, he was sick with malaria and exhaustion. The Red Cross put him in a taxi and sent him to Armidale, not far out of Perth, where we were living with my mother. My brother saw him first — my father's elbow sticking out of the window of a dusty old Holden cab which was bumping up the driveway — and ran towards him, yelling and screaming across the paddocks so that the rest of us thought the bull had escaped and we all came running too.

I had forgotten all this until I began telling Tom — remembering now how we all cried and laughed, and how my father wept when he had to tell my godmother Yette and my aunt Doreen he had no news of their husbands, his friends.

Because he was so sick with malaria, my father was only allowed to stay one night. Nine months later, my brother David was born. My mother was forty-three. Meanwhile, my father had joined the Australian army, which effectively meant he was away from us for long periods of time. The Americans dropped a nuclear bomb on Hiroshima, followed by Nagasaki. Japan surrendered.

'But how did you get back to England afterwards?' asked Tom, who had been listening, engrossed.

I told him how we were repatriated in 1946 to an England weakened by war, high unemployment and food rationing, and how my father was unable to get a job. No one wanted to employ a fifty-six year old rubber planter in the middle of an English winter.

I stretched my legs. I was getting cramp. Tom pulled me to my feet and we continued our walk, with the dog once more galloping ahead of us. I continued my story.

'A relative had said he might be able to find my father a job selling farm tractors so we went north and ended up in the cheapest house we could find, just outside Sheffield in Yorkshire. This was black, scar-faced country dominated by open-cast coal mining. The job didn't eventuate. My father tried to buy and sell second-hand cars with the minute amount of war compensation money he had received. The unsold cars piled up outside our front door in the cold and the sleet and the snow, and there they stayed.'

'Did he know anything about cars?' interrupted Tom.

'No,' I said sadly. 'He was great on Browning, but didn't know a ball bearing from a wing nut.'

'So what happened?'

Ah, I thought, what happened? I told Tom how, as winter dug in and those crippled second-hand vehicles my father had bought became covered in snow, they loomed at us like prehistoric monsters every time we opened the front door. My older brother had enlisted in the British Army and been posted to Sudan by this time. My father decided to go north, to Manchester, hoping to find work there. My mother and I and my brother, David — who was about three — stayed behind. My mother had to persuade the high school in Sheffield to waive my fees.

We had rented the house in Yorkshire unfurnished and my mother collected bits and pieces from junk stores to furnish it. Once she went to an auction and came back with ten commode chairs. 'They went for nothing,' she said apologetically. 'I thought we could fill up the chamber pots with flowers.'

She bought a second-hand sewing machine and made curtains and loose covers for sofas and chairs. I don't know how she was able to do this when she had never been taught and said she did not *wish* to be taught. I suspect it was her determination to do things her own way. She made cakes and jam, and we sold them by the side of the road. She started designing textiles and illustrations for Christmas cards. She was collecting a portfolio, she said. Two days after the landlord and the bath-tub incident, my mother decided she'd had enough of our poverty.

'If you're in a hole, there's no point in staying there,' she said impatiently. Her voice meant business. Within twenty-four hours, she had sold her sewing machine, bought a lovet-green suit with a nipped-in waist and a long flared skirt — a Christian Dior look-alike — and left a neighbour in charge of me and my brother. She put her portfolio of drawings under her arm and caught the train to London. By the end of the week, she had a job as a design consultant at a leading textile firm.

'Even though she hadn't done any work like that before?' said Tom.

'Even though she hadn't done any work like that before. From then on our lives started to go right again.'

Heavy drops of rain were starting to fall, and the clouds rolling in from the sea were growing dark. I shivered, and said I thought it was time to go. Tom and I walked along the sandy beach track to home. Our conversation had stirred up for me the unhappiness of that time in England immediately after the war, and I was beginning to fall into a melancholy mood.

After Tom left, I continued thinking of my mother and how beautiful she had looked when she was very young — the youngest student at the Central School of Art — and then how she looked a few years later, standing hand in hand with my father, eyes downcast, dark hair a cloud about her face, wearing a smoky grey dress which fell from a yoke and was loosely girdled below her waist and pinned with a large French fabric rose. It looked apricot in colour, but the photograph was sepia-coloured and faded, so it was difficult to tell. My father in a suit, clean-shaven, tall and handsome. Both of them tall and handsome. Future unknown.

The capacity to move in the face of adversity, to find a way through: this was my mother's gift to me. 'Rrrr-resilience.' I spoke the word out loud and this time Bibi the dog did not thump her tail. Even as I write this I am aware that our family traumas were — and still are — small, compared with the sufferings of many. But somehow or other, in those five years in Australia — in rural Armidale and in Perth — I found a strength that I did not possess before. The milk-sop timid child, sheltered by the ever-present English nanny, grew up. Perhaps it was having to struggle with the problems of gawky adolescence.

Almost certainly it was because my mother trusted and believed in me. She hugged me often and our greetings developed a ritual that consisted of her twisting her mouth first to one side and then the other, as I kissed her on both cheeks. 'The wind will change,' I used to warn her as I grew older.

Almost certainly it was also because, in coming together in Australia, we formed our own small tribe. There were three mothers; five children (including my baby brother); my father, who came home only occasionally, wearing army uniform and silently pleased that when his second son was born, all the younger soldiers had cheered him. (My father had his own kind of resilience, but I did not appreciate it until much later in his life.)

In Australia, we had a freedom we might never have known had we stayed in England. Galloping horses along the beach — we worked for nothing at the local riding stables so we could exercise their horses. Running through bush-land on our way to school. Learning to surf in the mindless blue of Cottesloe beach. Lamingtons, meat pies and rainbow cake — which always looked better than they tasted. Outdoor movies, or cinemas, sitting in deck chairs, bougainvillaea purple against a darker purple sky. Freedom and innocence. News of the war filtered through to us but, as children, did not touch us much until every now and then a friend's mother, also from Malaya, might hear that her husband had died in prison camp, and our mothers would go visiting with flowers and cake and lowered voices. If my father were home on one of his brief stays he would lock himself in the lavatory, staring into the mirror, saying, 'Why me? Why did I escape and they die?'

I won a scholarship to the only selective high school, Perth Modern School. I made friends. I had windswept hair. I became good at tennis. My relationship with my father, which had been a difficult one because I had not grown up with him and he felt like a stranger, began to mellow.

Then something happened that threatened my new-found world. My father was home from the army on weekend leave and we were sitting round the kitchen table. My mother had made apple cake with runny icing, the dog was snoring, my baby brother was in his playpen. It was a peaceful domesticated scene until my father said in his rather abrupt way, 'How would you like to go back to England?'

'I'd *hate* it,' I said with passion, stabbing a fork on the table top. A move to a new school in England would be my fifth in five years. I wanted permanence. I wanted … I wanted … But it was no use wanting if everything was to be taken away.

I waged a silent rebellion. For the rest of that term I worked very hard and came top at the end-of-term exams — just to prove I could do it. For the next term, I cheated at every possible opportunity — just to prove I could also do it. I alternated my good and bad behaviour. I courted disaster. I was warned my scholarship would be taken away. But I didn't care. It was the only way I could exert some kind of control over my life at a time when everything else was out of my control.

Thinking about this part of my life made me realise that much of my resilience was developed during those Australian years. I remembered how, at the beginning of our voyage back to England, some kind of epiphany occurred. The children and parents on this journey had been invited to a gathering in the stern of the ship, a farewell to Australia. I nearly stayed away, such was my sullen mood, but my mother looked so hurt and worried that I slouched along behind her, dragging my feet and hanging my head. A large, embarrassingly jolly man, who looked like an ageing boy scout, started up a stirring rendition of *Waltzing Matilda*. The ship's engines began to thrum beneath us, the sea turned phosphorescent, and we sang, all of us, and as I watched the lights of Fremantle slip into the distance, I felt an unexpected surge of gratitude for the independence I'd gained in Australia.

14

A question of age

The news about Robert was getting progressively worse. I have long had a cavalier attitude towards ageing, but since Robert's illness, my mind kept returning to Katherine Hepburn's famous remark, 'Old age is not for cissies.'

When we first met, only a few months earlier, Robert had been sixty-nine, and I a year younger. I reflected that a small child might have found us exceedingly old. When I was forty, one of my sons, aged four, squinted up at me through a fringe of blonde hair and asked — with some anxiety — 'Are you very old?'

'No,' I said firmly, 'I am not very old.'

'Oh good,' he said, 'You still smell quite fresh to me.'

Now I wasn't so sure.

A few years earlier, I had been asked to write a book about ageing which I called *Coming of Age* — not realising until too late that Simone de Beauvoir had already written a book called *The Coming of Age*. It was about the same time that new, old-age proponents like Deepak Chopra and Betty

Friedan developed passionate arguments that life over forty-five could be wonderful. What's Friedan on about, I thought? Forty-five is easy. It's eighty-five when things get dodgy.

Friedan stated that the 'age mystique' hobbles us in much the same way as the feminine mystique hobbled women. Just as darkness is defined as the absence of light, so is age currently defined as the absence of youth — downhill all the way to incontinence, senility and the nursing home. Friedan argues vehemently for 'acceptance, affirmation and celebration.'

I wrote my own book at a time when I ruefully needed to confront my own ageing. I remember standing in the London underground and seeing an insurance poster: 'You can avoid the collecting tin, but you cannot avoid old age.' Instead of rushing to take out an insurance policy, I felt angry. I was not yet ready to sail into my twilight years.

I escaped to Italy to finish the book on ageing, and settled into a villa near my younger brother David. It was supposed to be an old stone villa, but because funds were tight I ended up with a 1940s stucco maisonette, with barley-sugar columns and purple Formica on the kitchen benchtops. In my bedroom hung a plastic Madonna who glowed in the dark. I think she was painted with phosphorescent paint.

'I am very old,' I wrote with a degree of flamboyance (even though I was merely sixty-three). 'I sit in a small room in Italy watching the rain beat down on sodden trees, while a cat yawls at my feet. The cat appeared unbidden on the day I arrived, and has lost much of its hair and most of its teeth. It smells. I would like to kick the cat because I am here to finish this celebratory book about old age and not to be reminded of decrepitude.'

The rain was relentless. Grapes fell in bruised purple heaps before they could be harvested, and I played a tape of the mad scene from the opera *Lucia de Lammermoor* very loudly while I read about the biology of ageing. My taste buds were declining, bone loss accelerating, kidneys and bladder packing up, body fat piling on, discs shrinking, tendons stiffening. I felt deeply depressed.

I went for a walk on my brother's farm — the brother my mother gave birth to in Australia when she was forty-three. David is thirteen years younger than I am — not very old. We squelched in brown mud through woods full of mushrooms and truffles and golden salamanders. On my way up a steep little hill, I realised I had been clinging to tree trunks and branches, terrified I might fall. My balance was probably going, I thought. I might have osteoporosis. I might break a hip. My brother was staring at me, amazed, and then he laughed and gave me a huge shove so I half fell and half raced to the bottom of the hill where I too collapsed with laughter. I shouted with joy. I was not old, I was young, young, young! I raced home and gave the cat its regular antibiotic injection. It purred and sat on my lap for the first time. Its mange had improved, its breath was tolerable. I named it Vittorio.

Later, I walked out into a fragrant garden and found a few brown-skinned pears still left on the trees. Blackbirds shook water from their feathers, the sun shone, I opened a bottle of red, life was too good to be in a crisis about ageing.

So here I am, several years later in Sydney, writing this book about resilience and secretly worrying again, mainly about Robert's illness getting worse, but also about the fact that I too might be moving into the firing line. Could there be a sag in my own resilience? Defiantly, I went for a swim. It was cold.

• • •

Dr George Vaillant, the American psychiatrist who said that we all know what resilience is until we try to define it, has written a book called *Ageing Well*. In this book he says that resilience, forgiveness and joy may have more to do with successful ageing than regular exercise or handfuls of anti-oxidant pills. Vaillant, who is a professor at Harvard Medical School, completed the longest and probably the most important study into ageing ever undertaken — one which set out to discover how we could stay healthy throughout life. He studied the lives of 824 people over six or more decades and found that emotional and psychological factors may well have more to do with successful ageing than lifestyle factors, stress and genes.

'To be healthy is much more than just an absence of disease. It's also a state of mind,' he writes. 'An ability to experience the biological ravages of time without actually feeling unwell. In other words, people can present symptoms of ill health without believing themselves to be unwell.'

He identified four human qualities which help older people become 'the happy well and not the sad sick.' The first is a future orientation — to anticipate, plan and hope. The second is a capacity for gratitude and forgiveness. The third is being able to imagine the world as it seems to others — to have the capacity to love, and to have empathy for others. The fourth is the ability to interact and connect with people, accompanied by a belief that the world is a safe place and you are not a victim of other people's circumstances.

But the world *isn't* always a safe place — ask those who are savaged by wars or famine, or those who are victims of AIDS in countries that cannot afford even the most basic of care. Simone de Beauvoir, in her book on old age, gave another example of environmental influences on ageing when she reminded us that in societies based on tradition and stability — like ancient China in the Confucian era — wisdom was highly valued and old people were treasured. But as soon as conditions changed and became unstable, old people began to be regarded as a nuisance. Society needed good fighters, and age gave way to youth.

Old people may once have been savaged by rejection and neglect. Now they are endangered by a relentless optimism which, while admirable, might well bring about its own feelings of inadequacy. I, for one, don't want to be rolled in a marshmallow of euphemisms. I decline to be known as a 'senior citizen', 'a tribal elder' or a 'golden oldie'. I would loathe to end my twilight years in a sunset village. I do not want to be universally caring and sharing. And I am not growing older. I am growing *old* — a fact which I state quite mildly, but in protest against the 'ain't-it-wunnerful' brigade.

Resilience grows from facing reality, not languishing in fantasy land. At a time when age is 'busting out all over', I make a plea for respecting differences in the way people choose to live their lives. Some people will want to jump up and down on trampolines, or plunge into aqua aerobics. Others will choose to isolate themselves. Some will struggle with poverty or sickness that needs more than heated swimming pools to relieve the pain. Some will be mellow and benign of temperament; others will want to rant and rage. Some will join the soy milk brigade; others might want to follow Noel Coward's advice: 'The secret of youth is a mixture of gin and vermouth.'

Several people have profoundly influenced my own vision of age. Barbara Wace, my mentor and friend, was one of the first women war correspondents for American Associated Press and, later, an eminent travel writer. She was eighty-five when she travelled by bus for eleven weeks through outer Mongolia, carrying a gold-topped walking stick and a backpack. Her parties in her one-room flat in London were legendary, and rocked with people of all ages from babies to ninety plus. Now she is ninety-five, and lives in a home for 'indigent gentlefolk' just outside London (only the English could have homes for indigent gentlefolk). She still wears her blue jeans and carries a cane with a carved parrot's head, given to her by an African chieftain. When I visit her, we drink bourbon and discuss everything from euthanasia to Prime Minister Blair's tiresome grin. She says being old has allowed her to be more ascerbic, and quotes that doyenne of women journalists, Martha Gelhorn, who was still snorkelling well into her eighties and used to dismiss people she found boring by saying, 'Come again, when you have a little less time.'

I watched my father grow from being a thin, withdrawn and disappointed man to a glorious eccentric after he was diagnosed with lung cancer at the age of seventy and lost most of one lung. He made a remarkable recovery, showing he must have been very strong. It also challenged his previous, somewhat acerbic, attitude to life, as if he'd had a wake-up call to enjoy what was left. He climbed the Swiss Alps, went surfing at Bondi, bought so many second-hand books that the walls of his bedroom were lined two- and three-deep, and drove an old London taxi cab wearing a variety of assorted head gear, reciting poetry and singing Victorian music hall ballads. When he and my mother went out together, she paled beside his new-found warmth and playfulness. For a while, I was angry that he hadn't been more amiable earlier in his life.

• • •

My mind came round full circle to Robert, this man I loved who was now so ill. One morning I woke at about four o'clock with a strong sense of foreboding. Each day another bud of hope about our future was being nipped. We had originally hoped to have six months in Hawaii — good, long time. Then it had been scaled back to three months — not fantastic, but still a reasonable amount of time. 'We could even go to concerts and movies and trips in the country,' Robert had said. Then it became obvious he wasn't going anywhere but bed, which might be in a hospital, not his home. Time was rapidly diminishing.

That afternoon, I received an email from one of Robert's friends, Francesca Firstwater. He had already told me that she was part of the circle of friends who had helped Robert through his last battle with illness. She lived in Spokane in a place with the improbable name of Tum Tum and had worked with indigenous peoples from different parts of the world:

Hallo Anne, I wish you to know you are warmly invited into our healing circle and hope that I can offer support and strength to you in this time with Robert. My guess is that we might need you as much as you might need us. My sense is that Robert does not have that much time left, so please listen to what you need from this time with him and follow your heart. I do look forward to meeting you and building a friendship. Sincerely, Francesca.

Francesca's message gave me strength. Up till then I had felt useless. By saying I was needed, she helped me feel I had a place to go. A few days later, I woke in that strange blank space before dawn and knew I must leave that very same day. I was on the plane a few hours later.

Before I left, my son Josh hugged me and said, 'You have an honour to do, it's going to be hard, but you will be all right. Has Robert any family?'

'Yes, two sisters, one is in England and the other is in Canada. I don't know very much about either of them.'

'Don't worry, you'll know as much as you need to know. Just trust yourself. But don't forget, you are accompanying him on his journey, it is not your journey. When you return to your own life, people who love you will be waiting for you.'

15

Spokane

There is snow on the ground when I land at Spokane, which is the second largest city in Washington State — population 200 000 — and lies somewhere between Seattle and Minneapolis, Salt Lake City and Calgary, and two hours drive from the Canadian border.

In a tourist brochure I read on the plane, I learned that Spokane was founded in 1873, and grew prosperous from mining, agriculture, timber and railroads. Later I found it had managed to keep many of its fine old civic buildings dating from the turn of the century.

'You'll like it,' Robert had told me. 'It's not my home, but I've come to realise it's a good place to live. There's a symphony orchestra, good jazz, beautiful roses — oh, and a wonderful bookshop.'

The airport is smallish and the tourist shop is stocked with good quality winter gear — jumpers, ski jackets, socks and woolly caps. People rugged up in heavy coats are greeting one another as I stand alone, wondering in which direction to turn, until I see three smiling women carrying a large placard on which is written in purple, 'Welcome Anne!' They introduce themselves as Susan Virnig, Francesca Firstwater and Michele Holbrook, who says she is married to Ryan Holbrook, Robert's surgeon.

I look to them for news. They tell me it isn't good. Robert is not rallying as well as they had hoped. Snow crunches beneath our feet as we make our way to the car, and then, from the car to the hospital. Someone takes my arm, my breath blows in white clouds, the ground is white, the hospital is white, everything is leached of colour.

Robert's thin, white face lights up into a smile of joy when I walk into his hospital room. When I bend to kiss him on his mouth, tubes get in the way. Tubes everywhere, a tube in his nose, tubes in his frail bruised arms, blood in one tube, mucous out of another, feeder tubes looped into flasks and bottles that bubble and gurgle. A catheter bottle dangling from the bed. Hands like grass rustling on white sheets. He is thin, so thin. A body possessed, taken over, punctured, gowned, labelled, and a dark-haired, cheerful nurse saying, 'How are your feet?'

'They're odd,' Robert says.

'How do you mean odd?'

'Well, they're not even.'

His humour is still operating. He turns his face to me, 'Rub my feet a little.' His feet are cold and so are his hands, although the room is warm from central heating.

The others make way for me and, after I have rubbed Robert's feet, I sit by his side for a while, holding hands. He keeps smiling at me, in spite of all the tubes.

Several people now seem to be in the room — Susan, Michele and Francesca, who brought me to the hospital, and now Bob Stilger comes forward and envelopes me in a hug. He is a bearded, chunky man with stubby fingers; he wears a large turquoise ring, speaks with a slight stammer as if he is anxious to get out the right words, and yet has a funny and relaxed manner. I warm to him, especially when he thrusts a coffee in my hand. There is one other new face, Amanda Butcher, who helps Robert and Bob in their work: a young woman with enormous dark, intelligent eyes. I feel a little overwhelmed, meeting everyone in this crowded hospital room. What was it Robert had said earlier — 'Talk to them like you do me, say anything you want, they'll listen. They're well trained. They trained me.'

Susan takes me to Robert's apartment, which is on the second floor of a grey two-storey building surrounded by gardens and trees. Behind the apartment is the Cathedral of St John the Evangelist, a large and handsome church, suitably buttressed and spired. 'Use it as your landmark and then you won't get lost,' she says, and I think to myself that she doesn't know me. I once drove halfway down the South Island of New Zealand before I found I was going the wrong way. But Spokane seems to be a manageable size, and I like the fact that from Robert's windows I can see the city spread out before me.

Robert's sitting room is large and comfortable with piles of books, a television, a music system and, in the kitchen, a cupboard stocked with nourishing food. This surprises me. I have grown accustomed to Robert's indifference towards food. 'We bought food for him,' Susan says wryly. 'That was the easy part. Getting him to eat it was the hard part.'

In the centre of the dining-room table is a vase filled with eucalypt leaves, kangaroo paw and Christmas bush — how on earth did they get Australian flowers in mid-winter in Spokane? I am touched by their thoughtfulness.

I return to the hospital later that afternoon. People drift in and out of the room. Robert sleeps, talks with me, deals with business matters with Bob. There is an unreal quality about our meeting. Everything is in parenthesis as if we are waiting, and I am a visitor on this ship of sickness; a visitor who has to leave when darkness closes in outside, though inside the lights still burn and the ship ploughs on carrying its cargo of human distress.

That night, when everyone has gone home and I am alone in this strange city, in a strange apartment, I feel displaced and miserable. I make myself hot milk. I prowl round the apartment. I switch on the television and switch it off again. When eventually I return to bed, I lie on my back and hold a stern conversation with myself. If resilience is strengthened by a sense of belonging, then I have to find a way to make this place my home, and as quickly as possible.

My mother always used to say she could make a home anywhere, provided she had a jam jar full of flowers from a hedgerow. I don't know how she thought she would always be able to find a hedgerow, and I certainly can't find any in Spokane at two o'clock in the morning, but there is my vase of Australian flowers, and photographs of my family, stuffed in my wallet. I have also set up my computer, which winks and blinks at me throughout the night.

This need for home lies deep within all of us. It's hard to be resilient if there is no safe base from which to journey forth. But home doesn't have to be brick walls and a picket fence. I comfort myself with this thought. Nomadic people carry their homes with them. Aid workers make themselves at home in some of the most remote or dangerous places in the world by simply pinning up photographs, bringing along pieces of cloth, musical instruments, toys, favourite drinking mugs — anything that will help ground and nurture them.

Interestingly enough, this same need is found among homeless people, who regard their park benches and doorsteps with proprietorial fierceness. They learn survival techniques and behaviour codes; stake out their networks; ride the trains at night; sleep in caves, tents, parks; find abandoned cars. I learned all this the hard way, from those years when Jonathan lived on the streets and I would spend fruitless hours trying to find him. I also learned of the loyalty of street people. Some of them came to Jonathan's funeral, and put flowers and twigs and leaves on his grave. Only recently, a man with a sunken face and long grey hair called out to me from a park bench and said he knew Jonathan. 'He was a good boy, your boy, always looked after the others, even if 'e was a bit mad. Couldn't help it, I s'pose. Nice to see you again, love. Take care.'

And as I remember that man, and his words of kindness, I think how punitive we are in our attitude to homeless people. For a while in the mid 1990s, I chaired a Commonwealth Advisory Committee on Homelessness, and this reinforced my awareness that we don't like to see homeless people on our streets. We think they're strange, or smell, or might do something unpredictable — particularly if they look a bit different from us. They make us feel guilty. They depress property values — yet, paradoxically, the rising value of urban property has been responsible for making many people homeless. Street people like the city. It's where they belong, where they have their friends and favourite haunts. They know the drop-in centres, the all-night cafes, the places where they can get an occasional bed, the places where they merit respect. Yet here I am, in this comfortable apartment, snug in bed — Robert's bed — feeling homesick.

Stop it, Anne! Remember that man who lived in a drainpipe in Sydney's Centennial Park? It must have been a large drainpipe. The mental health team knew where to find him and the post office delivered his mail there. Inside the drainpipe he had a comfortable nest. He said that at night he could wriggle out of the drainpipe and look up at the stars.

Then a well-meaning but meddling officer from some newly formed bureaucracy moved him to a huge block of apartments in the outer suburbs of Sydney where, when he woke up in the morning, he saw a brick wall instead of the sky. Instead of his mates, other itinerants, he had commuters rushing off to work, looking at him askance. He was lonely. I am not suggesting that a drainpipe is an ideal home (even a real estate agent might find it hard to pitch a sale), but it was what this man knew, where he felt safe, and where he had the company of friends. I worry if I see homeless people on our streets in case they are sick, or vulnerable, or hungry; but if living on the streets is what they wish, I respect their right to be there.

I am wide awake again, stalking round Robert's flat, looking down at the few lights which are still blinking, realising that having a home, a place of belonging, is more than just having a roof over your head. I have heard stories of people dying from starvation and loneliness in one-roomed flats.

Most of us crave a place where we are welcomed and known. Nowadays my immediate community and extension of my home is the cafe up the road. It's the place where I take my work, or go to escape my work. More than that, it's somewhere I can gossip about the bad-tempered woman who won't agree to a common waterpipe, the all-night party in the flats opposite that brought out the police, the woman who pulls up all the community trees and how her vandalism might be avenged. I know when someone's dog has bone cancer, and might have to be killed ('euthanased' is the word that vets now use). I am grateful when someone tells me they spotted a man trying to break into my car. The cafe is not just a source of local information and entertainment, it also nourishes me — and not just with Portuguese custard tarts. It gives me a secure feeling that this is where I belong.

So that now, here in Spokane, this is how I must operate — get to know my neighbourhood, open myself up to Robert's friends, find out about this city, be curious, come to feel that this is home. For me this will be important in the days ahead. It will help me to be resilient.

Time passes in a blur, and all the while Robert is struggling between life and death as one calamity follows another. First it is asthma as his lungs fill up with fluid. Then it is shitting. He has a blocked intestinal tract and this will kill him unless it can be cleared. A young Chinese gastro-enterologist asks everyone gathered around his bed if we are family. Yes, we all say. He tells us they have cleared the blockages with a new treatment, but his intestinal tract has tumours which are affecting his peristaltic movement.

'I have moved mountains,' says Robert.

'Take your lavatory humour outside,' says Bob. He puts his arm around me, then looks at Robert. 'You chose well Robert.'

'I told you we were right together.'

I look at Robert's arms, bruised from injections and drips. Some kind of brown fluid is draining into him — or is it out of him — but his hands are warm, complexion better, voice stronger. He manages to smile when the orderly comes to take him to the x-ray room.

It is less than two days since I arrived but it seems like two months. My body and mind are already tired. Bob is strained. 'I am trying to get the pieces together,' he says.

Susan looks concerned. 'You are doing just fine, the best you can do is just fine, it's heroic.'

'We need to put more attention into Bob,' Susan says to me later. I've got a lot of time for Susan. There is something very honourable and thoughtful about her. I suspect she is clever — later I find she has an armful of degrees. She and Bob met during their senior year in college when they were studying in Japan and kept up a long-distance relationship until Bob managed to lure her out to Spokane.

Bob has a list of alternatives to be used in Robert's treatment: Reiki, massage, cranial massage, reflexology, acupuncture, guided meditation, a homeopathic cancer specialist, bees and honey and medical intuitives (what on earth are medical intuitives?). I glance at him. He does look tired, this man whose father was a tree-trimmer in Portland and whose first job was in the fields picking beans and strawberries when he was eight. Whether the family ate meat or not depended on whether his father was able to shoot a deer or an elk. Bob worked his way through college, and said that despite their different backgrounds, he and Robert saw many things in remarkably similar ways. I had already noticed how they seemed to be able to finish each other's sentences and had a similar kind of humour.

Robert returns from the x-ray room. He is still walking, but it takes a big effort to lift himself onto his bed. 'I must walk each day. Yesterday I couldn't walk.' He clears his throat and assumes the expression of a man about to take control.

'One, I have decided I will not work anymore; two, no visitors except all of you — but I don't want you to give up the rest of your lives in looking after me.'

'I will not work anymore,' is a huge step for this man.

Saturday morning, still less than four days since I arrived. Robert had a bad fever last night. We assemble in the hospital, Bob is already there, leather hat on the back of his head, clutching a coffee.

Later Robert and I spend time alone together, holding hands. 'Tell me if there is anything I can do for you?' I say.

He looks thoughtful. 'Yes, it would help me to know what you are getting from this, because it must be hard.'

I don't know what I reply. Something like, 'You're giving me your love and you're allowing me to give you mine.' Or is it simply, 'But I love you.'

I can remember the words of others more easily than my own, mainly because at night I make notes about what has happened during the day. I do not keep a regular diary. I have never had the slightest interest in recording that I had dinner with Bill and Marge, or that I ate oysters with a chocolate brandy sauce. But when something challenging happens to me, particularly something that I don't fully understand, then I write it down.

Writing is an anchor. It helps me make sense of my life. At this point I need to make sense of my life. I have come to recognise that although dying might seem to be the antithesis of resilience, it lies at its very core.

Robert's systems are shutting down, and it matters that they shut down lovingly and well. Dying is hard work.

It requires its own kind of resilience — for Robert most of all, but also for those who are with him. We need to share this most profound of experiences and the universal questions it makes us confront. The meaning of life is connected inextricably to the meaning of death.

There is a pain in my chest and I am eating quantities of comfort food: porridge and bananas, thick slabs of bread sprinkled with sugar, hot milk. I am deeply tired. To the left of me is a pit of ash, the ash of self pity that I could easily fall into. There is also a black door, the door of depression that I could just as easily open. The door of anger is red — the odd flash of anger can fire my energy and give me the strength not to capitulate. When a friend rang from Australia a few hours earlier and said, 'You'll be all right, you're resilient,' I flared. How did she know I would be all right? Resilience seemed a label people kept slapping on me. Nobody wants to be resilient all the time, I thought, it's exhausting. We need times when someone else takes over for a while. Like in my mother's case.

It happened about a year after she had succeeded in bringing the whole family together again in London. But still my father hadn't managed to find work and he sank into a deep depression.

'Good morning,' we'd say hopefully, when we'd find him in his dressing gown, staring out of the kitchen window, with frost on the window panes, and not even a robin in sight to cheer him up.

'I can't find the slightest thing that's good about this morning, nor any other morning come to that,' my father would reply.

My mother was still the sole breadwinner, working in her demanding design job during the day, as well as sewing at night to make enough money to pay for my younger brother's schooling. One morning, like the best of heroines, she took to her bed and lay back on her pillows, weeping. We were aghast. We had never seen our mother weep.

The doctor was called. Jack was a close friend of both my parents and, after a while with my mother, he emerged and found my father in the kitchen, reading *The Observer* and sucking on an empty pipe.

'Bea's worn out,' Jack said. 'You'll have to get a job.'

My father put down his pipe. 'And where do you suggest I find one?' he said dourly.

'Anywhere, old boy,' said Jack. 'I don't care if it's digging ditches, any job.'

In three days my father had found work as a commercial traveller selling cheap and nasty Christmas cards. It was something he hated — he used to quote vociferously from Arthur Miller's *Death of a Salesman*. But it relieved my mother. She stayed in bed for three weeks, and then one morning, she rose, had breakfast, and went to work as if nothing had ever happened. Later, I came to realise she had a repertoire of responses to overload. They ranged from saying, 'Oh dear, oh dear,' in a low voice in which she would wring her hands like Lady Macbeth — to short sharp blow-ups of impressive anger. She reserved taking to her bed for the direst of times.

Not long after that, my father found a job he loved, working for an art-house publisher called Gordon Fraser who had headed up UNESCO radio during the war. Fraser only employed people he liked — I think he responded to my father's astringent sense of humour; he would hold business meetings in the London Zoo where he was a director and my father would tell us about gathering for meetings in the monkey house, or down with the lions and tigers.

My father's depression lifted. He was working with people he liked, he felt needed, he had control over his life. He bought a second-hand taxi cab and toured bookshops in the southern counties, singing songs in a Cockney accent:

Wot a marf 'e'd got,
Wot a marf.
When 'e wos a kid,
Goo' Lor' luv'll,
'Is pore old muvver
Must 'a' fed 'im wiv a shuvvle …
Wot a gap 'e'd got …

Then he'd bound out of his cab and, striding into the next chintzy bookshop on his list, switch to something more appropriate like a Shakespearean sonnet. Years later I'd reflect that sometimes, when resilience flags and we are locked in self doubt, we need a kick up the bum from a loving friend.

Ryan, Robert's surgeon, has arrived, reminding me more and more of the actor Robin Williams. He is a chunky man with short brown tousled hair and a serious face which quickly becomes humorous. Ryan grew up the fourth of seven children, the black sheep of a family which had been a member of the Church of Jesus Christ of Latter-day Saints almost since its inception. Ryan's father ran hospitals, a some-what autocratic man against whom Ryan at first rebelled —

then he had something he described as a profound spiritual experience and he returned to his family and served a mission for the church. He became a surgeon and had a clinical research fellowship at Harvard. He came to Spokane with his wife Michele and their children to start a cancer treatment centre at one of the hospitals — he wanted to bring the best possible cancer care to a small city, believing everyone deserved the best. Ryan has a quiet, alert dependability. I suspect he is easygoing with everyone except himself. Like Robert, he works too hard.

Robert's face comes alive when he sees Ryan. He tries to heave himself up in the bed. 'I have a sense that some of the pieces are fading from me,' he says, as Ryan pulls up a chair next to him and takes his hand. 'I no longer have much interest in what is around me, and whether this is the morphine or because I am dying I do not know. My pain is bad, my body is filling up with fluid, I have a lot of discomfort. Life is not much fun, and unless it improves I do not want to stay around much longer. I am interested in the quality of my life, not the quantity.' He lies back on the pillows after this outburst, and takes a deep and painful breath. 'No life-saving measures, is that clear everyone? These guys are rough, they break bones to keep you alive. It is not a good thing.'

I look at his poor frail body and think, 'No, it is not a good thing.' Then I look at his eyes — they are grey-green — and see he is struggling to maintain control, not of death but of what happens to him while he is still alive. I want to ask if he is frightened, but this is not the time. I want to take away his discomfort, but I am unable to. I want to weep, but I must wait till later. The men are having a practical discussion, and it is not the right place for tears.

It is becoming obvious that Robert is moving towards a place where he will have to choose between pain and a morphine haze, and that's what Ryan is discussing now: the morphine patch, the morphine bolus, the pain consultant who is due to arrive any minute. Acupuncture could help. Maybe.

Robert listens to the options and says in a voice that brooks no arguments, 'I want as little intervention as possible.'

Now they discuss feeding options: juices, ice cream, tea: green, black or peppermint. 'I have no interest,' says Robert. 'We can't do macrobiotic stuff at this stage, it's too late.'

They move to the possibilities of saline solution, nutrition packs or a feeding tube. 'A small operation to insert the feeding tube, a small anaesthetic,' says Ryan slowly and clearly. 'But you might be in a coma afterwards and be worse off than you are now. I think you are too frail.'

Robert nods, as if he is making a decision about the weekly shopping. I am impressed by the thoroughness of the discussion. Robert then announces he wants to go back to his apartment. He says this with authority, even though his voice is weak. 'It's my home, and I want Anne to be there with me.'

I feel a lurch of panic. I'm not sure I can cope with this kind of responsibility, even though of course Robert should go home. My eyes light on Francesca who I know is a nurse — perhaps she could help! But there is a problem. She is already looking after Bob Stilger's very sick mother. Bob says he can find someone else for his mother, and everything is settled with remarkable ease.

There is a pause, while Robert closes his eyes. When he opens them again, he looks at us and asks, 'How are you doing?'

16

The Wolverine Poochpack

I am alone in the apartment, awaiting the arrival of Robert from the hospital. In a surreal way, it feels as I am awaiting the arrival of the groom. In the room which was to have been my study, all the accoutrements of death and dying have been methodically assembled. On top of an ordinary grey filing cabinet I pick up an innocent-looking piece of paper and read:

Death Notice:

Turn oxygen off and remove nasal canala
Close eyes and mouth
Lower head of bed and place arms at his side
Wash face clear of secretions
Fix covers and pillow
Make presentable for group to visit
Call Bob 994 1317, he will contact everyone else.

So why does seeing it there in black and white make me feel sick? Is it because the printed words obliterate all hope? Or because those bald instructions send me into a panic? What if Francesca has to leave for some reason and I am on my own, and Robert dies? What if I do something stupid? I might manage to close his eyes and mouth, wash his face, fix the covers and the pillow, but will I be able to lower the head of the bed? What if I press the lever the wrong way so that he springs up like a jack-in-a-box, and stays fixed in rigor mortis? This is bleak comedy, and I don't like it.

The hospital bed comes first. It looks too short for Robert. 'It was too short for my granddaddy, Ma'am,' says the young orderly with ginger hair and freckles who carries it in. When he sees the dismay on our faces, he promises to get the extra-long model, but not till the following day.

Next he brings the equipment. Three oxygen cylinders — one big, one medium and one portable cylinder, which is a spare. The cylinders will send out a beeping alarm if they are accidentally kicked or if the filter needs cleaning. 'This is how it sounds,' says the young man, giving a restrained kick.

Half an hour later two male nurses arrive, carrying Robert on a stretcher. He looks alarmed as they lift him to the bed, his breathing is heavy and his body is still linked to tubes. He is accompanied by Bob, Susan and Francesca, who will be staying with me in the apartment

Linda brings up the rear. Linda, the home nurse, stockily built with a flat sense of humour, a good smile and a firm handshake. Her hair is blonde and straight, she wears white ankle socks, and is of an indeterminate age. She says she will be calling by once a day. I gaze upon Linda with gratitude.

Bob decides he should perform introductions for Linda's

benefit. 'This is Anne, Robert's good friend from Australia.'
He squeezes my hand.

'Well, fancy that! My, oh my, I have a friend called Joan
who lives in Sydney. You wouldn't know her, I suppose?
Joan Yates? No, oh well.' She gets straight to work. 'Yes
Ma'am, this is the morphine bolus and here's how it works,
and there's a morphine patch — you gotta watch these drips,
and the thin little tubes up his nose. The feeding pack is this
plastic pack of milky-looking stuff and it contains everything
he'll need. It's better than a feeding tube.'

Robert's eyes are closed.

Susan and I pace around the feeding pack, which is in a
sexy-looking black zippered bag, inexplicably called the
Wolverine Poochpack. Susan has a look of fierce concentration on her face; I am feeling inadequate.

'The wolverine of death has arrived.' That's what comes
into my mind. It is *not* what I say, but my mind keeps dealing
in wisecracks. I assume it is distress.

Francesca looks at the feeding pack in a matter-of-fact
kind of way. This woman is obviously used to Poochpacks.
She pushes back her long dark hair. 'Does it make waste
matter, yes or no?'

'Why I knew a woman who had a colostomy and was on
one of those, and a woman with a fistula, and it sure made
stools, yes Ma'am.' Linda smoothes the pale green cellular
blanket over Robert's bed. She looks tired.

Oh God, I think, being so ill really does take away all
dignity.

'It's okay,' Robert says to everyone at large — and, as if he
can read my thoughts, 'I have no embarrassment about this
sort of thing. I'm just grateful everyone is here.'

You are full of such interesting contradictions, I think.

Completely open, with that hugely infectious laughter of yours — yet I have also seen you draw back, alarmed, as if everyone is coming too close.

Francesca has said Robert reminds her of a thoroughbred horse, one that gallops up for attention, allows its nose to be patted, and then suddenly rears up and gallops away. But not today, not on his homecoming and, since our time away together, never with me. Right at this moment, his room is filled with people, all fussing round him; our major focus is on managing his illness. Robert's pain relief is to be managed in two ways: through intradermal morphine patches, placed high on his shoulders, which have a slower time release than the IV or intravenous solution, which is self-administered via a pump. A beeper reminds him when he needs another dose. Once he has the morphine button or bolus in his hand, he insists on taking off the morphine patches. I have a strong feeling he is determined to stay conscious right to the end.

Saline solution and Lasix are two more fluids dripping into his body; Lasix is a diuretic administered intravenously and intended to decrease fluid retention. The fluid build-up spreads across his abdomen and can also spread down his legs to his ankles which are encased in white elastic stockings with holes for the toes. Fluid pressure gives him pain and discomfort. Over his feet he has short blue and black bed socks.

I look at all the equipment, try to remember the instructions, and thank God Francesca is here. In refugee camps and war zones I have held children who are dying. I've been in operating theatres during amputations. I have nursed my own children and learned to be strong. But my adherence to regimes and detailed instructions leaves much to be desired. I am the kind of person who leaves reading glasses in the refrigerator and forgets if I have taken one pill or five. I worry I might show the same kind of vagueness.

Next day, the new bed arrives, seven feet ten inches long. The same young man with the ginger hair carries it in. 'My granddaddy had to have one of these — remember I told you — the first one was way too short.'

Michele arrives with another honeycomb blanket and more sheets for this new extra-long bed. She has come from the clinic she runs for Ryan, and from the demands of four children. She reaches down and kisses Robert. She is pretty and charming and I warm to her, but then I warm to all of Robert's Healing Circle. Michele says she is fifth-generation Californian and has an honours degree in Bio-behavioural Psychology. She was in the process of applying to medical school when she found out she was expecting her third child. 'A husband in surgical residency training, a wife in medical school and three pre-schoolers didn't seem like a recipe for success on any of those counts, so in the end I chose not to attend medical school.' Poor health has haunted her since her youngest son's birth.

That first night, Robert sleeps while everyone congregates in the kitchen, eating the food that friends have brought — Cajun chicken, salads, boxes of pastries, large polystyrene cups of coffee. Coats, shoes, bags and scarves are piled in the hallway. It is beginning to look like a teenager's sleepover party. Would that it were.

When everyone has gone home, Francesca and I sit and listen to the gurgle of the oxygen cylinder, the gurgle of the rain outside, and the gurgle of Robert's lungs. His eyes remain closed. I look at Francesca, long legs stretched out in front of her, her eyes shining, and decide she reminds me of that poem by Anna Wickham about the quiet gentleman who wants to sit and dream, but his wife is on the hillside 'wild as a hill-stream'. She thinks that's delightful and presses me for more.

'I am a quiet gentleman, and I would sit and think; but my wife is walking the whirlwind through night as black as ink.'

'Oh boy, that's me,' she says, this woman who was born in Indiana, third child of seven; was raised in a large extended family community on land belonging to her grandparents; and was married at nineteen to a young lawyer of African and native American descent. Francesca has had three husbands and two children, worked with abused women and children, run several mental health programs and owned and operated two small businesses.

'Anything more you want to know about me?' she teases, and gets up to move a vase full of gerberas which is hiding Robert from our view.

Even though it is mid-winter, flowers keep arriving in test tubes of water — with crystals to keep them alive — and in baskets lined with moss. Lilies and candy tuft and small pink rosebuds, pink and white stocks, gerberas, phlox and roses.

Robert watches Francesca for a while, then says, 'I love gerberas, twist them around so I can see them. Throw away the dead flowers.'

Prayer and healing symbols arrive from all over the world, particularly from Robert's American Indian friends: prayer knots and prayer beads, a red-tailed hawk's feather, a stone wrapped in a red cloth and a little bag of ash. I read the instructions with curiosity. It says to put it on the tongue or on the third eye. Robert says drowsily, 'Try the third eye. It's in between the first and second.'

A medical routine becomes established. A friend, Meg Wheatley, sends a poem: 'We have come to love you strongly, old dragon.' Bob had told her Robert looked like a dragon as he blew into his nebuliser, a colourless plastic dispenser with a mouth-piece for dispensing a medication called albuterol into the lungs, making it easier for him to breathe. We need to rub his back, shave him, do his teeth, clean his mouth and ears, straighten the mattress. We take it in turns.

'I am not concerned, do what you will,' he says, 'and thank you.' He says that while we busy ourselves looking after his needs, he feels he is drifting out to sea, slipping further and further away.

Around him is this community, this small group of people ministering to his needs, weaving bands of love, each in our different ways: one of us asks the questions, terrier-like in her insistence, braving disapproval; one of us tackles the hospital doctors, despite being uncomfortable about it, and carries the burden of organisation without complaining; one person needs to check if everything's being done okay — 'Am I doing it right, is it okay?' Sometimes our roles reverse or change with the ebb and flow of our need for tolerance and humour, our willingness to be vulnerable, our recognition that without honesty we will be lost. It is also essential that we are honest with Robert, this man who is moving so swiftly towards his death. Just as Robert's death is unfolding from the patterns of his life, so are our lives becoming shaped by his death.

I put on Schubert's String Quintet in C, but while it is balm for me, it is an intrusion for Robert. Some music is too complex for him to bear — a single instrument is better than orchestral, and sacred music doesn't go down too well (I think he feels we are hastening him towards the end). If it weren't so loud, I have a hunch that *When the Saints Go Marching In* might cheer him most of all. Cartons of food still keep arriving from friends and neighbours. As I pack away the food, I recognise that we sometimes minimise the blessing in these acts of kindness.

Francesca sits on the window sill, framed by a clear blue sky. 'My sense is there are too many invasions on Robert, who is such a private person,' she says. 'When I worked with him, I always had to move slowly. If I took his hand and held it too strongly, he would withdraw it. It's okay Anne, you can hold his hand, he won't withdraw it from you. But we must be careful we don't intervene just because we are desperate to be doing things, we must give him the space he needs and has always needed. My role is just to be a hand-holder, not the fixer that I usually am, to respect the spirit and the soul of the man. Fixing is not what the soul wants.'

Soon visitors have to be kept at bay and only Robert's closest friends come in small regulated numbers. Emails keep arriving from all over the world. Ever since Bob Stilger sent out a message that Robert was ill, there have been hundreds of messages:

Dear Robert, I just wanted you to know that all your vision, your efforts, your writings, your compassion and your immense ability to care so deeply have been and will continue to be an inspiration to so many of us ...

We read some of the emails to Robert, who looks pleased, but then he says he wants to concentrate on the few closest people in his life. I reflect how often this happens: we start off wanting to engage with the whole world but, at the end, as our focus diminishes, it can only hold those we love.

I am sitting by his bed and Robert reaches out to take my hand. 'Remind me of those days on the island together,' he says. I realise with distress how weak his voice is becoming.

'Remember the little yellow bird that was building a nest outside the dining room hut?' I say. 'And waking up together to see that water, so blue and calm, and all those little row-boats pulled up on the shore?'

He nods — as well as he is able to nod, propped up by so many pillows. If he lies too flat, it is harder for him to breathe.

'I remember our reciting poetry,' he says.

I remember the poetry too. We discovered we had learned the same poetry at school: 'My name is Ozymandias, King of Kings' (said with great bravura) ... 'Do you remember an inn, Miranda? Do you remember an inn?' ... 'Does the road wind up-hill all the way? Yes, to the very end.'

We would play a game, starting with a couple of lines, and challenging the other to finish. 'I shoot the hippopotamus, With bullets made of platinum, Because if I used leaden ones, His hide is sure to flatten 'em.'

'Cheat,' Robert had said. 'Cheat, I'm sure you never learned that at school.'

That had been my last offering, and now here in this room, Robert looks as if he is ready to play again.

'Western wind, when wilt thou blow, The small rain down can rain?' He is looking at me expectantly.

'Christ, if my love were in my arms And I in my bed again,' I say softly.

Touched, and heartened by this shift into a happier world, we decide this will be our night out — Robert, Francesca and me. Bob has brought us a pile of videos — a schmaltzy romance, *Sleepless in Seattle*, a couple of Charlie Chaplins and some old Marx Brothers. We drink cocoa and munch biscuits, while Robert blows on his nebuliser and dozes in between laughter, which exhausts him but brings a sparkle to his eyes.

'Laughter improves immune systems,' he says drowsily.

'One minute of laughter equals ten minutes of aerobic exercise,' is my contribution — I hate aerobic exercises. Then I recall a travel anecdote that has always made me laugh — a notice from a Bucharest hotel lobby: 'The lift is being fixed for the next day. During that time we regret you will be unbearable.'

We giggle feebly and Francesca goes out to the kitchen and comes back with a carton of coffee ice-cream and a packet of marshmallows. Robert has a spoonful of the ice-cream. 'Any more and it'll kill me,' he says, and we roll around in laughter again. Robert remembers one of Woody Allen's movies in which he leaves his oncologist's office elated with the good news he doesn't have cancer. He capers down Park Avenue, rapturously embracing the life he had expected to lose. 'It's not the dying that worries me,' he explains. 'It's being there when it happens.'

This time our laughter is more restrained. I realise that while it's all right for Robert to tell that story, for Francesca and I it would have been venturing on dangerous ground. It's *his* dying, not ours. At the last Paralympic Games, the competitors gave themselves public nicknames no one else would have dared to use. Blind athletes called themselves The Blinkies. Winter Olympians were Hoppies. The Shakeys were those with a neurological disability. The sprint cycling team, Bits and Pieces. The 4 x 100 metre relay team, The Missing Bits. Then there were the Wheelies for those who couldn't walk, and the Walkies for those who were amputees. The sitting volleyball team called themselves The Crabs. It's this kind of humour that allows people to reclaim their lives and move out of the victim role.

Robert's drowsy comment about laughter improving

immune system response was right. Perhaps the most celebrated and well-documented case of humour helping to reverse the effects of stress-related illness is the story of American writer, Norman Cousins, who managed to 'reverse' his severe form of inflammatry arthritis (ankylosing spondylitis) with humour — he booked a room in a private hotel, moved there with his nurses, and went on a non-stop Marx Brothers movie feast.

None of this is new. It was written in the Proverbs (17:22): 'A merry heart doeth good like a medicine but a broken spirit drieth the bones.' And a famous seventeenth century physician, Dr Thomas Sydenham, believed 'The arrival of a good clown exercises more beneficial influence upon the health of a town than of twenty asses laden with drugs.'

The arrival of *three* good clowns, wearing silly wigs and red noses, brought laughter and relief to the children of East Timor after the militias went on their killing rampage in 1999. Dr Peter Spitzer (aka Dr Fruit Loop), who is the co-founder of Australia's Clown Doctors, says their mission was to help children find their smiles again. In one orphanage, they visited a young girl who had witnessed her father and brother massacred, and her mother raped and killed. The director of the orphanage later told them the child smiled for the very first time during their visit.

'Humour is a third kingdom where the spirit becomes tough and elastic,' wrote Herman Hesse, long before resilience was the province of academic research.

Humour and resilience are now a subject for academic discourse and research. Ann Masten, from the University of Minnesota, who has written prolifically about resilience, says that a trait of resilient people is a sense of humour — it helps relationships and is invaluable for coping with life's adversities. Then there's the tricky business of defining humour. Some kinds of humour can be damaging — like ridiculing people. Good-natured, healthy humour allows people to laugh with each other and not take themselves so seriously. It's a way of establishing connections, defusing conflict, and coping with pain and anxiety.

Enough. Robert has now fallen asleep, the lovely Francesca is tidying up, and my head is nodding. I look at Robert lying there in his extra-long bed, his body and face wasting away, but his spirit still strong, and I am filled with gratitude for this brief time we still have to share. Who'd have thought the very best Saturday night out would be cocoa, marshmallows and the Marx Brothers by the bed of a dying man?

17

Spirit

It is important to keep myself well. There is no point in having a resilient spirit if the rest of me falls apart. Inside this apartment I am cut off from the world outside. I go walking in the snow to feel the weather, to know I am connected to the earth. My fingers grow numb from cold and my nose is red. I catch a glimpse of myself in a shop window and laugh because I look like a clown. Leaves are still falling from some of the trees and I watch the clouds scudding overhead, see the snow melting. Reassure myself I am still alive. Just before I reach the apartment I manage to pick a few red-berry branches from the tree and smile at a rather cross-looking neighbour who has just poked her head out of the window.

Inside the apartment, Francesca is singing. She makes up songs about frogs, about ants, about death and love, about whatever comes into her head, and sings with a vibrancy which is electrifying. She says she doesn't know what's going to emerge until she opens her mouth; it comes from her spirit.

Francesca frequently uses the word 'spirit' and I wonder what it means to her. I've come across the same word again and again in my reading on resilience — it's a hard one to define. I ask Francesca how she would define it. She takes a deep breath and sits on the floor to think for a moment before she says, 'It's love that is always greater than the love that sits inside me; it's where all of my longings can fly and go deeper and wider; it's me as the creator and the created; it's everyone and everything; it's what I live for and what I'm willing to die for.'

She pauses, and Robert opens one eye. 'Well done.'

She laughs. 'But you haven't heard it all … it's the next unknown that begs me onward and horrifies me all in the same moment.'

'That I can understand,' he says dryly, and then begins to cough so we have to go and hold his body and plump up the pillows.

'It's a booby-trapped word.' He waves a long, thin finger in the air. 'People get embarrassed. Or they try and confine it to a church.'

I wonder about this. I don't get embarrassed, but I do find 'spirit' a perplexing word. To me it's about mystery, about that underlying connection of all life, that expansiveness into the infinite. When I try to describe it I think immediately of an experience I had in the Ogaden desert in Ethiopia. It was a time of great famine and we were filming nomadic tribespeople who had travelled long distances to a distribution of food. On the way, many people had died. Bodies were wrapped in shrouds waiting to be buried, upright and deep down in the sand so they wouldn't be eaten by jackals. Children staggered towards us with sunken ribs and skeletal heads. The sand was punctuated with the bleached white bones of animals. In the midst of this devastation, a group of emaciated young women appeared, dressed in long skirts of faded yellow and red. They fluttered around us like dying butterflies, weaving patterns of gentle beauty.

An old man said, 'They dance with their skin and bones. They tell you thank you for telling their story, thank you for saving their lives.'

I felt wonder at their generosity and shame because we couldn't save their lives. All we had were three stale sandwiches and a bottle of water in the back of our jeep. But in return for bearing witness, we had seen how their spirit transcended their weakened bodies in an exquisite act of grace. In Western society, we struggle to reconcile such encounters with our rationalist, materialist outlook.

One scientist who isn't afraid of the word 'spirit' is neurologist and author Oliver Sacks. Sacks is one of those rare types: a man blessed with an understanding heart and poetic voice whose books frequently portray the human spirit transcending its bodily limitations. In his books, Sacks introduces us to people with the most extraordinary perceptual disorders, who nevertheless manifest enormous resilience as they re-order their differences, accept them, even love them. Sacks had originally thought of deafness as an impairment and an impoverishment; his original conceptions were radically overturned when he encountered the rich language, community and culture created by Deaf people.

Again and again Sacks shows us that human limitation is a matter of perception; mystery is ever present. There is the artist who felt suicidal when he became colour blind after a sudden brain injury, but who found the world acquired such a beauty and significance of its own that he turned down the offer of restoring colour to his sight. A man who had severe frontal lobe damage which made him indifferent and insensitive to life found the full scope of his sensibility whenever he sang. Many people with Parkinson's disease, who tended to freeze or make small stuttering steps in the advanced stages of their illness, were able to dance beautifully to music. A Hare Krishna patient with a brain tumour was unable to function unless he was singing a jingle or swaying to music. Art, music, poetry, dance — all things creative — seemed to extend the mind's physical and mental flow.

Sacks talks about discovering 'our unknown and un-expected strengths, the infinite resources for survival and transcendence which Nature and Culture, together, have given us.' I reflected this was similar language to that used by social scientists like Emmy Werner and Ann Masten when they wrote about 'innate self-righting mechanisms', and the 'everyday magic of ordinary normative human resources.'

At this moment, a bleak thought overcame me, and one that could not be fixed with 'everyday magic'. Here was Robert, a man with meaning in his life, with spiritual strengths and boundless optimism, who was getting sicker, thinner and weaker every day. His mind was desperately trying to control his body, but not succeeding. I felt some kind of guilt — as if we were letting him down in some way by not supplying sufficient hope. I found it hard watching him desperately seek to be in control, not just of his life, but of his dying.

'I do not want to lose my mind,' he said, tapping his forehead. He was hanging on to his mind for dear life, forfeiting morphine, refusing sleep, determined not to lose control. The effort of moving his arm made him grimace. Tubes still entered his body from all directions. Once, in the middle of the night, I imagined he had slipped away and some great sea creature with octopoid limbs had taken his place. His breath was now harsher and more laboured, making him difficult to understand. But not on this occasion.

'I do not want to lose my mind,' he repeated, pushing away the morphine bolus that lay by his hand. I leaned against the side of the steel bed and looked at his body, his feet almost touching the end, the skeletal thinness of his frame.

I remembered my little French godmother, Yette, who was so small she almost disappeared in the bed in which she died. Yette was ninety-six, and was being looked after in her daughter's house in Wales after suffering several strokes. It's a place I always visit when I return to Europe, a huddle of old grey stone farm buildings nestled into rolling fields. Yette's bed was turned so she could look out of her bedroom window onto the view. It was a valiant gesture because her last stroke was massive, and for the last few days her eyes had been closed and her body curled up like a baby. Such a small body, barely drawing breath. Dying, the doctor said. He also said she wouldn't regain consciousness. He hovered for an awkward moment by the door.

'Probably you would prefer to let her die in hospital,' he said, his face slightly pink.

Unexpectedly, from the bed in the corner of the room came a strong voice, pitched firmly in the French accent that had stayed with Yette all her life.

'Thank you, I prefer to die at 'ome.'

Where did that come from, that voice of authority, making the last important decision about her life, when her mind was massively damaged by her stroke? What mysterious processes allowed her to proclaim, 'I prefer to die at 'ome'?

Many years ago, when I was making a documentary about

children with severe disabilities, I filmed a child who had been born with very little brain function. Her body and her limbs were limp like a rag doll's. She could neither talk, walk, nor sit up unaided. One afternoon, I watched her set out across the floor of the children's home where she lived, propelling herself on her stomach from one corner of the room diagonally towards the other. On the first two occasions a helper lifted her off the floor and carried her back to her cushions in the corner. Each time, she screamed with rage. The third time, she set off again with her head down and her forearms and elbows moving her along at increasing speed. We watched her, curious to see where she would go. When she arrived at a bookcase in the opposite corner of the room, she reached up, panting with exertion. She grasped a large thin book, with a brightly coloured spine, and pulled and tugged until it fell on the floor, almost hitting her nose. Her mission accomplished, she squealed and laughed with delight, thumping the book with her hands. Her face was rapturous.

'Can she read?' I asked the nurse.

The nurse shook her head. 'No way, but she must've seen the other children take books and decided she should have a go.'

Just as with Yette, I wondered about this mysterious life force which propelled her to make such an extraordinary and difficult journey.

And what about when people develop Alzheimer's disease and their brain cells are damaged beyond repair? What then is left? This was an issue which had vexed me for many years, ever since my proudly independent mother developed this illness, as had her own mother and one of her maternal aunts. Did anything of my mother's essential self remain, imprisoned inside the disease? The same conundrum challenged John Bayley when his wife, eminent English author, Iris Murdoch, fell ill with Alzheimer's. As Iris Murdoch's language began to disappear, it was her sounds of love that survived the longest. Even when she had no words left, she made loving little sounds and held her husband's hand. With my mother, it was her love of beauty that remained. She clung to this as if it were the last remaining shred of her humanity.

When eventually we had to hospitalise her, because it was unsafe to leave her at home, at first she fought us. She said she was lost in a fog, and I must rescue her and take her home. She cried and I cried. But gradually she settled and became well-known in the wards — always well-dressed, always carrying her black patent handbag, occasionally wearing a hat and her pearls. She loved the beauty of the walled garden just outside her ward, which could be locked so residents could not escape. She hated the ugliness of the wards themselves. Sometimes she would sweep through the dining room and at an opportune moment, tug at the corner of a table cloth so that baked beans and fish fingers cascaded on to the linoleum floor.

'Table cloths should be white linen,' she would announce imperiously. 'Not plastic.' Sometimes it was the ugly curtains that raised her ire, and she would yank them down, or remove another resident's clothes, saying brown cardigans were ugly and slippers should not be worn in the house. Like the Queen, she rarely relinquished her handbag. (It was usually full of lipsticks and apple pie.)

I shiver, even though it is warm inside. This has been a difficult day. What began with pondering the meaning of resilience when you're dying, quickly became lost in puzzling about the meaning of life. The oxygen cylinder is gurgling away, the snow has started to fall again, and Bob arrives with some groceries for us, and with Robert's papers. Robert has asked him to get his business affairs in order.

'Who said dying is hard work?' murmured a voice from the bed.

Robert's death has assumed a raw sense of inevitability. This is becoming an extraordinary journey, for which there are no maps and no guidelines — for who is to say how to behave when you are dying? How can you have hope when death has already marked you? Do you fight, drawing on a will to survive? Do you become philosophical, saying, 'death lies waiting for us all'? Do you become angry like Dylan Thomas and 'Rage, rage against the dying of the light'? Or do you try to honour those final days of your life, however difficult they may be? Noble words, but hard to hold onto when you know the end is likely to be messy, painful and undignified.

What is my role, I who usually have such an abundance of hope? Why am I behaving as if this man whom I love will die? What is there left if I don't have hope? I look at the others and know that, almost certainly, most of them think the same as I do. It distresses me. I want to prove the power of love — but I have been there twice before, with the illness and death of my mother and of my son. I would go there again if I thought it might succeed but, try as I may, I cannot believe it will. For a while, I feel like a traitor, as if I might be sending messages into the ether which could damage Robert's recovery.

I know that hope and optimism figure strongly in the literature on resilience. Resilient people are hopeful about overcoming problems in their lives. Each success helps build optimism and confidence. 'If you're in shit, there's no point in staying there,' said my mother all those years ago on that farm in Western Australia. Each time she met a problem, she found a way to move through it.

Hope is the value which keeps us human in the face of the unthinkable; its importance is enshrined in folklore, in contemporary psychology, in Greek mythology. When Prometheus stole the fire from heaven and Zeus, in revenge, sent Pandora to earth to bring misery to the human race, Pandora brought with her a box containing every ill known to human-kind. When she opened the box, they spread across the world. In the face of disaster only hope remained.

Hope is the balm we need when things go wrong: 'I hope you'll get better', 'Don't lose hope', 'Hope for the best.' It gives us reason to stiffen the sinews, summon the blood, prepare for what's ahead.

Then, at some stage (and usually it's a gradual process) we have to start distinguishing between realistic hope and illusory hope. Realistic hope gives us wisdom to under-stand the past, and energy to plan for the future. Illusory hope hinges on fantasies that something or someone will magically make things better. At some point, resilient people stop trying to control the uncontrollable. They put aside unrealistic hope, because it no longer helps. I no longer hold onto my hope for Robert, but I am desolate it has gone.

Back in the apartment, Robert makes a huge effort to raise himself to a position where he can look me in the eye. 'I'm not going to give in. I want to live for you.'

Apparently the appropriate reply is to tell someone *not* to hang on. 'It's all right to go': that's what you are supposed to say. But when it's a matter of *this person's* life or death, there is no appropriate reply — every life is different; so is every death.

'I want to live for you,' Robert repeated, and blew on his nebuliser like a dragon snorting clouds of smoke. I did not have the heart to say, 'Don't live for me'; it seemed like a rebuttal. Instead, I said, 'I know you do.'

18

Yours truly, Annie

Two children have just arrived by Robert's bedside, Annie and Kate. One is aged about twelve, the other is about seven. Robert holds out his arms to them, and I notice that even though he looks so ill, with his hollowed eyes and gaunt frame, the children are not frightened to come near him. They dump their school-bags, kiss him and sit by his bed. He looks so pleased to see them, and then I notice his eyes are filled with tears. He has already told me he finds it hard to accept he will not see Annie or Kate grow up.

Annie, the older of the two, is the only child of Bob Stilger and Susan Virnig. For some time she has looked upon Robert as her grandfather. She has dark bright eyes, delicate features and a quick intelligence. Robert has taught her a card game called Racing Demon which everyone plays at ferocious speed, and Annie always wins — she is quicker than anyone else. I know she has brought a pack of playing cards with her today but she realises at once there will be no more games and leaves the cards stowed in her school-bag. A few days earlier she had made a special card for Robert and he thanks her and says it is beautiful. He asks if I can see it and she nods. When Robert passes the card to me, I see a picture of a cruise ship, and underneath the words, *Bon Voyage, I love you Robert*. I read:

Dear Robert,
Your presence has been a marvellous gift to us all from the very first day you came to Spokane. You've graced us with your presence for so long it will be odd without you puttering around people. I'll miss you cheering at my soccer games and keeping my dearest Father in line, something even the most knowledgeable of us (me, of course) can't do. I want you to know that I'll miss you and that I love you and I'm glad you were able to live in Spokane even if it was only for two years. I love you, Your Granddaughter, Yours truly, Annie.

This card will also serve as a coupon for one hour of violin concerts and juggling shows, provided by Annie and Amanda. Made for Robert by Annie.

Annie does indeed juggle. From the moment I met her she has been juggling, flipping three and sometimes four coloured balls in the air, catching them, flipping them again, on and on. I've wondered if she is trying to juggle away her distress.

Kate pulls out her own card. She is the only daughter of Ryan and Michele, who have three sons, all older. Kate is one of those sunny children, with straight fair hair and a wide smile. Her card is made from brown paper and she has stuck a large purple heart on the front:

Dear Robert, I don't want you to die, but if you do I will miss you. Love Kate. I love you.

I recognise Robert's delight at seeing Annie and Kate, and realise how much they will miss him. He gives them his love and undivided attention, even though he is so ill. Friendships like these are important to children as they grow up. They happen out of mutual enjoyment and respect and have their own integrity, quite separate from parental love. I think of my godfather Leo, and of all he gave me while I was growing up. He did so not out of a sense of duty but because he *liked* me. Of course my parents loved me. That's what parents were for. Of course Leo loved me. That was his godfatherly responsibility. But that he actually *liked* me, that was fantastic.

Leo was an engineer who built bridges and turned the experience into poetry. He was a rotund and smiling man, half Italian, half Irish, with gingery white hair, a gingery white moustache, and arms that were always carrying books and food. He spoke six languages, and collected young people like a pied piper — teaching them how to cook and eat Italian food, how to enjoy museums and art galleries, and how to go on unexpected adventures, like catching the first London bus that came along, simply to see where it would go. Every Saturday he would fossick in second-hand book-shops with my father, while a small trail of young people followed behind. He had an innocent enthusiasm about him which turned every encounter into an adventure.

Another significant person in my adolescence was an artist called Elise Blumann who lived down the road from us all those years we were in Perth. Elise wore red velvet cloaks and daring fishnet stockings. She held salons to show her paintings and to talk about art. She served wine on silver trays and reminisced about Europe 'in former times'. I was eleven, and she was my friend.

Elise had been a successful painter in Europe until she and her husband, Arnold, an industrial chemist, fled Nazi Germany in 1934, and eventually settled in Perth in 1938 where they built a house on land that ran down to the edge of the Swan river. Here they had a huge garden which was mainly bush. Wild grass and rushes grew near the river's edge and became nesting haunts for ducks and stately black swans. The house was reminiscent of Bauhaus architecture, with a white-washed courtyard sheltered by grapevines. The Blumanns had only just finished the house when England declared war on Germany and when Elise's husband, Arnold, was arrested along with all other 'aliens' and interned. His neighbours started referring to him as 'Schmidt the spy'.

Elise made friends with my mother because she saw her buying Oxford English Marmalade in the local corner store and decided she must be a civilised human being. After that, she made friends with me. She would invite me round for tea and apple cake, or tea and ginger cake or, as I grew older, a glass of white wine. Hers was the place where I sought refuge from the squabbles of our precarious life. She gave me books to read and talked to me about art and music and what was happening politically in the world. She took me into the hills and taught me about the bush and plants and birds. She explored the outback and talked about the rock paintings she had seen and Aboriginal culture and people she had met. She paid for me to have French lessons with her younger son Charles — as a result I can still recount Aesop's fables in French. When she asked if she could paint a study of my hands, I was thrilled at the honour of such a request. Only adults would have their hands painted, not little girls.

The fact that such an interesting and charming woman enjoyed my company would have been enough in itself to boost my self-esteem. But she also opened my eyes to a world which was then being devastated by war, and which I mightn't have known about till much later in my life. Our mothers were too fraught to do more than minister to our basic needs.

We remained friends right up to the time of her death. She was well over ninety when I heard she had suffered a series of small strokes, so the next time I visited Perth, I went to see her. When I arrived at her house it looked the same as when I was a child. I rang a Cambodian temple bell at the front door, which was opened by a nurse whose uniform was an unappealing shade of pink.

'Mrs Blumann is a vegetable,' the nurse said brightly. 'She won't know you, pour soul.'

I wondered what sort of vegetable Elise would choose, and decided probably an artichoke because of its rich inner heart and the complexity of its beautiful green leaves, tinged with purple.

The nurse had said Elise was in the garden so I wandered outside into an open space of trees and low-lying bush. I had to put my hand to my eyes because the light was so bright I could barely see where Elise was sitting. She was wrapped in a magenta and orange shawl. She always loved brilliant colours. She wore a straw hat and a scarf tied over the hat which pulled it into the shape of a bonnet. Her head was slumped down to her chin, and she looked as if she were dozing. When I walked up to her, she straightened herself and her expression became animated. Her face was old and wrinkled but still brilliantly mobile with high cheekbones and green-flecked eyes. She held out both her hands. 'Anna,' she said. And then curled up again into a ball.

For a while I talked nervously to fill the silences before I realised it would be better just to sit quietly by her side. Once I said, 'Do you get bored sitting here?' and she waved her arms at the view as if my question were foolish. A black swan went gliding by, followed by a phalanx of fluffy little cygnets.

Just before I left, I asked about her retrospective exhibition at the Art Gallery of Western Australia the year before. It had won widespread acclaim, perhaps the most she had ever received.

'I heard it was brilliant,' I said. 'I'm so glad they gave it to you.'

She lifted her head into an imperious pose. Her eyes were fierce and her voice strong.

'It was my due.'

I had told Robert about Elise when we were in Queensland talking of our childhoods. 'You and Elise would have enjoyed one another,' I told him. 'You share the same zest for life.' ('Darling, he is a gentleman,' Elise would have said of Robert, beaming at him with approval.) And then she would have offered him some wine and asked if he knew Europe 'in former times'.

There was no wine in Robert's flat and, on this particular evening, I badly wanted some. Robert had cut out alcohol when he first became ill, and I had decided during this period of stress, it might be better if I also gave it a miss. Francesca slipped out to get a bottle for us, and we took it into the room that was once Robert's study — the one now full of medical gear.

Francesca had first met Robert two years earlier, just before his cancer operation. Bob had insisted Robert go and visit Francesca, as there was a chance he wouldn't survive the surgery and Francesca was trained in working with people who were very ill. Francesca had listened to Robert telling her he was fine, just fine, but when she questioned him on this, he vehemently stuck to his point.

'Yet I knew he had cancer. He was about to have this operation which might kill him. His wife had left him. His work had folded. He had no home. He had lost so many things. But he wasn't able to talk about it. His talk was out there. Not here,' and she touched her heart. 'He has changed so much in the two years since his illness and since we've had the Healing Circle. It's almost as if, right at the end of his life, he is at last able to get in touch with his feelings, to become wholly real.'

I uncorked the bottle of wine (it happened to be Australian) and poured us both a glass as I told Francesca about Annie and Kate's visit earlier that day. She nodded. 'He'd love that.'

Night is closing in and I look down on the city spread out below, grey buildings, grey rain-washed streets, drops of rain on the red rowan berries outside the window, rain glistening on the telephone wires. Someone has left their lights on in a red car, parked just below. Inside, Robert sleeps and Francesca is sitting on the floor in the room next door, reading the medical list and eating a biscuit known as a Wheat Thin. They are indeed very thin and we usually manage to work our way through a whole packet by morning.

I hear Robert's voice and go to him. He reaches out an arm. 'Pull up a chair so I can look at you. Sit by me, hold my hand. We had our honeymoon, didn't we and we will have it again. I have fantasies about sex, I need to see your body and touch you and make love with you.'

This is so touching and so strange in this room with all the bottles and tubes, and the hospital bedstead, and this man who is dying, wanting to make love, making me feel I am being loved. For one wild moment I think about getting into bed with him, just to hold and comfort him, but there is too much gadgetry and the bed is too narrow. He is also so fragile and in so much discomfort that holding hands is about all he can bear.

Then Bob arrives with newspapers under his arm, and two flasks of coffee which he puts carefully on the low table that is already overflowing with everyone's gear, including one of Annie's juggling balls which she has left behind. Bob beams at the sight of Robert and I sitting there, still holding hands, and comes and puts his arm on my shoulder.

'Thank you for giving Anne to us,' he says to Robert.

Robert says confidently, 'She's not yours, she's mine!'

By the following night, Robert is very sick, and everyone gathers around his bedside. We stand in a circle, holding hands as if to keep death at bay. After a while, his breathing grows easier and the others leave.

That night I dream Francesca and I are in an old-fashioned sedan car, driven by two men wearing Humphrey Bogart raincoats and hats. One minute we are in the middle of heavy traffic, the next we have turned into a country lane with green fields dotted with sheep and lambs. A powerful black stallion with a shining coat comes galloping up to us, tossing his head and racing with the car, showing off his beauty and strength.

The car stops and we are guided underground, down a long dark tunnel. Ahead of us we can see a glimmer of light. One of the men says we are going to see the black stallion ride through the gates to freedom.

Outside the tunnel, we find the stallion is prancing round and round a paddock with an open gate. The stallion gallops up to the gate, then baulks and rears and turns away. He does this several times. The man says, 'Before he leaves, he will have sired an exceptional foal which will be given to the judge.'

Francesca suggests that because the horse is nervous we should jump on his back and ride through the gates with him. This next time, he gallops straight through and I wake with a start.

The dream was so vivid that, for a moment, I am confused and don't know where I am. It's still dark outside, the oxygen cylinder is making its usual gurgling noises, and when I stumble to the door of Robert's sitting room, I can see Francesca asleep on the day-bed by the window. Robert isn't asleep. He is sitting upright in his bed, no longer leaning on his pillows, and by the night light at the side of his bed, I can see that his face is radiant. Almost luminous. He tells me he woke from a deep sleep feeling he would get better. By now, Francesca has also woken and we sit around Robert's bed as I tell them both my dream.

'We must meet tomorrow morning,' Robert says. 'Call everyone together.' He makes it sound like a clarion call, and for a moment I wonder if I'm still dreaming.

'Can you sleep again?' I ask, stroking his forehead. 'Yes,' he says, 'yes, I can. But don't forget to call the meeting. And ask Ryan if he will come. Tell him I'm much better. He won't believe you.'

Ryan comes round quite early — before his morning rounds, and when he checks Robert's body, he finds the fluid has receded; his abdomen, ankles and feet are no longer bloated; his white T-cell count is nearly normal. I know that just before death there is sometimes a rallying, but this is more like a rocket launch than a rallying.

When Michele arrives, bringing home-made biscuits and fruit, Robert holds out his arms to her. 'I'm so much better,' he says. 'Ask Ryan. And listen to Anne's dream.'

As soon as the others arrive, we sit around Robert's bed while I tell them the black stallion dream. When I finish, Robert takes over. He has the same kind of energy as the Robert of old, as if he were at one of his public meetings, teaching and questioning an audience full of people. He seems to be on some kind of high. 'Think about how you can integrate the black stallion myth into your lives,' he says. 'Not collectively, but as individuals. Keep it simple. Money and institutions are not the issue. Nor are life and death. The dream is about finding the joy behind the fear and confusion, to be able to sit in the "not knowing", and be patient until you know.'

That night, I write the dream down. It came from my own subconscious but because we are all in such a state of heightened awareness, I feel some kind of collective alchemy is also operating. Dreams don't respond to intellectual interrogation, and I recognise the need to put this one away — at least for a while.

Next day I wake in the grey light of early dawn. When I go to Robert's bed I can see he is again fading. His breathing is harsh and I feel apprehensive.

The following night, I have a second dream in which Robert says, 'We will have a marriage.' As he speaks, the room begins filling up with people of every age and nationality until the whole world is there. I think, 'I have nothing to wear,' then I find a dress of wild silk, decorated with poppies and sheaves of wheat. When I look down at my feet I am wearing enormous boots which are growing out of the earth, sprouting wild grasses and flowers and covered in mud.

I realise I am entering the strange underworld of Robert's illness, dreaming nearly every night, moving into different states of consciousness, while at the same time Robert seems to be shifting in and out of different parts of his own consciousness. I feel as if our dreams are being shared in some way.

The next morning, Francesca comes into my room and says, 'I woke up and knew that the bear of death was very close.'

Robert stirs and asks for his back to be rubbed. 'I'm sorry to be a nuisance but I'm going to ask all the same. See how well you've all taught me.' I rub him gently. The skin on his back is paper-thin and tender. 'How are you going?' I ask. 'I think I'm slipping back again,' he says, grimacing with pain. He takes my hand and kisses it.

Ryan arrives at the end of the afternoon after a whole day in surgery. He has been the most kind and caring of doctors, giving information quietly and slowly, allowing Robert to make the decisions and as far as possible to stay in control. When he sees Robert and hears his laboured breathing he runs his fingers through his thick dark hair and looks rueful. There are tears in his eyes. Francesca is standing by the door. 'I wish this happened more often; they say the world will not be healed till men have filled the oceans with their tears.'

'I want albuterol,' says Robert, but his hand is too weak to hold the nebuliser and the valve leaks.

'But you don't need it, Robert, your breathing is clear, your skin is a good colour.'

'I want Anne.' He is silent for a few minutes then continues: 'I want to say that I do not like drifting in and out of consciousness. In order of preference, I want to come fully into consciousness, as I was yesterday when we all met. If that is not possible I want to be fully sedated, but I do not want to be given anything that will impair my body's capacity to recover. I want to live through my seventies. I don't want to go through the gates yet, whatever they are, is that clear?'

Robert, oh Robert, you are trying so valiantly to keep in control, to sound lucid as you give us all directions. But I know from your eyes you feel the game will soon be lost.

Annie enters the room where I sit by Robert. Her eyes go straight to the bed, her gaze is direct. Her mother explains, 'Robert can hear what you say, tell him goodbye and bon voyage.'

Annie shifts her gaze and looks away, 'I'll say that next time.'

Her mother says gently, 'The hard thing to learn is that sometimes there isn't a next time.'

Annie bites her lip.

19

Across the gulf

Robert is fading. He does not speak, so I do not know what is going on in those long harsh silences broken only by his heavy breathing. His eyes are half-closed but spring wide open if anyone makes an unexpected move. Illness now possesses him and it is difficult to reach across the gulf without violating some kind of sacred boundary. It's as if he's approaching a place we cannot possibly understand and he wants to be left in peace to get on with it.

The leaves on the rowan tree outside are falling and the berries now lie red on the ground. Francesca gazes out of the window, ruffling her long dark hair with her hands. 'When I was a little girl I saw a tree in mid-winter which was bare, but one branch, and one branch only, still had some leaves. I tried to shake them down, but they wouldn't fall, so I climbed up the tree and pulled on the branch, and then I hung from the branch, but they still wouldn't fall. But when I told this story to Robert a few days ago, he did not like it. I think he felt I was hurrying him to his death, or somehow questioning the way he was fighting death every step of the way. Now I realise I was wrong; Robert has to die in his own time and his own way.'

I thought about my great aunt Kate, the one who became a clairvoyant. She chose to die in her own time and in her own way. Great Aunt Kate was still fiercely independent in her eighties, but in the last two or three years of her life she had begun having dizzy spells. She refused to go to a doctor — her time had not yet come, she said. No, she wasn't bored or lonely because she talked with Cyril at least once a day.

'Cyril, my lover,' she used to challenge us, rolling a cigarette, tucking in the stray tobacco with care.

'Is he in heaven?' I asked, as the smoke curled around her head, her eyes still bright, her expression one of tart amusement.

'Scraped in.' She said that each day she told him to behave, because when she died she would be unwilling to put up with the discomforts of joining him in hell.

Soon after that conversation, Aunt Kate became increasingly fragile, until she seemed to waft away. At her doctor's urging she reluctantly agreed to come and live with us in London. My mother and I went to collect her, and found an envelope propped against the front door. It contained instructions about where to find the front door key, and a note.

'In spite of your kindness, dear Barbara, I have decided it is time to join Cyril, even though he doesn't deserve it. Please let yourself into my flat. You will find everything in order.'

Kate was lying small and frail in her narrow bed, wearing her best dark-red crêpe dress, a hat trimmed with dark red flowers, and lace-up shoes with cuban heels. Her nose was powdered, her handbag neatly placed by her feet, her hands crossed over a photograph of the errant Cyril. Her face looked just as determined in death as it had been in life. She had taken no drugs, nor violated her body in any way.

Robert was rambling. He held up both long thin hands, saying, 'This is called con-sequence. There is a plan, a frame, a context. Thumbs up, please. Communicate. Repeat.'

We tried to follow his movements.

'Thumbs up, please. Thumbs up means "yes". Down means "no".'

We lowered our thumbs. He continued, adjusting the green blanket, wincing as he tried to change positions.

Suddenly I needed to get out, to clear my head, to think through what was happening inside that room where Robert lay dying. I went for a walk down the hill outside the apartment, holding on to the iron railing where the path became suddenly steep, past the stone wall, the fir tree, its branches spangled with rain, and a maple tree, stripped bare. Under my feet were sodden drifts of coppery leaves. As I shuffled through the leaves I puzzled my way through the various stages of Robert's dying.

At one level — and from the very beginning — he had known he was dying — or his cognitive self had. At another level, through his dreams and mine, he had shifted into an awareness of the immortality of self — probably the morphine also helped to induce some of these euphoric states. Yet now came the struggle. In these altered states of consciousness, was he able to look down on himself? Look down on his poor, discoloured body that he could scarcely move, yet did not want to abandon.

'My T-cells are fighting my cancer cells,' he had rambled, 'yet both of them are part of me. Curious. Very curious.'

When I return, Robert is lying back in his bed, a puzzled look on his face. He is talking to Francesca. He turns towards me and wiggles his fingers, acknowledging my arrival.

'What can you give to make me strong?' Robert is asking. 'I feel as if I am caught half way out of a window, as if I am out of my body, and I do not like it.'

Francesca takes his hand. 'Do you want me to be honest with you? Your soul, your spirit is really strong and clear, and I admire you for that. It wants to live.'

'I want to live,' says Robert.

'But your body is doing something else. Your body is no longer willing to go on living, Robert, it's dying.'

Robert looks at me, almost pleadingly.

'Is that what you think, Anne?'

'Yes,' I say reluctantly. 'Yes, and I wish I didn't.'

'Get Ryan.'

'It won't help,' says Francesca gently, as she wipes a damp cloth over Robert's forehead. 'Getting Ryan won't stop the dying process, Robert. It has gone too far. Your body has to die, like the trees and the fields and the earth; they are alive and then they die.'

Ryan comes half an hour later. He pulls up a chair and asks Robert how he's feeling. The trust and closeness between these two men is exceptional. I have a feeling it shifts Ryan into places his professional training would normally require he hold back from.

Robert says, 'All these things you talk about, being born, going back — is that what's happening?'

Ryan nods.

Robert tries to sit up. 'Then we will have to hope for a miracle,' he says in a determined way.

Ryan shakes his head. 'Robert, it's not the right time for

miracles. You are seventy years old, you have done your deeds, it is time to die.'

Robert makes an even greater effort to sit upright in the bed. He clears his throat. 'Right then, how shall I do that?'

Now he sounds more like a small child, wanting to prove himself, to get the answers right. So many layers of living inside him — inside us all. What was it Walt Whitman said? 'I am large, I contain multitudes.'

Francesca waves a hand towards the bags and bottles that have become conduits for Robert's life. 'You could remove the TPI bag,' she suggests softly.

I am holding my breath, squirming at the direction the conversation is taking.

'Will it hasten my dying?'

'Yes, it will,' says Ryan.

He looks at me. 'This will be very hard on Anne.'

I think, Yes, it will be very hard on me, but far harder on you. I glance down and see I have dug my fingernails into my palms, leaving red marks.

Robert holds out his hand to me, and says, 'I love you. Dying is not what I would have chosen but I have no choice but to accept.'

I nod. Tears are flowing down my cheeks.

Robert squeezes my hand. 'It's all right. I haven't gone yet.'

We all laugh, weak laughter mingled with the tears. He asks if we will move his bed towards the window so he can see the rowan tree, and then he dismisses us, showing yet again that iron will of his not to let go, not to break down. 'Now go, I'll see you in the morning.'

Francesca and I do not go. Sometimes it feels as if we will be here for ever.

Early the following morning Robert is looking better. I have thrown away the dead roses from beside his bed, the sky has cleared, and the others arrive. Bob has his hands full of cappuccinos, Susan brings fruit, Michele has some drawings from Kate, and Ryan enters, unwrapping his long red scarf and giving it to Robert who has held out his hand.

'I don't want to die,' says Robert. 'I know that's what we decided, but I've changed my mind.' He gives us a look of defiance, before folding his hands over his bed covers as if to say, 'And that's that. Challenge me now, if you dare.'

I notice that his skin, usually so pallid from lack of oxygen, even has a slight flush of colour.

Francesca smiles. 'It's fine to change your mind.'

'I have changed my mind. And I reserve the option to change it again. What do you think I should do? I want to hear from all of you before I decide.'

I recognise that part of his behaviour relates to the amount of morphine he is now taking. It is becoming increasingly difficult for him to maintain a consistent train of thought.

Michele says it might make it easier if we talk about what we believe happens after death. We go round the room. Two of us believe they will be united in heaven with those they love; two talk about mystery and moving into light; two say they honestly don't know. I am one of these. I think of Robert Frost's words, 'Forgive, O Lord, my little jokes on Thee, And I'll forgive Thy great big one on me.' It's not that I don't believe in anything — like radical English theologian Don Cupitt, former Dean of Emmanuel College, Cambridge, I believe passionately in the whole mystery and beauty of life. I just have no idea of what happens once we die.

Bill Houff, a friend of Robert's in Spokane, a research scientist and a Unitarian Universalist minister, has written one of the best books I have read about spirituality, *Infinity In Your Hands*. He says that perhaps the impasse of not knowing is inevitable because the finite mind can never understand the infinite.

While my thoughts are wandering, the issue of the TPI feeding pack is obviously still troubling Robert. I say, 'The fact that you are hesitant means maybe it's too rushed. You're right — there's no need to hurry your decision.'

'I can increase the morphine if you want,' says Ryan, 'but that will make you woozy.'

'No, no, no.' Robert's voice is firm.

'You could leave it and do nothing,' I suggest.

'No, no, I have decided to stop the TPI. Send for saline.'

Ryan says, 'Okay, if you're sure, we'll set things in motion.'

Robert asks, 'If you cancel the TPI and I change my mind, can I get it again?'

'Of course,' says Ryan, 'Of course, any time.'

'Can I drink?'

'Yes, for sure.'

As soon as Robert starts dozing, I leave the room and go to the kitchen where I howl. Howling is more comforting than crying. Howling comes from deep within. Later that night, I read from James Elroy Flecker's poignant Arabian story of love and death, *Hassan*, the part where Rafi says, 'The sunlight changes on the wall from white to gold. It is evening. Our time has come.'

Robert seems more peaceful. The TPI bag has been replaced by saline, and he is dozing much of the time, drifting in and out of consciousness. I find my way to the cathedral on the hill, just behind the apartment. It is a fine stone building, built in gothic style, its heavy doors keeping out the cold. I find it hard to push them open as I haven't much strength in my arms. A wedding rehearsal is in process and a group of young people are surrounding the altar, rehearsing events for the following day. At first I am glad. I listen to the music soaring upwards, I think it is Mozart's *Poave* — then I become suddenly angry. Angry for Robert having to die and angry for me being left behind. 'It's unfair,' I want to call out, and to stamp my foot like a child. Tears are running down my face, but I can't find my way out. All the doors seem to be locked and I am trapped in this rehearsal for a wedding, while across the road the man I love is dying.

The next day is Sunday and Robert is very scratchy. He tells us his feet and legs are sore, his back, his arms too. His face lights up when Ryan appears.

'No bolus, no sleeping pills. I want to stay awake.'

'Saline?'

'No, nothing.'

Francesca sings and Robert asks her to stop. No, he doesn't want music. He doesn't want water. He wants nothing.

'Nothing,' he repeats.

It feels as if he is moving into bleak places, the kind that Virginia Woolf described as the 'wastes and deserts of the soul'. I remember being warned this might happen by a friend of mine, Petrea King, who works professionally with people who are dying. 'Don't tiptoe round people if this happens,' she said. 'If you behave like this, you'll scare them; at some level, they'll know you're not being real.'

Some time late that night Bob looks in. Robert flickers his eyelids and appears to drift off into that space which is somewhere between sleeping and waking.

'Warriors, we were warriors,' says Bob in a sad voice. 'Two days ago, he was fighting to stay alive, now he is fighting not to die.'

After Bob has gone, Robert gets querulous. Every two minutes he rings his bell, wanting something. 'Speak ... don't speak ... come ... go away ... move the TPN ... I want sedation ... I don't want sedation .. I want saline ... no, I don't want saline.'

He hears Francesca observe he is doing it hard and he cuts in, sharply, 'Be specific, how am I doing it hard? What context? How could I do it better? You're not the one who's doing it.'

She nods, and says, 'That's right. I'd be making much more of a fuss than you.'

Perhaps it is not death but dying we fear, that terrible loneliness that ultimately we have to face alone.

I am back in my childhood, and those horrible dreams I had where I became a large iron file, grinding myself away with sounds that made my teeth ache. Smaller and smaller, until the moment came when I ceased to exist. There was no more. But maybe dying is not like that at all — maybe it's just a cessation of life, gentle or sharp, now you see it, now you don't, no golden light at the end of the tunnel, no great white universe in which we fly away, hands folded, maybe calling out last minute messages through the ether, 'Don't forget to eat your lunch. I love you. Free the refugees.'

Whatever it is that happens or doesn't happen, we haven't made much of a fist about finding it out.

Robert wants his water moved, the flowers, the clock, his morphine bolus. The sheets need straightening. His feet want rubbing. His face is harsh. Has he realised there are no more trades he can make, no more bends in the road?

I bump into Francesca in the kitchen, we are both in search of Wheat Thins, anything to keep us going. All day and throughout this long and stressful night he has had us on the hop. Every two or three minutes he rings his buzzer, summoning us to his side.

Francesca snaps, 'If he doesn't die soon, I'll kill him.'

Robert's buzzer rings, strident and insistent.

'Maybe he was a tyrant in a former life, how about that? Maybe this is just a spot of regression.'

We begin to giggle like schoolgirls. In his room, Robert waves at his water. 'More!'

It is already full.

Francesca is standing behind me and whispers in my ear, 'I'll have to lie down soon or I'll fall down.'

He looks straight at us and rings the buzzer again, not once but three times, even though Francesca and I are standing next to him, even though I have held out his water which he chooses to ignore.

'Faces Forward,' he barks at us. It takes a tremendous effort for him to speak loudly, but this command would have done justice to a sergeant major. 'Faces Forward!'

'What did you say Robert?' For a moment, I am unable to understand and then I realise he means we mustn't talk behind his back.

'F is for Faces Forward,' he repeats.

I crack. 'And F is for Fuck Off Robert!'

He looks at me aghast. 'But I'm dying,' he says in a small voice.

'I know you are, I know you are, but you're behaving abominably, and it breaks my heart to see you in such a lonely, terrible place.'

'Am I really behaving badly?'

'Yes — but that's not the point, it's not being able to reach you, love you, me — all of us. Don't make it so hard on yourself, Robert.'

And then I am appalled. What right have I to tell him how to behave? I think.

'I want you to think very carefully about coming,' he had said on the phone before I left Australia, his voice already hoarse. 'I've not done this kind of thing before and it's going to be tough.' He was right. It is tough.

He is silent for a moment, then reaches out and takes my hand. 'Don't ever stop being honest with me. That's why I love you.'

The rest of the night is fretful. I snatch a couple of hours sleep and wake up after the following dream: a young man is leaning against the trunk of a tree, his back towards me. I put my arms around him and, as he turns, I see an arrow has pierced his heart. I pull it out, and while blood gushes forth from the wound he dies in my arms.

Days are lost in a swirl of flowers and messages. Someone talks again about the white light that comes with death. It isn't an image I can relate to, but then words sometimes obscure rather than clarify our inner meanings. If white light means mystery, this ending of a life, this room bathed in love and generosity, then I don't mind what we call it. But all the time this relentless force of dying refuses to be assuaged. The terrible pity of a body that is collapsing, every cough an assault on breathing, every movement bringing pain. Dying is hard work. I cross Robert's hands to pull him to a sitting position — that's how it's done. He tries to spit but nothing comes, because dehydration is setting in. The bed is uncomfortable; there are ructions in the mattress; each attempt to smooth it brings yet more discomfort. We need male energy; we, the handmaidens, are wilting.

I look outside the window and see it is snowing, but a few clusters of berries are still scarlet on the rowan tree, clinging to white-spangled branches. Robert looks at them and manages to smile. What was that short story by famous American short-story writer O. Henry, about the consumptive young woman who promised to stay alive until the last leaf dropped from a vine that grew outside her window? Every night her lover crept downstairs and painted a leaf on the wall that held the vine.

We have no wall, we have no vine. But we still have the rowan tree that has grown from seed, through spring, summer and autumn. And now it is winter. The beauty of this natural world must assume an exquisite poignancy to a person nearing death.

English writer, Denis Potter, wrote just three months before he died:

Beneath my window in Ross-on-Wye — when I am working the blossom is out in full. It's a plum tree … it's the whitest, frothiest, blossomest blossom that there ever could be. And things are both more trivial than they ever were and more important than they ever were, and the difference doesn't seem to matter … the glory of it, the comfort of it, the reassurance.'

And then, as if to reassert his well-known acerbity, he says, 'Not that I'm interested in reassuring people — bugger that?'

Robert says he is tired, so very tired. He has been struggling to maintain consciousness but feels he cannot continue much longer. He asks Ryan to give him more morphine, not to kill him but to help him sleep. He tries to pull himself up against the pillows and says with a dignified formality: 'I want you to say goodbye and thank you, and then I shall say goodbye and thank you.'

But he doesn't lose consciousness. He has this commitment to relate to each of us, his friends, and the incredible courage and determination to stay present, right through to his last breath. He hovers for about an hour, sometimes opening his eyes, sometimes closing them, his breathing getting worse. Then he heaves himself up into a sitting position again. He looks around at us; his eyes, once so inquisitive, now have a deep innocence. He winks at Michele. He squeezes my hand. He blows me a kiss. I look at his wasted body as he gasps, jerks upright, his teeth gritting skeletally, his breath held back, an automatic reaction. There are several jerks and spasms. His face looks like a Samurai warrior's. There is a death rattle, neither soft nor pretty, followed by such small sweet sighs, the body sinking back softly, gently turning his left shoulder, the gown slipping. The last breath wouldn't blow a feather. His head stops moving. He is dead.

Like a medieval painting, the light in the room is suddenly golden. Francesca is at his head, her face lit up so it also shines with the same golden light. Maybe it is the way we are looking at him, maybe I imagine, but this is how I remember it: this extraordinary luminous quality of the light. There is a low moan from all of us, a huddle, and a soft weeping.

We put down the bed and we wash Robert's face, put his legs and his arms by his side, and try to close his mouth — but it won't close.

'It wouldn't in life, it won't during death,' says Bob, his eyes filled with tears.

20

If you love, you grieve

An hour after Robert has died two mortuary assistants arrive, friendly young men dressed in grey flannel trousers and dark grey jackets with blue ties. They are not as sepulchral as some of the undertakers I've met — black-suited and po-faced. These are more like the young men who work in the downtown organic store.

When Robert's body has been carried away, we stay in his apartment recalling stories of his life and of the past few days. At the same time, I try to remember all that comforting stuff about death — that it is part of the cycle of life, that we are dying from the moment we are born — but it doesn't help. One minute we had sat with a man who was thinking, moving, feeling. Then the man died, and in his place there was a body, warm for a few minutes and then alarmingly cold. Such a fine thread that connects us to life. Such a brief moment of time that takes that life away. Although I had all that time to prepare for Robert's death, I still went into some kind of shock. At the same time I felt immensely tired.

When Jonathan died, well-meaning friends informed me in kind and sensible voices about the various stages of grieving — ideas which have evolved from the pioneering work of Kubler-Ross — but it doesn't work in any neat order, not in my experience, anyway. We all react differently to the death of someone we love. Culture, temperament, beliefs, age, experiences that have gone before influence the way we feel and behave. My natural reaction is not to deny my grief, and to know that the more I have loved someone, the greater my pain will be. But it will settle — gradually, and over time.

Allan Kellehear, Director of the Palliative Care unit at La Trobe University in Melbourne, says, 'I think we don't fully understand or appreciate how diverse grief is. You fall in love in a thousand ways, and you grieve in a thousand ways.'

In African countries, I have walked in processions of wildest grief, with mourners beating their breasts, prostrating themselves on the ground, and expressing their sorrow with such intensity they sometimes move into states of altered consciousness. In England, I remember funerals where not one moist eye was seen, but as soon as formalities were over, the tears would flow. Australian funerals are also fairly stoical affairs, yet at the many services in remembrance of those who lost their lives in the Bali bombings of 2002, it seemed as if there had been a cultural shift. Australia showed its openness to grief. Churches were packed. Men wept openly. People from all religions joined the services, as loss began its long and painful transition into memory.

For some people, initial grief is a raw and unpredictable pain. For others, pain filters through more slowly, a little at a time as the body can bear. After my parents died, I felt chilled, as if I had been moved to the front line of the family and now there was no one ahead to comfort and protect me. When my son died, there was a wildness about my grief, a sense that something so unnatural had occurred. Children are not supposed to die before their parents. Two young policemen gave me the news. They came to my office at the Film and Television School, where I was Director. I'd had a sense of foreboding that Jonathan wouldn't live much longer, but even so, I wasn't prepared for the terrible shock. I heard myself utter a raw and primitive cry that seemed to come from the centre of the earth. With Robert there was deep sadness, but without the wildness.

After we had all taken some kind of meal together, Francesca offered to stay one more night with me, but I needed to be alone. I wanted time to sift through what had happened, and how I felt about it. Our culture has not always dealt kindly or wisely with death. We can be impatient with grief, often giving unstinting support for a brief while and then withdrawing, saying brusquely that it is time to get on with normal life again.

Australian psychotherapist and author Stephanie Dowrick says:

The truth is, though, that after any great loss there is no such thing as normal life. When life returns, 'normal' will feel different. Profound grief is not something we get over. In time, we get on, sometimes noticing with surprise how much life is still giving to us even while it has been taking so much away.

Freud calls the work of mourning and melancholia a ritualising of grief, a means of making death more bearable.

From wakes and memorial services to gatherings round the kitchen table, we are honouring death while at the same time trying to stumble back and find meaning in life. We sat around a lot in those days after Robert died, talking about him, talking about death, drinking tea: Indian tea, china tea, jasmine tea, tea made of orange blossom and dandelions, tea with cloves and cardamom; tea interrupted by visits from friends and neighbours, and phone calls from salesmen wanting us to join their industry of death.

'Mr Theobald is dead? Oh, Mr Theobald is passed away, my deepest sympathies, Mrs Theobald I presume?

'No, no, I am not Mrs Theobald, but Mr Theobald is dead.'

I do not like the term 'passed away'. Once I made a television documentary about the funeral industry called 'Everyone a Customer', and ever since meeting 'king pin' sales representatives who sold plots in lawn cemeteries while they talked about the 'dear departed' I have been savage about euphemisms of any kind. But this is simply my own personal reaction. Euphemisms help some people get through difficult times.

I was glad Robert died at home. I was grateful I was there. It is strange that although we have just lived through a century of deaths, wars and genocides, not many of us have seen a dead body. Most people in the Western world die in hospitals. A friend and colleague of mine, Australian broadcaster Phillip Adams, says this is 'rather like living in a forest and being denied the sight of a fallen tree.'

I remember the first time the fact of death was denied to me. An eighty-year-old woman, wearing a faded pink satin dressing jacket, was propped up with pillows in the middle of a row of twenty beds. I had gone to interview her about nursing home conditions. I tried to work out if the view from her bed provided anything more than bedpans and temperature charts. Could she perhaps catch a glimpse of a tree, a corner of blue sky? I did not think so. She was embarrassed because I had found her without her teeth. She said she felt undressed. At her request I scrabbled around for the missing teeth in her bedside drawer, but when I turned round, holding the teeth in a crumpled handkerchief, I saw that she had died — silently, as if in mute protest at the indignities that age obliged her to endure. I called a nurse and said timidly, 'I think she is dead.'

I do not know *how* I knew she was dead. I did not take her pulse and she was my first corpse, not to put too fine a point on it, but I just knew she was dead. The nurse responded by pushing me out of the room as if some terrible indecency had occurred, too shocking for me to observe. Yet I had felt the need to linger, to hold the old lady's hand, to take in the mystery of a life which had suddenly and un- ceremoniously ended. Instead, I went down to the hospital canteen and drank three cups of tea: tea when babies are born and tea when people die.

All manner of strange things occur after death, as if the land on which we stand suddenly moves. Someone has gone, but we have no idea where. Dust to dust, ashes to ashes, pft, that's it? Or is there a Buddhist sea of universal consciousness that takes us in, and then reincarnates us, delivers us back to the shore? What to make of those darkened corridors of transition, at the end of which some people claim they see a golden light? Whatever our culture and our belief system, we are only certain of one thing, the person who has just died has died, and is not going to return in earthly form. At first, this is one of the hardest things to accept. I find myself looking at the empty space in the middle of the room where

Robert's bed has been. I think of the energy and ideas and excitement he brought into my life. Someone said perhaps the experience of being with Robert when he died also gave us the chance to be reborn, perhaps into a more spiritual existence. I did not feel reborn; I felt like a clod of soggy, wet earth.

It had snowed heavily during the night, snow powdering the trees, snow thick on the streets and the rooftops, on the windows of the cars. Even the rowan berries outside Robert's window were now frozen and had changed to a deeper, crystallised red so they looked like a Christmas Day confection dusted with icing sugar.

Every time I turned on the television I heard Christmas carols. 'Joy to the World', sang a plump young woman with dark red lipstick and some kind of tiara sitting uncomfortably on her bouffant hair. Up until Robert's death I had kept myself physically well, but now my whole body ached. I found it hard to get out of bed, my eyes and my head throbbed, a heaviness held me down, and my heart was sore. Why the heart, I wondered, that throbbing muscle of blood and tissue — why not my spleen or my liver or my left arm?

Sometimes Annie was practising the piano or the violin; sometimes we played Racing Demon. She wasn't juggling as much. One day, a large square green plastic box was delivered to the house: Robert's ashes. An older man brought it, plonking it down and saying cheerfully, 'He sure was a big guy, yessir, nearly didn't fit him all in, had to pack him down some.'

The box did not seem to bear any relationship to Robert, and I looked at it askance.

I went for a walk with Annie, Bob and Susan, and Annie began jousting with me in the snow. We raced and pushed each other — I was determined not to fall over. It seemed important to stay on my feet. We played pool. She won. Table tennis. I won. That night, the bed was cold, the snow had turned to sleet. My thoughts kept returning to the box, the green box of ashes, the box that contained Robert.

'Don't hold your anger in,' says everyone, including me. *Don't hold your anger in*, but in this apartment with its paper-thin walls, what am I supposed to do with this surge of rage I suddenly feel? If I yell, I'll bring out the neighbours who are already furious with me because yesterday I let the hand basin in the bathroom overflow and sent a deluge of water running down the walls of the flat below. In my dreams, the green box of Robert's ashes keeps appearing before me, spinning round and round in space. Where are you, I ask Robert, and why have you left me weeping? Why did you open up my heart again and then leave me with such indecent haste? I can't remember you, not your face, nor your touch, nor even your voice.

Dreams of every kind are coming with increasing frequency as if there are no barriers between my conscious and unconscious mind.

In one dream, I am in the turret of a castle in India, listening to a minstrel who is singing in the street below about people who are poor and sick and alone. I call out that I want to help, and throw down the contents of my purse — eight dollars and thirty-five cents. He counts the money and looks up in wonder, 'But you have given me so much.'

'I have given you all I have. Don't go!'

But he is already moving away, his voice growing fainter until it disappears.

I wake from this dream and go to my computer which sits on Robert's desk, its light blinking and winking. I begin typing. What do I expect, in this witching hour of night? That miracles will transpire, that out of the ether a message will come bouncing into my lap? Do I really expect this? Yes, like the child who writes a note on Christmas Eve when the moon hangs full and white, I indeed expect miracles. In the morning, when the grey light of early dawn fills an empty room, I switch on the computer, but I already know the screen will be blank.

Grief opens up. Like a sudden storm, it deluges me, as raw and painful as when it all happened. When this happens, I weep. Sometimes I weep alone. Sometimes I find comfort from others. I walk. I go into the countryside.

Bob comes with Robert's silver ring. He had taken it off when Robert was in hospital and kept it safely; now he gives it to me and says this is where it belongs. And his hat. I want to take Robert's Akubra hat back to Australia. I know it is too big for me, but I think somehow I might make it fit.

I thought often about the briefness of our time together, and I veered from sadness to recognising that life itself is so fleeting it sometimes seemed a miracle we enjoyed even this.

In the immediate weeks after his death, Robert seems to have exited the universe. I have no sense of his presence. I wait. I observe. I try to comfort myself with the words of American poet and funeral director, Thomas Lynch: 'This is what happens around the world; if you love, you grieve, and there are no exceptions.'

21

In retrospect

I am at home now, in my house near the sea, with the dog, Bibi, asleep at my feet and small boys skateboarding noisily outside my window. Soon they will go home and I will play some Bach, and then later I will meet Jane for dinner. Life has returned to its normal beat, almost as if nothing had ever happened — but not quite, because I am different. Am I wiser? Not necessarily. Sadder? No, I don't think so. I am sad that Robert died, but my view of life is no sadder. In fact, it is happier because I feel blessed to have had the love Robert and I shared, however brief. I think of a Zen poem that I have always loved: 'The morning glory, which blooms for an hour, differs not at heart from the giant pine, which lives for a thousand years.'

I stayed on in Spokane for six weeks after Robert's death. I felt I needed time alone in his apartment, and time to deepen my friendship with the people I had met and grown to love. When I came home, family and friends helped me ease my way back into life. It took some time. At the beginning, I felt as if I had been dropped from a great height and shattered into pieces.

My life and Robert's became intertwined in ways I could not have imagined at the outset of writing this book. Our ideas and our experiences influenced one another's. Being with Robert gave an extra dimension to my writing; as I wrote, I felt my boundaries extend and the book seemed to develop an existence of its own — the mounting pages representing my growing understanding. When Robert became ill, it felt as if everything conspired against love. Yet our being together even as he died somehow defied despair, reinforced his spirit and mine. Not for one moment did I regret our coming together.

Looking back I can see that, initially, I thought of resilience as a quality that some people possessed and others lacked. Somewhere, fairly early on in my reading, I realised that resilience was much more than that, and infinitely more complex. Resilience is the life force that flows and connects every living thing, continually prompting regeneration and renewal. Robert's work was about honouring and using that life force for our greater good: finding ways of working and living together that won't destroy ourselves and the world in which we live. His enormous optimism prompted increasing numbers of people to commit themselves to building a more caring and responsive society — people who, like me, are alarmed by the degradation of our planet, by wars and violence, by the gap between rich and poor, and by the growing numbers of children around the world who will suffer because adults will not make the world safe for them.

The world's resilience is weakened if it receives too many blows. Each time we move into states of discord, whether with each other or with our environment, we damage our capacity for regeneration.

Ultimately we are each responsible for ourselves and for the kind of societies in which we live. Even the smallest of steps can bring change. I believe at the deepest level a yearning for good lies within all of us. In essence, we share the same longing for peace and love, the same need for respect, the same fear of pain and suffering, the same desire for joy. Our lives are connected and are part of a far greater whole. If we recognise this, we can transform our notions of self to embrace each other and work together to create a wiser, gentler world.

One night, not long after my return to Sydney, I was on my own at a friend's house overlooking Pittwater, listening to a recording of the opera Tosca. As the music swelled to a climax, I heard an echo of the song from my dream: the minstrel's song about the poor and the lonely. It started softly, a fine thread behind the music, then grew to fill the room until it was the only sound I could hear. It was so elemental, so overpowering, that I had a sudden sense of losing my soul — as though I, my 'self', no longer existed. I called out in anger and was almost immediately overcome by a completely different feeling — that my soul was growing to fill everything and everywhere and all sense of time and space had disappeared. I felt at peace.

Perhaps such experiences happen at times of intense grief or joy. Perhaps at these moments our subconscious minds are able to break through the confines of everyday life, and remind us we are part of a much bigger existence, one that has no boundaries. 'Grief never leaves you,' I once heard writer V. S. Naipaul say, 'but it mutates into a deepening awareness of the greater capacity for love, and an extra-ordinary awareness of the interconnectedness of life.'

Notes

In time the wind
Pythian IV, *The Odes of Pindar*, trans. C. M. Bowra, Penguin
    Books, London, 1969.
It may not be
Jeanette L. Johnson, 'Commentary: Resilience as Transactional
    Equilibrium' in Meyer D. Glantz and Jeannette L. Johnson
    (eds), *Resilience and Development, Positive Life Adaptations*,
    Kluwer Academic/Plenum Publishers, New York, 1999,
    p. 227.

1. IN THE BEGINNING
'I won't give in
Oral evidence given at Early Childhood Special Education
    Conference, July 1976, for Royal Commission into Human
    Relationships, reported in Anne Deveson, *Australians at Risk*,
    Cassell Australia, Melbourne, 1978, p. 382.
'Until we reach our limits
Polly Young-Eisendrath, *The Resilient Spirit*, Allen & Unwin,
    Sydney, 1997, p. 7.
'We all know perfectly
George Vaillant, *The Wisdom of the Ego*, Harvard University Press,
    Cambridge MA, 1993.
When Australian author Geraldine Brooks
Geraldine Brooks, *Year of Wonders: A Novel of the Plague*, Penguin
    Books, Melbourne, 2002.

Noel Pearson insists that
Noel Pearson, *Our Right to Take Responsibility*, Noel Pearson
& Associates Pty Ltd, Cairns, Queensland, 2000, p. 5.
According to a recent United Nations Report
The State of the World's Children 2003, UNICEF Publications,
New York, December 2002.
'toxic society'
Interview with Fiona Stanley by Victoria Laurie in 'How to
Grow a Baby', *Weekend Australian Magazine*, 13–14 October
2001, p. 25.
'drifting further out
John Ralston Saul, *The Unconscious Civilization*, Penguin Books,
Melbourne, 1997, p. 36.
'Resilient people and companies
Diane Coutu, 'How Resilience Works', *Harvard Business Review*,
May 2002, pp. 2–7.
'We must expect everything
Seneca, *Naturales Qauestiones 1 & 11, Epistulae Morales XCL 15*,
trans. T. H. Corcoran, Loeb-Harvard, 1972, p. 87.

2. THE DEFROCKED ECONOMIST
Jung described this experience
C. G. Jung, Memories, *Dreams, Reflections*, Fontana Press, London,
1995, Chapter XI, pp. 330–50.

3. EVERYDAY MAGIC
Sweet are the Uses of Adversity
William Shakespeare, 'As You Like It', Act 2, Sc. 1. in *The
Complete Works Of William Shakespeare*, Oxford University
Press, London, 1954, pp. 217–42.
'He would bring a sandwich
Interview with Norman Garmezy by Jon E. Rolf in Glantz and
Johnson (eds), *Resilience and Development, Positive Life
Adaptations*, pp. 5–14.

They believed that
Norman Garmezy, 'Stress, Competence, and Development:
Continuities in the Study of Schizophrenic Adults, Children
Vulnerable to Psychopathology, and the Search for Stress-
Resistant Children', *American Journal of Orthopsychiatry*,
vol. 57, no. 2, April 1987, pp. 159–74.

'Mental illness steals
Mona Wasow, *The Skipping Stone, Ripple Effects of Mental Illness on
the Family*, Science and Behaviour Books, 1995, pp. 11–33.

'In my child's mind
Carmel Williams, 'Bathing Rosa', *Weekend Australian*,
14–15 August 1999.

I remember longing
Gloria Steinem, 'Ruth's Son', *Ms Magazine*, vol. 46, 1983,
pp. 47–50.

'keepers of the dream
Norman Garmezy, 'Vulnerability Research and the Issue of
Primary Prevention', *American Journal of Orthopsychiatry*,
vol. 41, no. 1, January 1971, p. 114.

Numerous clinical case studies
Norman Garmezy, 'Stress, Competence, and Development',
American Journal of Orthopsychiatry, vol. 57, no. 2, p. 165.

'loved well, worked well
Emmy Werner, 'High risk children in adulthood: A longitudinal
study from birth to 32 years', *American Journal of
Orthopsychiatry*, vol. 59, no. 1, 1989, pp. 72–81.

'an innate self-righting mechanism'
E. E. Werner and R. S. Smith, *Overcoming the Odds: High risk
children from birth to adulthood*, Cornell University Press, Ithaca,
New York, 1993.

myth of the golden child
F. Beauvais and E. Oetting, 'Drug Use, Resilience, and the Myth
of the Golden Child' in Glantz and Johnson (eds), *Resilience
and Development, Positive Life Adaptations*, pp. 101–6.

Even as late as 1995
S. E. Buggie, 'Superkids of the Ghetto', *Contemporary Psychology*,
vol. 40, 1995, pp. 1164–5.
'law of the hammer'
A. Kaplan, *The Conduct of Inquiry, Methodology for Behavioural
Science*, Chandler Publishing, San Francisco, 1964.
Simply put, the law's basic postulate
Norman Garmezy, 'Stress, Competence, and Development',
American Journal of Orthopsychiatry, vol. 57, no. 2, p. 164.
This recognition of the inherently dynamic
Michael Rutter, 'Psychosocial resilience and protective
mechanisms', *American Journal of Orthopsychiatry*, vol. 57,
no. 3, 1987.
What began as a quest
A. S. Masten, 'Ordinary Magic, Resilience Processes in
Development', *American Psychologist*, vol. 56, no. 3,
pp. 227–38.
Even the most basic
A. S. Masten, 'Ordinary Magic', *American Psychologist*, vol. 56,
no. 3, p. 235.
'Most people, most of the time
Robert Theobald, 'The Healing Century', six-part series
broadcast on ABC Radio National, April/May 1998 (for
transcripts: http://www.abc.net.au/rn/events/theobald.htm).

4. SHAPING BRAINS
The extent of early brain
Justine Ferrari, 'Body Parts', *Weekend Australian*, 4–5 May
2002.
The first scientists to discover
Hubel and Wiesel's Nobel Prize for their discoveries
concerning visual systems was shared with
Roger W. Sperry for his discoveries concerning
cerebral hemispheres. Information about Hubel and

Wiesel's work from the Nobel Assembly Karolinska
Institute, press release 9 October 1981, and D. Hubel
'A Big Step along the Visual Pathway', *Nature*, vol. 380,
1996. p. 197.

'It is an area
Loretta McLaughlin, '2 at Harvard Share Nobel in Medicine'
in Boston Globe, 10 October 1981. For further reading on
early brain plasticity see M. Cynader and J. F. Mustard, 'Brain
development, competence and coping skills', *Entropy*, vol. 1,
no. 1, Toronto Founders Network, 1997.

The adopted children from Romania
'Turning Point — What's Happened to Romanian Orphanage
Children?', 45-minute video produced by ABC Network
USA, 1997. Further information: Trudy Rosenwald,
Adoptions International, aiwa@multiline.com.au

'Broken bones will / The systems in the human brain
Bruce Perry, 'Incubated in Terror: Neurodevelopment Factors in
the Cycle of Violence' in J. Osofsky (ed.), *Children, Youth and
Violence: The Search for Solutions*, Guilford Press, New York,
1996, pp. 124–48. See http://teacher.scholastic.com/
professional/bruceperry/bonding.htm

… one third were doing very well
Elinor Ames, 'The Development of Romanian Orphanage
Children Adopted to Canada', Final report to the National
Welfare Grants Program, Human Resources Development,
Canada, available through http://www.bcadoption.com/
articles/attachment/ames.htm — or full report: Children from
Romanian Orphanages, Box 1353, Southampton, Ontario
NOH 2LO, Canada.

Similarly positive was a British study
M. Rutter and The ERA study team, 'Developmental Catch-up
and Deficit, following adoption after severe global early
privation', *Journal of Child Psychiatry*, vol. 39, no. 4, 1998,
pp. 465–76.

Rutter wondered whether
M. Rutter, 'Resilience in the Face of Adversity', Medicine Meets
   Millenium, World Congress on Medicine and Health,
   21 July–31 August 2000. See http://www.mhhannover.de/
   aktuelles/projekte/mmm/germanversion/d_fs_programme/
   speech/Rutter_V.html
The search for effects
Ann M. Clarke and Alan D. Clarke, *Early Experience and the Life
   Path*, Jessica Kingsley Publishers, London, 2000.
going back to the Royal Commission
Royal Commission on Human Relationships, Final Report,
   vol. 4, AGPS, Canberra, 1977, pp. 156–94.
In fact, child abuse and neglect
D. Weatherburn and B. Lind, *Social and Economic Stress, Child
   Neglect and Juvenile Delinquency*, New South Wales Bureau
   of Crime Statistics and Research, Sydney, 1997.
dramatised documentary
'Do I Have to Kill My Child?', 1976, broadcast Channel 9,
   distributed by Film Australia, Sydney.
Take another scenario
'A Waiting List as Long as Your Arm', 1 in 6-part ABCTV
   documentary series, *Faces of Change*, broadcast 1983.
Research corroborates
J. M. Gaudin, N. A. Polansky, A. C. Kilpatrick, P. Shilton,
   'Family Functioning in Neglectful Families', *Child Abuse
   and Neglect,* vol. 20, no. 4, 1996, pp. 363–76.
J. Garbarino and D. Sherman, 'High-risk neighbourhoods and
   high-risk families: the human ecology of child maltreatment',
   Child Development, no. 1, 1980, pp. 188–98.
one of the pioneers/Mustard says
Fraser Mustard, *Early Years Study Report*, a report into the
   relationship between brain development in early childhood
   and later health and life outcomes. See http://
   www.founders.net. Also Dr Fraser Mustard, The Canadian

Institute for Advanced Research, 180 Dundas St. West, Suite
1400, Toronto, Ontario, Canada M5G 1Z8.
The most famous study
John R. Berruta-Clement, *Changed Lives: the effect of the Perry
Preschool program on youths through age 19*, Ypsilanti,
Michigan, The High/Scope Press, 1984. See also
Lawrence J. Schweinhart, 'How the High/Scope
Perry Preschool Study Grew: A Researcher's Tale',
published online by the PhiDelta Kappa Center for
Evaluation, Development, and Research at
http://www.pdkintl.org/ edres/resbulpg.htm.
See also High/Scope's website at www.highscope.org

5. A GREAT WORLD TO BE IN

One of the most useful models
Urie Bronfenbrenner and S. J. Ceci, 'Nature-nurture
reconceptualized: a bio-ecological model', *Psychological Review*,
vol. 101, no. 4, 1994, pp. 568–86.
There is a mass of evidence
Colin Blakemore interviewed by Deborah Smith in 'Machine
Gene', *Sydney Morning Herald*, 1 August 2002.
'emotional intelligence'
Moira Rayner and Mary Montague, 'Resilient Children and
Young People', a discussion paper based on a review of
international research literature, published by Policy and
Practice Research Unit 1999, Deakin Human Services
Australia, Deakin University.
American author Judith Rich Harris
Judith Rich Harris, *The Nurture Assumption*, Bloomsbury,
London, 1999.
Resilience literature stresses
Ann S. Masten and Douglas Coatsworth, 'The Development of
Competence in Favourable and Unfavourable Environments',
American Psychologist, vol. 53, no. 2, pp. 205–20.

'One of the largest studies
Thomas G. Plante and Dustin A. Pardini, Religious
Denomination, Affiliation and Psychological Health: Results
from a Substance Abuse Population. Paper presented at
American Psychology Association's Annual Convention,
Washington DC, 4–8 August 2000. See APA's website:
http://w.w.w.apa.org/releases/faith.html
One of the largest studies/heathenism is a health hazard
Harold Koenig, The Healing Power of Faith, Science Explores
Medicine's Last Great Frontier, Simon & Schuster, New
York, 1999.
According to the Medical Journal of Australia
H. G. Peach, 'Religion, spirituality and health: how should
Australia's medical professions respond?', Medical Journal of
Australia, vol. 178, no. 2, 2003, pp. 86–8.
All things by immortal
Francis Thompson quoted in William H. Houff, Infinity in Your
Hand, Skinner House Books, Boston, 1990, p. 24.
'When it comes down to it
Janine Shepherd in P. Traynor, Roads to Recovery,
Allen & Unwin, Sydney, 1997, pp. 31–5.
'The remarkable attitude/'I had spent
Martin Seligman, The Optimistic Child, Random House,
Sydney, 1995.
resilient people are formed
Michael Rutter, 'Psychosocial resilience and protective
mechanisms', J. Rolf, A. Masten, D. Cicchetti,
K. Nuechterlein, and S. Weintraub (eds), Risk and Protective
Factors in the Development of Psychopathology, Cambridge
University Press, New York, 1990, pp. 181–214.
It's called Yes, We Do Have Future Choices
Robert Theobald, We Do Have Future Choices, Southern Cross
University Press, Lismore, 1999.

6. FAMILIES — WE ALL HAVE 'EM

An online bulletin from
Fostering Resilience in Children, Familial Environmental Factors, Ohio
State University Bulletin, pp. 875–99. See
ohioline.osu.edu/b875_3.html

'Parents are the bones
Peter Ustinov, *Dear Me*, Little, Brown & Company,
New York, 1977.

'being the parent of an adolescent
Andrew Fuller, *Raising Real People, Creating a Resilient Family*,
ACER Press, Melbourne, 2000.

'securely attached' children
Ann S. Masten and J. D. Douglas Coatsworth, 'The Development
of Competence in Favorable and Unfavorable Environments',
American Psychologist, February 1998, p. 208.

Emily Werner's famous research
Emmy Werner and J. L. Johnson, 'Can We Apply Resilience?',
Resilience and Development, Positive Life Adaptions, p. 263.

One would be in less danger
Ogden Nash from 'Family Court' in *Handbook of 20th Century
Quotations*, Sphere Books, London, 1984, p. 125.

'They fuck you up
Philip Larkin, 'This Be the Verse', in Neil Astley (ed.), *Staying
Alive*, Bloodaxe Books, 2002, p. 205.

In her book,
Pamela Kinnear, *New Families for Changing Times*, discussion
paper 47 for the Australian Institute, June 2002.

It is not the actual break-up
M. Rutter, 'Resilience in the Face of Adversity', *Medicine Meets
Millenium*, World Congress on Medicine and Health,
21 July–31 August 2000.

'a sometimes comforting
Thomas Moore, *Care of the Soul*, Harper Perennial, New York,
1992, p. 27.

The half-caste is

James Isdell, 1907, letter cited in Report of the *Inquiry into the Death of Malcolm Charles Smith*, by Commissioner J. H. Wootten, April 1989, in Royal Commission into Aboriginal Deaths in Custody, 1987–1991, National Archives of Australia.

I remember that day / 'They're looking in here

Maria Tomlins, 'Looking for That Familiar Face' in *Under the Mango Tree, Oral Histories with Indigenous People from the Top End*, published by Northern Territory Writers' Centre Inc., Darwin, N.T., 2001, pp. 25–31.

7. IT TAKES A COMMUNITY

feeding the poor

Elizabeth Windschuttle (ed.), *Women, Class and History, Feminist Perspectives on Australia, 1788–1978*, Fontana/Collins, 1980, pp. 53–72.

The right to self determination

Noel Pearson, *Our Right to Take Responsibility*, Noel Pearson and Associates, Cairns, Queensland, 2000, p. 5. See also: Indigenous Enterprise Partnerships, PO Box 7573, Cairns, Qld 4870 or mwinner@ozemail.com.au

Client one:

NSW Youth Drug Court case studies: extracts from speech given by NSW Premier Bob Carr at the Law Society, Sydney, 24 October 2002.

The story of Claymore

Brian Murnane and John Mant's stories in David Leser, 'It Takes a Village', *Sydney Morning Herald, Good Weekend*, 5 June 1999, p. 41. For further information: Claymore Benevolent Society, PO Box 171, Paddington, NSW 2021 www.bensoc.org.au

The story of Ben

The film about Ben and schooling for homeless children failed to raise finance and was never made.

The story of Rwanda
Rwanda material was used by various radio and TV news
  outlets immediately following the genocide, 1994.

8. VIOLENCE
'Behind the barbed wire
Martha Gelhorn, *The Face of War*, Sphere Books, London, 1967,
  p. 172.
'The conflict between the will
Judith Herman, introduction to *Trauma and Recovery*, Basic
  Books, New York, 1997.
Nothing belongs to us
Primo Levi,1958, *If This is a Man*, Abacus Books, London,
  1987, p. 8.
'Even epochal and unprecedented
Laqueur Thomas: *Review of Robert Gordon, Primo Levi's Ordinary
  Virtues: From Testimony to Ethics*, and Ian Thomson, *Primo Levi*,
  in *London Review of Books*, 5 September 2001
Precisely because the Lager
Primo Levi, *If This is a Man*, pp. 46–7.
'Here, listen Pikolo / 'like the blast of a trumpet / '...I close my eyes
Primo Levi, *If This is a Man*, pp. 115–21.
Where I wrote, 'I would give
Primo Levi, *The Drowned and the Saved*, Sphere Books, London,
  1989, pp. 112–13.
I almost never had the time to devote to death;
Primo Levi, *The Drowned and the Saved*, p. 120.
They are overcome
Primo Levi, *If This is a Man*.
A person with hope
John Berger, 'The Tree with Blue Eyes', in *Le Monde
  Diplomatique*, April 2000, p. 15.
Maria Pilar was twenty-one
Maria Pilar in *Transitions*, no. 3, August 1999, pp. 22–3.

The story of those prisoners/quoted interviews
Tim Bowden, 'Prisoners-of-War, Australians Under Nippon',
    16-part radio series, first broadcast ABC Radio 1984 (available
    on cassette through ABC Enterprises). See also: Hank Nelson,
    Prisoners of War, Australians under Nippon, ABC Books, Sydney,
    1985, 1990, 2001, p. 11, p. 46.
Next to us/aversion to
Primo Levi, *If This is a Man*, p. 77, p. 85.
I came across the work of
John Berger, 'The Tree with Blue Eyes', pp. 14–15.
'Some Advice to Those Who Will Serve Time in Prison'
Nazim Hikmet, 'Some Advice to Those Who Will
    Serve Time in Prison', from *Poems of Nazim Hikmet*,
    trans. Randy Blasing and Mutlu Konuk, Persea Books,
    Inc, New York, 1994.
'By writing I found peace
Primo Levi, 'Chromium', *The Periodic Table*, Abacus, London,
    1985, p. 150.
'I believe in reason/'Only in this case am I
Primo Levi, *If This is a Man*, p. 382.
Stephanie Dowrick, in her book
Stephanie Dowrick, *Forgiveness and Other Acts of Love*,
    Penguin Books, Melbourne, 1997.

9. THE PROBLEM IS THE PROBLEM
'In the process
Alan Rosen, '100% Mabo: De-Colonising People with Mental
    Illness and the Families', *A.N.Z. Journal of Family Therapy*,
    vol. 15, no. 3, 1994, pp. 128–42.
In 1998, I came across a paper
Sylvia Rockwell, 'Overcoming Four Myths that Prevent
    Fostering Resilience, Reaching Today's Youth', *The
    Community Circle of Caring Journal*, vol. 2, no. 3, Spring 1998,
    pp. 14–17.

Krissy

Krissy's story in ABC 6-part documentary series, 'Faces of Change', 1983, and in Anne Deveson, *Faces of Change*, ABC/Fontana, Sydney, 1984, pp. 25–65.

His psychiatrist lent him a book

George Vaillant, *Adaptation to Life*, Harvard University Press, Cambridge, Massachusetts, 1977.

In the old days/'Where should David go/'Now that was worth

M. Wasow, 'Strengths versus Deficits, or Musician versus Schizophrenic', *Psychiatric Services*, vol. 52, no. 10, October 2001, pp. 1306–7.

10. VALUES — WHAT HAPPENED?

Professor Bronfenbrenner

Urie Bronfenbrenner and S. J. Ceci, 'Nature-nurture reconceptualized'.

'every day magic

A. S. Masten, 'Ordinary Magic, Resilience Processes in Development' in *American Psychologist*.

'Many were concerned

Richard Eckersley, 'Future visions for children's well being' in M. Prior (ed.), *Investing in our Children: Developing a research agenda*, Academy of Social Sciences in Australia, proceedings of workshop, Melbourne, 29–30 May 2002.

Eckersley believed that

Richard Eckersley, 'Generation Wrecked', *Sydney Morning Herald*, 19 February 1999, p. 10.

children and adolescents were experiencing

Fiona Stanley, interviewed by Victoria Laurie in 'How to Grow a Baby'.

Eckersley states that such problems

Richard Eckersley, 'Generation Wrecked'.

'There hasn't been a change
Martin Seligman, on 'Life Matters', ABC Radio National,
16 August 2002, repeat broadcast of Seligman forum on
depression, recorded in Sydney 1994, transcript available:
abc.net.au/rn/talks/lm/stories/S648530.htm

A sobering lesson from Europe
M. Rutter and D. Smith, *Psychosocial Disorders in Young People:
Time trends and their Causes*, John Wiley & Sons for Academia
Europaea, Chichester, 1995.

One in forty schoolchildren
Michael G. Sawyer, Joseph M. Rey, Brian W. Graetz, Jennifer
J. Clark and Peter A. Baghurst, *Medical Journal of Australia*,
vol. 177, no. 1, 2002, pp. 21–5.

'We have been so used
Robert Theobald, *The Healing Century*, pamphlet based on
public broadcasts delivered in Australia, Canada and the
United States, 1999. (See earlier ref.)

we need to find meaning in life
Margaret Somerville, *The Ethical Canary*, Viking Australia, 2000,
pp. xi–xii.

In England, the two British researchers
M. Rutter and D. Smith, *Psychosocial Disorders in Young People.*

'It is essential that we develop
Joanna Macy, *World as Lover, World as Self*, Parallax Press,
Berkeley, California, 1991. The story of the workshop, south
of Chernobyl, has been told in several of Joanna Macy's
workshops.

11. THE BRIEFEST JOY

Oh, life is a glorious cycle
Dorothy Parker, 'Comment', *The Comic and Erotic Love Poems*,
The Currawong Press, Sydney, August 1980, p 9.

'*the most extraordinary aspect*
Deirdre Macken, 'Tour of the Nation's Psyche', *Australian Financial Review*, 25 October 1999, pp. 15–16.
Janet Holmes à Court
Janet Holmes à Court in Robert Theobald, *Visions and Pathways for the 21st Century*, Southern Cross University Press, Lismore, Australia, pp. i–v.
'*to know one's strengths*
Drusilla Modjeska, *The Orchard*, Pan Macmillan, Sydney, 1994, p. 64.

12. SHADOWS OF ILLNESS
'*It is in our spontaneous acceptance*
Alain de Botton, *The Consolations of Philosophy*, Hamish Hamilton Ltd, Penguin Books, Melbourne, 2000, pp. 75–9.
We live in the middle of things
Seneca, Praemeditatio in Alain de Botton, *The Consolations of Philosophy*, p. 91.
Our house is a happy house
Joe and Ethel Manfredotti, interviewed by John van Tigglen in 'Two of Us', *Sydney Morning Herald, Good Weekend*, 5 May 2001, p. 77.
I began researching my book
Anne Deveson, *Tell Me I'm Here*, Penguin Books, Melbourne, 1992, 1998.
'*pain ever young and active*
Colette, *The Blue Lantern*, Farrar, Straus & Giroux, New York, 1963, p. 10.
In a book called, Pain
Patrick Wall, *Pain: The Science of Suffering*, Weidenfeld, London, 1999.
Jenny Diski, writing in
Jenny Diski, 'Feel the Burn', Review of Patrick Wall, *Pain: The Science of Suffering*, in *London Review of Books*, 30 September 1999, p. 57.

'Did you ever read
Sogyal Rinpoche, *The Tibetan Book of Living and Dying*,
    Harper, San Francisco, 1992.

14. A QUESTION OF AGE
A few years earlier
Anne Deveson, *Coming of Age*, Scribe Publications,
    Melbourne, 1994.
new, old-age proponents
Deepak Chopra, *Ageless Body, Timeless Mind,* Random House,
    Sydney, 1993.
'age mystique'
Betty Friedan, *The Fountain of Age*, Jonathan Cape,
    London, 1993.
'To be healthy is much more
George Vaillant, *Ageing Well*, Scribe Publications, Melbourne,
    1993.
Simone de Beauvoir
Simone de Beauvoir, *The Coming of Age*, Putnam, London, 1972.

16. THE WOLVERINE POOCHPACK
that poem by Anna Wickham
Anna Wickham (1883–1947), 'The Tired Man' in *Poetry of the*
    English-Speaking World, Readers Union with William
    Heinemann, London, 1957.
Perhaps the most celebrated
Norman Cousins, *Anatomy of an Illness*, Bantam, London, 1981.
And a famous seventeeth
Dr Thomas Sydenham in Craig Hassed, *New Frontiers in*
    Medicine, Hill of Content, Melbourne, 2000, p 76.
'Humour is the third kingdom
Herman Hesse quoted in S. J. and S. Wolin, *The Resilient Self:*
    How Survivors of Troubled Families Rise Above Adversity,
    Villard Books, New York, 1994.

a trait of resilient people is a sense of humour
Ann S. Masten, 'Humor and competence in school-aged
  children', *Child Development*, no. 57, 1986, pp. 461–73.

17. SPIRIT
One scientist who isn't afraid
Oliver Sacks, *Seeing Voices*, Picador, London, 1991.
'our unknown and unexpected strengths
 Oliver Sacks, interview with Rachael Kohn, 'The Spirit of
  Things', ABC Radio National, 3 November 2002.
'innate self-righting mechanisms'
Emmy Werner, 'High risk children in adulthood'
'every day magic'
Ann S. Masten, 'Ordinary Magic, Resilience Processes in
  Development', *American Psychologist*.
The same conundrum
John Bayley, *Elegy for Iris*, St Martin's Press, New York, 1999.

19. ACROSS THE GULF
'I am large, I contain multitudes'
Walt Whitman, 'Song of Myself', from J. M. and M. J. Cohen
  (eds), *Penguin Dictionary of Quotations*, Penguin Books, London,
  1960, p. 415.
'Forgive, O Lord
Robert Frost, *Complete Poems of Robert Frost*, Henry Holt & Co.,
  New York, 1949.
Bill Houff, a friend of Robert's
William H. Houff, *Infinity in Your Hand*.
'The sunlight changes
James Elroy Flecker, *Hassan*, Penguin Books, London, 1948,
  p.105.
'wastes and deserts of the soul'
Virginia Woolf, 'On Being Ill', *The Moment and Other Essays*,
  Harcourt Brace Jovanovich, New York, 1948, p. 11.
short story by American author
O. Henry (William Sydney Porter) 1862–1912.

'Beneath my window
Denis Potter, interview with Melvyn Bragg, 'Without Walls',
    Channel Four TV, London, 5 April 1994.

20. IF YOU LOVE, YOU GRIEVE
the pioneering work of
Elizabeth Kubler-Ross, *Death: The Last Stage of Growth*, Simon &
    Schuster, New York, 1986.
'I think we don't fully understand
Allan Kellehear, Director of Palliative Care at La Trobe
    University, Melbourne, interviewed by Rachael Kohn in
    'Good Grief', The Spirit of Things, ABC Radio National,
    26 August 2001.
'The truth is, though
Stephanie Dowrick, 'A time to mourn', *Sydney Morning Herald,
    Good Weekend*, 27 October 2001.
Freud calls the work of
Sigmund Freud, 'Mourning and Melancholia', 1917, in the
    *Pelican Freud Library II: On Metapsychology: The Theory of
    Psychoanalysis*, Penguin Books, London, 1984.
'rather like living in a forest
Phillip Adams, in conversation with the author.
'This is what happens…if you love, you grieve
Thomas Lynch, 'Embalming Father' in *London Review of Books*,
    20 July 1995.

21. IN RETROSPECT
'The morning glory
Alan W. Watts, *The Way Of Zen*, Vintage Books, New York, 1957,
    p. 124.
Grief never leaves you
V. S. Naipaul

Reading suggestions

Bayley, John, *Elegy for Iris*, Picador, New York, 2000.

Bouby, Jean-Dominique, *The Diving Bell and the Butterfly*, Fourth Estate, London, 1997.

Bringing Them Home, Report of the National Inquiry into the Separation of Aboriginal and Torres Strait Islander Children from their Families, Human Rights & Equal Opportunity Commission, 1997.

De Beauvoir, Simone, *The Coming of Age*, Putnam, London, 1972.

Deveson, Anne, *Tell Me I'm Here*, Penguin Books, Melbourne, 1998; *Coming of Age*, Scribe Publications, Melbourne, 1994; *Australians at Risk*, Cassell, Sydney, 1978.

Dowrick, Stephanie, *Forgiveness and Other Acts of Love*, Penguin Books, Melbourne, 1997.

Duff, Kat, *The Alchemy of Illness*, Virago Press, London, 1994.

Friedan, Betty, *The Fountain of Age*, Jonathan Cape, London, 1993.

Fuller, Andrew, *Raising Real People, Creating a Resilient Family*, ACER Press, Melbourne, 2000.

Hassed, Dr Craig, *New Frontiers in Medicine*, Hill of Content, Melbourne, 2000.

Jung, Carl G., *Man and His Symbols*, Picador, London, 1978.

Levi, Primo, *The Drowned and the Saved*, Michael Joseph, London 1988; *If This is a Man* and *The Truce*, Penguin Books, London, 1987.

Macy, Joanna, *World as Lover, World as Self*, Parallax Press, Berkeley, 1991.

Moore, Thomas, *Care of the Soul*, Harper Perennial, New York, 1992.

Neill, Rosemary *White Out, How Politics is Killing Black Australia*, Allen & Unwin, Sydney, 2002.

Pearson, Noel, *Our Right to Take Responsibility*, Noel Pearson and Associates Pty Ltd, Cairns, 2000.

Resilience and Development, Positive Life Adaptations, Glantz, Meyer D. and Jeannette L. Johnson (eds), Kluwer Academic/Plenum Publishers, New York, 1999.

Rinpoche, Sogyal, *The Tibetan Book of Living and Dying*, Rider Books, San Francisco, 1992.

Royal Commission on Human Relationships, vols I-V, AGPS, Canberra, 1997.

Sacks, Oliver, *Seeing Voices*, Picador, London 1989; also read: *Migraine, Awakenings, A Leg to Stand On, The Man who Mistook his Wife for a Hat, An Anthropologist on Mars* (all published by Picador).

Saul, John Ralston, *The Unconscious Civilisation*, Penguin Books, Melbourne, 1997.

Seligman, Martin E. P, *The Optimistic Child*, Random House, Sydney, 1995.

Somerville, Margaret, *The Ethical Canary*, Viking, Melbourne, 2000.

Tacey, David, *Edge of the Sacred*, Harper Collins, Melbourne, 1995.

Theobold, Robert, *We Do Have Future Choices* and *Visions and Pathways for the 21st Century*, Southern Cross University Press, Lismore, 1999.

Vaillant, George, *Ageing Well*, Scribe Publications, Melbourne, 1993; *Adaptation to Life*, Little Brown, Boston, 1977.

Williams, Mark, *Suicide and Attempted Suicide*, Penguin Books, London, 1997.

Young-Eisendrath, Polly, *The Resilient Spirit*, Allen & Unwin, Sydney, 1997.

Index

Aboriginal societies 9
Aboriginal children —
    removal 86
Aboriginal economic
    models 93
    Indigenous Enterprise
        Partnerships 94
    Indigenous Negotiating
        Team 9
Aboriginal leadership 9
Aboriginal life expectancy 9
Aboriginal self-
    determination 93
    wrongs committed against
        Aboriginal people 121
Adams, Phillip 261
adolescence 76
advocacy groups 127
age and ageing 189–94
AIDS see HIV/AIDS
alcohol and alcoholism 10, 66,
    69, 85, 146–7
Alzheimer's disease 228–9
Ames, Elinor 45
Amnesty International 113
anger 150–1
anthropocentrism 6
apology
    'to Australia's Indigenous
        people' 121
    'true' 120

Argyle Community Housing 97
Arneil, Stan 116
Arnott, Felix Archbishop
    (Royal Commission on
    Human Relationships) 4
art 125, 226
Auschwitz 117–19; see also
    concentration camps, Dachau;
    Holocaust

Bacon, Sir Francis 24
Baldwin, Jacob 68
Bangalore, India 26
Bayley, John 229
Ben's story 99–101
Benevolent Society 15, 93, 99
Berger, John 113
Blain, Jonathan 12, 26, 78, 120,
    138–9, 165, 170–1
Blakemore, Colin (experience
    genes) 62
Blumann, Elise 235–8
Bowden, Tim, *Prisoners of War,*
    Australia under Nippon 114
brain
    early childhood programs 53
    early stimulation and
        development
        animal 43–4
        human 43–51
    neuronal connections 43

plasticity (Hubel and Wiesel)
42–3
research and resilience 41
visual systems and the brain 42
Brew, Marc 3
Bronfenbrenner, Urie (bio-
ecological model) 61–2, 142
Brooks, Geraldine 8
Bunyan, John 28

Canadian Institute for Advanced
Research (CAIR) 49; *see also*
Mustard, Fraser
Centre for the Study of
Religion/Spirituality and
Healing, Duke University 66;
see also Koenig, Harold
cerebral palsy 68
Champ, Simon 122–8
change (social) 10; *see also*
Western society
charitable organisations 92
Chernobyl 150
children (in today's world) 10
Aboriginal children —
removal 86
Australian teenagers 145
characteristics of resilient
children 62–3
child abuse 46–9, 85
child development and
resilience (bioecological
model) 61; *see also*
Bronfenbrenner, Urie
child's peer group 65
childhood competence 30
children at risk (mental illness)
30–3
children in a toxic society 10
children's literature 27, 148; *see
also* resilience

early childhood programs and
early intervention programs
50–2
'golden child' 35
infant determinism 45
medicated children —
behavioural, emotional
problems 147
parenting 51
prematurity 53–5
protective factors 49
resilient children 35; *see also*
Garmezy, Norman
Romanian orphans 44–6
'securely attached' children 78
United Nations Report on
Children (*The State of the
World's Children 2003*) 10
see also New South Wales
Youth Drug Court 95;
Perry Pre-School Project
(US) 50
China 193
Chopra, Deepak 189
Civitan International Research
Center 37–8
Clarke, Ann and Alan, *Early
Experience and the Life Path* 46
Claymore Community 96–9
Coleridge, S. T. 117
Colette, *The Blue Lantern* 175
colonising — the experience of
the mentally ill 126–7
community 92
resilient communities 95–6; *see
also* resilience, family
connectedness 67, 79, 148, 268
concentration camps
Auschwitz 112, 117
Dachau 106
see also Holocaust

consumer movements 125, 127
consumerism 14
consumption 150
Coutu, Diane 11
Coward, Noel 193
creativity 226
crime, juvenile (Weatherburn and Lind) 47
culture of negativity 126–8
cystic fibrosis 67

Dachau 106; *see also* concentration camps; Holocaust
dance 226
Dante, *Canto of Ulysses* 111
David's story 136–8
de Beauvoir, Simone, *The Coming of Age* 189, 192
de Botton, Alain, *Consolations of Philosophy* 168
death 211, 260–2
deep ecology 150–1
depression 10, 70, 119, 145, 148
age of onset 145–6
'epidemics of depression' 145
Descartes — Cartesian mind-body split 36–7, 176
Deveson, Anne
Coming of Age 189
'Do I Have to Kill My Child?' 47
'Everyone a Customer' 261
Tell Me I'm Here 170
'They Smell Different' 71
Diski, Jenny 176
Down's Syndrome 63–4
Dowrick, Stephanie, *Forgiveness and Other Acts of Love* 120, 260
dreams 240–3

drug abuse, addiction 10, 62, 132, 140, 143–4
drug courts 95
drug summit 143–4
drugs
medication 8, 136
neuroleptic medication 29

Early Years Task Force, Ontario Canada 49; *see also* children; Mustard, Fraser
East Timor 221
survivors 108–9
Eckersley, Richard 144–5, 149
emotional intelligence 62
empathy 192
environmental degradation 149
Ethel and Joe 169
Ethiopia 224–5
Evatt, Elizabeth (Justice) 4; *see also* Royal Commission on Human Relationships
euthanasia 142
'everyday magic' 23, 38 142, 226

family 74, 85
break-up 146
diversity 85
dysfunctional 77
influence 75
mythologies 83
nuclear 84
poverty 77–8
quality time 85
values 85
Firstwater, Francesca 198, 215–16
Flecker, James Elroy, *Hassan* 251
forgiveness 119–20, 192; *see also* Levi, Primo
Fraser, Gordon 207
Fraser, Malcolm 70

'free market' economics 18
Freud, Sigmund, *Mourning and Melancholia* 260
Friedan, Betty 190
friendship 113–14, 117, 235; *see also* mateship
Fuller, Andrew, *Raising Real People, Creating Resilient Families* 76
futurists 16–17
future orientation 192

Garmezy, Norman 29–30, 34, 126
Gelhorn, Martha 106, 194
genes — experience 62
gratitude 192
grief 151, 256–60

Harris, Judith Rich, *The Nurture Assumption* 64
hate 119–20
Hawke, Bob 143
Healing Circle 164, 215
Henry, O. 256
Hepburn, Katherine 189
Herman, Judith 108
heroin 133
Hesse, Herman 221
Hikmet, Nazim 117–18
HIV/AIDS 8, 128, 192
Holbrook, Kate 234–5
Holbrook, Michele 198, 215, 234
Holbrook, Ryan 198, 208–9, 234
Hole, S. R. 26
Holmes à Court, Janet 155
Holocaust 34; *see also* concentration camps
home 200
homelessness 99, 138, 201–2
hope 66, 98–9, 113, 125, 148, 230–1

Houff, Bill, *Infinity in your Hands* 250–1
Howard, John 120
Hubel, David (and Wiesel) 42–3
Human brain 40; *see also* brain
human psyche 128
human rights movements 34, 92
humour 220–2
Huntington's Chorea 67

Idi Dada Amin 60, 107, 141
individual
    holistic view of individual 147
    individual self-interest 149
    individualism 149
    rampant individualism 148
innate self righting mechanism (Werner and Smith) 35
International Catholic Migrations Commission 109
International Year of Disabled Persons (1981) 68
Isdell, James 86

Jake's story 131–5
Johnson, Jeanette L. xi
Joy 138, 157
Jung, Carl 20

Kaplan, Abraham, 'law of the hammer' 36
Keating, Paul 121
'keepers of the dream' (Garmezy; children) 34
Kellehear, Allan 259
Keynes, John Maynard 18
King, Petrea 252
Kinnear, Pamela, *New Families for Changing Times* 85
Koenig, Harold 66

Krissy's story 129–31
Kubler-Ross, Elizabeth 259

Laqueur, Thomas 110
Larkin, Philip 84
Levi, Primo 109–12, 117–20
    The Drowned and the Saved 111
    If This is a Man 119
Lidz, Theodore 171–2
Lind, Bronwyn (and
    Weatherburn) 47
Love 45, 156–7, 192
Lynch, Thomas 265

Mack, Tuisila 98–9
Macken, Dierdre 154
Macy, Joanna 150–1
Malaya (Malaysia) 182
mandatory sentencing 11
Mandela, Nelson 5
Mant, John 96
marijuana 132
Martineau, J. 24
Maslow, Abraham 146
Masten, Ann (everyday magic)
    38, 142, 221, 226
materialism 144
mateship 115
McGill Centre for Medicine,
    Ethics and Law, Canada 148
mental health
    Australian Mental Health
        Consumer Network 124
    health service —
        consumer 124
    Human Rights Enquiry into
        Mental Illness 122
    Mental Health Council of
        Australia 123
    mental illness 30–4
    National Alliance for the

        Mentally Ill (US) 172
    National Community
        Advisory Group on Mental
        Health 123
    paternalism 126–7
    Sane Australia 124
    schizophrenia 12, 29–3, 122,
        124–6, 136–8, 145, 170
    Schizophrenia Fellowship of
        NSW 123
    spirituality 126
middle class
    families 77
    therapists 77
Miller, Arthur, *Death of a
    Salesman* 207
modern society 8
Modjeska, Drusilla,
    The Orchard 157
Montague, Meg 62
Moore, Thomas 86
More, H. 24
Murdoch, Iris 229
Murnane, Brian 96–8
music 226
Mustard, Fraser 49–51
mystery 224–5
myth 128
    myths that prevent the
        fostering of resilience
        (Rockwell) 128–9

Naipaul, V. S. 268
Nash, Ogden 79
National Alliance for the
    Mentally Ill (US) 172
National Centre for
    Epidemiology and Population
    Health, Canberra 144
Native Title Act 9
negative bias 127

negativity 122
  culture of 126–8
Nelson, Hank 114
New South Wales Youth Drug
  Court 95; *see also* children, drugs
Newton, Isaac 36
Nguyen-Gilham, Viet 109

old age 189, 191
Organisation for European
  Economic Cooperation 16
Oxford English Dictionary 26

pain 175–6
parental psychopathology 146
Parker, Dorothy 153
paternalism 127
Pearson, Noel 9, 93
Perry Pre-School Project (US)
  50–1; *see also* children
Perry, Bruce, *Incubated in
  Terror* 44
Pilar, Maria 113
Pindar ix
Pinochet 113
plague 7
poetry 226
Pol Pot 141
Potter, Denis 256
poverty 77–8
precision bombing 7
prisoners of war 114–17
  *Prisoners of War Australians under
  Nippon* (Bowden) 114
Proverbs (17:22) 221
Prozac 147
psychosis 32, 145
psychosocial disorder 149
public good 149

quality time 85

Rayner, Moira 62
Reconciliation Convention
  1999 9
Red Cross 182
refugees 142
relational competence 64; *see also*
  children
resilience 2, 6, 10–12, 24–9,
  62–3, 267
  bioecological model of child
    development and resilience
    61–2
  characteristics of 62–3
  children 35
  children's literature 27–8, 145
  communities 14, 91–8
  comparative examples 7–8
  concept of 28
  connectedness 67, 79, 148, 268
  definitions 23, 24, 37
  disability 68
  earliest use 23, 24
  ecological systems 14
  emotional intelligence 62
  emotional maturity 62
  'everyday magic'
    (Ann Masten) 23, 38,
    142, 226
  family influence 75
  genetics 62
  Harvard Business Review 11
  international literature 62
  life force 267
  myths that prevent the
    fostering of resilience 128–9
  personality characteristics 60–6
  relational competence 64–6
  religion and spirituality 66
  research discipline 29–39
  resilient youth 64
  risk, stress and resilience 48

'securely attached' children 78
stock market 23
Ritalin 147
risk 48–9
  risk factor 48
Rockwell, Sylvia 129–38
Rodnick, Eliot 30
Romanian orphans 44–6; *see also*
  children
Rosen, Alan 126–7
Rosnan, Ros 172
Royal Blind Society 5
Royal Commission into Human
  Relationships 4, 47, 85
Rutter, Michael 46, 49, 70,
  146, 149
Rwanda 102–4

Sacks, Oliver 225–6
Sane Australia 124; *see also*
  mental health
Saul, John Ralston 10
schizophrenia 12, 29–33, 122,
  124–6, 136–8, 145, 170
Schwager, Jane 15, 20, 93, 266
self-determination 93
self-interest 149
self righting mechanism (innate)
  (Werner and Smith) 35, 226
Seligman, Martin 68–9, 148–9
Seneca 13, *Preameditatio* 167–8
Shakespeare, William, *As You
  Like It* 28
Shepherd, Janine 67
Singapore 1, 159, 181–2
Sisyphus 38
Smith, David (and Rutter,
  Michael) 146, 148–9
Smith, Ruth 35
Somerville, Margaret, 148
sommersi 109

South Africa 5
spirit 223–5
spirituality 66–7, 126, 224–6
Spitzer, Peter (Dr Fruit
  Loop) 221
Spokane, US 73, 197
Stanley, Fiona 10, 52, 145
Steinem, Gloria, *Ms Magazine* 33
Stilger, Bob 72, 164, 199, 204
stress 17, 48
suicide 118, 144
  suicidal ideation,
    behaviours 145
  youth suicide 10, 145; *see also*
    children
Sydenham, Thomas 221

teenage deaths 10; *see also*
  children, youth suicide
Telethon Institute for Child
  Health Research 10
Theobald, Robert 14-22, 26,
  55–7, 70–3, 140, 147–8, 150,
  154–5
  'enlarging the framework' 148
  The Healing Century 147
  *Visions and Pathways for the 21st
    Century* 155
  We Do Have Future Choices 71
Thomas, Dylan 230
Thompson, Francis 67
Tomlins, Maria 86–8
torture 108–9, 113
  United Nations Convention
    Against Torture 1987 108
toxic society 10; *see also* Western
  society
trauma 108

Uganda 107, 128
UNESCO 207

University of Canberra
  Conference 154
Ustinov, Peter, *Dear Me* 76

Vaillant, George 6, 134–5
  Adaptation to Life 134
  Aging Well 192
  The Wisdom of the Ego 6
values 141, 148–9
  moral values 149
  see also family values
violence 106–9
Virnig, Annie Stilger 233–4, 244
Virnig, Susan 72, 164, 178
voyeurism 128

Wace, Barbara 193–4
Wall, Patrick, *Pain the Science of
  Suffering* 176
Wasow, Mona, *Skipping Stone*
  31–2, 136–8
wealth 145–7
Weatherburn, Don (and Lind) 47;
  see also child abuse; crime,
  juvenile
welfare 92–4
  mutual obligation 92
Werner, Emmy 35, 79, 226

Western culture 126–7
  of negativity 127
Western society
  change (social) 10, 16
  lifestyle 144
  modern 8
  modern Australia 86
  quick fix society 147
  social decay 149
  social equity 18
  toxic society 10
Wheatley, Meg 216
Whitman, Walt 249
Wickham, Anna 215
Wiesel, Torsten (and Hubel)
  42–3
Williams, Carmel 32
women, changing roles 129
World War Two 109, 114, 159
writing 119, 205

Young-Eisendrath, Polly 6
youth 10, 144–5
  alienation 144–5
  suicide 10, 144–5
  unemployment 144
  see also suicide

zeitgeist 17